The Working Class
in American Literature

ALSO EDITED BY JOHN F. LAVELLE

Blue Collar, Theoretically: A Post-Marxist Approach to Working Class Literature, (McFarland, 2012)

The Working Class in American Literature

Essays on Blue Collar Identity

Edited by JOHN F. LAVELLE and DEBBIE LELEKIS

McFarland & Company, Inc., Publishers
Jefferson, North Carolina

This book has undergone peer review.

LIBRARY OF CONGRESS CATALOGUING-IN-PUBLICATION DATA

Names: Lavelle, John F., 1950– editor. | Lelekis, Debbie, editor.
Title: The working class in American literature :
essays on blue collar identity / edited by John F. Lavelle and Debbie Lelekis.
Description: Jefferson, North Carolina : McFarland & Company, Inc.,
Publishers, 2021 | Includes bibliographical references and index.
Identifiers: LCCN 2021033355 | ISBN 9781476673066 (paperback : acid free paper) ∞
ISBN 9781476643830 (ebook)
Subjects: LCSH: American literature—History and criticism. |
Working class in literature. | Social classes in literature. |
BISAC: LITERARY CRITICISM / American / General |
SOCIAL SCIENCE / Social Classes & Economic
Disparity | LCGFT: Literary criticism.
Classification: LCC PS173.W65 W67 2021 | DDC 810.9/352623—dc23
LC record available at https://lccn.loc.gov/2021033355

BRITISH LIBRARY CATALOGUING DATA ARE AVAILABLE

ISBN (print) 978-1-4766-7306-6
ISBN (ebook) 978-1-4766-4383-0

© 2021 John F. Lavelle and Debbie Lelekis. All rights reserved

*No part of this book may be reproduced or transmitted in any form
or by any means, electronic or mechanical, including photocopying
or recording, or by any information storage and retrieval system,
without permission in writing from the publisher.*

Front cover image © fran_kie/Shutterstock

Printed in the United States of America

*McFarland & Company, Inc., Publishers
Box 611, Jefferson, North Carolina 28640
www.mcfarlandpub.com*

Table of Contents

Preface
　JOHN F. LAVELLE　　　　　　　　　　　　　　　　1

Introduction
　JOHN F. LAVELLE　　　　　　　　　　　　　　　　3

The "giddy hows-wife" Revealed: Classifying Humor in Sarah Kemble Knight's *The Journal of Madame Knight*
　TERESA M. CORONADO　　　　　　　　　　　　　13

Twain's Antithetical Discourses in *Adventures of Huckleberry Finn* and *The Adventures of Tom Sawyer*
　JOHN F. LAVELLE　　　　　　　　　　　　　　　28

Violence, Labor and Collective Action in William Dean Howells' *A Hazard of New Fortunes*
　DEBBIE LELEKIS　　　　　　　　　　　　　　　　47

Writing the Spectacle of the Human Zoo: Literary Slumming and the Animalized Other in *Maggie, A Girl of the Streets*
　KAILEY HAVELOCK　　　　　　　　　　　　　　63

Social Radicalism in Sherwood Anderson's *Winesburg, Ohio*
　DEBORAH GIGGLE　　　　　　　　　　　　　　80

Losing Control: Contrasting Identity Constructs in Jean Toomer's *Cane*
　CHARLENE TAYLOR EVANS　　　　　　　　　　100

"One had to have castes": Class, Culture and Ideology in *American Tragedy*
　ADAM NEMMERS　　　　　　　　　　　　　　　121

Table of Contents

The Sun Also Rises for Some: Hemingway's Exploration of the
  Ideologies of Social Class in *The Sun Also Rises*
    JOHN F. LAVELLE *and* DEBBIE LELEKIS   141

Accidents of Birth: A Class Study of Faulkner's Colonel John Satoris,
  Emily Grierson and Abner Snopes
    MICHAEL J. FINNEGAN   157

The Root and the Link: Talismans of Class-Consciousness in
  Douglass' *Narrative* and Ellison's *Invisible Man*
    MARK HENDERSON   169

Haunted Privilege: Uncanny Estates in Flannery O'Connor
  and Shirley Jackson
    JASON MARC HARRIS   182

About the Contributors   211

Index   213

Preface

John F. Lavelle

The genesis of this book comes from the opportunity afforded us to expand and take the ideas in my first book, *Blue Collar, Theoretically: A Post-Marxist Approach to Working Class Literature* in new directions. *Blue Collar* lays out a new (for literature anyhow) concept of class based on sociological studies of humans and society first championed by Max Weber and others and mostly ignored in literary circles. This first book interrogates Marxist construction of class, seeing it as faulted at its base. The book lays out theories that contend that classes come in and out of existence based on Pierre Bourdieu's theory of social fields. It adds to this theory the idea of a power locus around which people compete through what Jean-François Lyotard calls performance, by what Bourdieu would call the presentation of cultural, symbolic, and social capital. Sociologists call the construction of classes within a social field—the act of separation—in-grouping/out-grouping, through what Bourdieu calls *distinctions* in the book by the same name and in subsequent books, *differences*.

Thus the purpose of this second book is to extend the ideas from the first book in real-world practical ways and to address the real problems with approaching class through economics by showing the complexity of class relations and at this time, in a relative way, the real danger of relegating class to economics. As this book is getting ready to go to press, there is great unrest in this nation because of the systemic disenfranchisement and subornation of a large part of our population due to the color of their skin. Marxism would have us believe it is due to their relation to the means of production or being in the lower class. *Blue Collar* contests this hypothesis and contends that the problems are due to class separation. While economic class separation subordinates skin color to economics, there is little doubt it is the *difference* in skin color which has allowed others, through out-grouping on a national scale, to systematically exclude them from life chances that cause their economic and other situations. While *Blue Collar* made an attempt to include race, sex, gender, sexual orientation, and other signs of *differences*, as markers for separation, the book did not go far enough. This collection, through its interrogation of texts, however, does.

Through many discussions with our editors, Debbie Lelekis and I decided to solicit papers concerned with class separation from all eras of American literature, colonial to contemporary, to test the theories from the first book. What we hoped to find was evidence of the workings of class and class separation throughout literature. We based our premise on the proposition put forth in the first book that texts are artifacts of their time and ideologies, whether dominant or subordinate. We believed if one looked at class sociologically or in a Weberian construction of class, the act of separation, whether physically violent or socially violent, would be present in the texts. What was discovered through the essays was that the class act was much more prevalent than we'd even thought. While reading through the submissions we realized that the first book needed to expand its concept of what class might entail, that it is the dominant act of society, and that is a socially violent act, sometimes physically violent, in that it denies people for one reason or another access to personal power, which then denies them access to life chances.

Thus, although this book mirrors the ideas of the first book, it carries them into the real world by interrogating texts from almost all the periods of American literature from the eighteenth century to the present day. The focus and scope are intentionally large to allow for examples of class throughout American literature reflecting an American social context. The purpose of the book is twofold: to put into practice the theories and ideas of the first book, establishing a base upon which we can begin to discuss class as it really exists, and its second purpose is to bring awareness of the true workings of class separation in society. It contends, as does my first book, that Marxism diagnoses the symptom and not the disease, in that it contends that the relationship to the means of production determines life chances instead of the reverse. It shows the class act to be the prevalent act of separation within society, and it finally asks if, in America, we are paying the price for ignoring this fact.

Introduction

John F. Lavelle

Marxism's definition of class proposes that classes are based on the relationship to the means of production. This relationship has usually been operationally defined through economics or agency within capital and labor; the former deals with the disparity of wages to profit or, as Marxists put it, the share of the surplus labor. This leads to the latter, a concern with the proletariat's rights as producers. However, this configuration of class has been contested by sociologists since at least Max Weber.

Marxism, although somewhat planted within the nascent economic theories of the time, greatly deviates from it in a philosophical turn. Weber is considered by some as the father of modern sociology, his theories based on strict observations. Sociological or Weberian theories might suggest that Marxists, since Marx, have been putting the cart before the horse, in the assumption that one's relationship to the means of production creates class structure and, as Andrew Lawson suggests, "what grows out of a capitalistic mode of production [is] exploitation and domination" (11). Thus Marxists believe class is a modern phenomenon.

We now know, through observation and research, that humans, even before they were humans, were communal animals with a class hierarchy. We still observe this in our closest evolutionary relatives, the other great apes. All have distinct class hierarchies. Why would proto-humans be the exception? Zoologists have shown that complex hierarchies exist among any species of animals that congregate together whether in a pack, herd, group, or tribe, proving that social class separation comes before and is the cause of economic class separation.

The major problem endemic in the construction of class as a grouping of heterogeneous people bonded together by economics is that it is only an abstract construction used mostly for political purposes and does nothing to explain how class actually works. Marxist class separation is based on a mindset steeped in modern political economics, i.e., capitalism, socialism, and communism in the Marxist sense. Marxism contends that, other than the first epoch of humanity, we have basically been stuck in a class, and we must struggle to improve our lot through revolution in one sense or another. It asks almost nothing about how class separation came about other than to say that certain productive hunters forced their will on the others. This idea depends on the exceptionalism of humans to all other animals in that seemingly we were not human, and then we were. Darwin's *On the Origin of Species* had been out for eight years before the publication of *Das Kapital*. At that time, evolutionary theories were hardly popular, contradicting most established knowledge based, one way or another, on the exceptionalism and privilege of humankind grounded in religious thought directly or indirectly.

Due in part to the ideological concept of "American exceptionalism," which contends that, as Americans, we live in a classless society, the study of class in America as economic stratification was, from the beginning, doomed, and with the movement away from class, the social inequities of race, sexual orientation, gender, sex, and ethnicity were taken up to explain the out-grouping of different people not due to their relationship to the means of production. This movement is mainly due to the study of class contained within the constraints of Marxism. In his book *The Working-Class Majority: America's Best Kept Secret*, Michael Zwieg comes close to suggesting class is a struggle for agency within social fields when he states, "Invisible force fields of power are built into structures that hold society together" (10). In discussing the "ruling class" he states, "The ruling class is bound together into a coherent social force by common networks and institutions" (17). He comes close to constructing class and the class dynamic sociologically as a social construct, but he avoids stating it is ideological in nature, and thus avoids having to come to terms with separations based on race, sexual orientation, gender, sex, and ethnicity.

Separation is not a new phenomenon. It has come down through history as a social stratifying act, many times codified within culture, religion, and laws of a society. Thorstein Veblen, an American economist and founding father of the institutional economic school, avoids all mention of the capitalist class in his seminal book *The Theory of the Leisure Class*. However, as the title contends, he does see a dominant class: the leisure class. Veblen states "it is for this [leisure] class to determine, in general outline, what scheme of Life the community shall accept as decent or honorific; and it is their office by precept and example to set forth this scheme of social salvation in its highest, ideal form" (124). This ideological viewpoint today is often alluded to as privilege, which depends on difference and distinction within a social field, with its criteria defined through social and sometimes physical struggle by those actors within that field. What is being contested within the precepts of privilege can be stated as a judgment of worthiness or unworthiness.

This metanarrative of privilege originates from one of two core ideological metanarratives coming down to us from history. The first, privilege, is better known as "the great chain of being." It is both social and religious in nature, that is to say religions have helped set up and maintain this idea through a stratification of beings from God or gods, through demigods or angels/saints, heroes and kings (two positions very much contested in their ranking). In feudal times (and one might say with our classed society and constant war we are still in those times) the ranking included (or includes) other lords, specialized fighting men (a rank very diminished as war changed), merchants (rich business people), all those very wealthy people, sometimes scholars, trades people, all other free people, and then those common people given no agency relegated to the lower classes through out-grouping. Historically, within all these ranks, there has been a sub-rank dependent on sex and/or birth. Examples of the struggle in ranking within privilege can be seen throughout history as far back as the *Iliad*, *Oedipus*, and *Antigone*. We see it in many early Byzantine paintings. In *Blue Collar, Theoretically: A Post-Marxist Approach to Working Class Literature* and in this book, we argue that class is endemic in literature.

The other major ideological metanarrative comes to us from humanism: the idea that all people are equal and thus start out the same. This notion contends that neither birth nor rank are criterion for justifying one's position within a field of power, but rather moral or immoral actions. This ideology, equalitarianism, unlike privilege, defines a person as moral or immoral through his or her actions, or as Friedrich Nietzsche contends, good or evil. This concept, although sporadically present throughout history (as in several books of the Old and New Testament) has only been a real and systemized concept for a few centuries and, in fact, is a radical concept counter to naturalism, that the human mind is capable of reason, able to change and control the baser instincts through the use of a reasoning brain. It also concludes that society might have certain natural laws similar to physics, one akin to Newton's law of action/reaction. Today we might also think of it within chaos theory. Out-group enough people, deny them access to life chances, and at some point in the future, there will be a tipping point as Marx alluded to in his belief in the proletarian revolution (although Weber has a much more complex scenario which actually played out between the two world wars allowing for the rise of Hitler). However, today we have met a tipping point with the systematic out-grouping of Black people in the United States. Black people in the middle class or higher have been constantly harassed by police and out-grouped through white privilege. This brings into question economics, specifically the relationship to the means of production, having any significant role in the systemic racism experienced today.

Social classes are not only mutable social arrangements but may have complex and multiple gradations and permutations, and they may come into existence and go out of existence. Social class permeates everyone's everyday lives in one form or another through the struggle for access to life chances, such as access to safe shelter, education, and job opportunities to name but a few. Sociologists contend the struggle is access to agency, more commonly known as power. Social class separation is, in part, a physically violent act within a social field through what Pierre Bourdieu first calls *distinctions*, which he later calls *differences*. Bourdieu also develops the idea of the social field as the field of power. Social fields or fields of power have a locus of power. In or near this locus, certain people hold power, dispense power, and gain power.

Theoretically, every human being is born with the same agency: the ability to act upon his or her environment freely. When humans enter into communities, they give up some of this agency for the benefit of the community. However, humans, even before being humans, were communal animals, and thus agency has always been distributed unevenly. A person, when born into a community, gives up an amount of his or her agency/power to a governance whether established by law or ad hoc. Practically, though, as Louis Althusser contends, even before a person is born, "the individual is interpellated as a (free) subject in order that he shall submit freely to the commandments of the Subject, […] in order that he shall (freely) accept his subjection, […] in order that he shall make the gestures and actions of his subjection 'all by himself'" (Althusser 123). How much power is given to or taken away depends on their social class.

Governance is a set of prescribed rules, whether written or traditionally oral, and persons with the right of responsibility to enforce these rules. Governance, in its basic form, is the holding of the legitimate right of violence, whether that is physical, social, or psychic. This governance, whether state, village or ad hoc organization, redistributes this agency/power to other organizations and finally to individuals. The nation-state, then, redistributes to the province, state, or district, all the way down to the village and those social organizations such as the PTA. They do this through written laws or rules. In a democratic nation such as the United States, one might think laws would be put in place to guarantee that agency would be redistributed equally. While these laws do exist, many laws have been enacted to do exactly the opposite. For example, most school aid is distributed by the property value of a school district. This gives those districts with higher property values, i.e., neighborhoods of wealthier people, better schools, and conversely worse schools in poorer neighborhoods, denying access to certain life chances and ensuring advantages to those already advantaged people.

However, most class separation takes place within ad hoc social fields or fields of power that, although existing in potential, come into actual being in each social situation. Each person is not only a member of many social fields but may exist in several at the same time and be in different positions to each locus of power. A field of power, in the end, is a battleground for advantage in the struggle for access to life chances and, in the least, is an act of social violence of out-grouping, often done through either physical violence or the threat thereof. Considering what may be lost or won by excluding others from certain advantages, it is truly as violent an act as separation by force. In a Marxist sense of class, the struggles involving exclusion by race, sex, sexual orientation, and gender must be thought of separately from class or the class struggle, since it is the proletariat against the petit bourgeoisie and the bourgeoisie. In a sociological configuration of class, social position determines economics through access to life chances. These struggles involving exclusion by race, sex, sexual orientation, ethnicity, and gender become central to class struggle, and they are five of the major class distinctions or differences used to out-group.

These social fields come into existence at a specific place and time and either dissipate quickly or are formalized into permanent existence by law and cultural traditions, but mostly through ideology. Ideology works through metanarratives that provide the narratives in which people construct their reality. "It is through narrativity that we come to know, understand, and make sense of the social world, and [...] constitute our social identities" (Somers 606). In "Symbolic Pollution" Mary Douglas contends, through narratives, we develop prototypes and stereotypes. "We select from all the stimuli falling on our senses only those which interest us and our interests are governed by a pattern-making tendency" (Douglas 156). "All our impressions are schematically determined from the start" and through these belief systems (ideology), people form prototypes of what is sacred or profane (Douglas 156). In her seminal book *Purity and Danger: An Analysis of the Concepts of Pollution and Taboo* Douglas states:

> We have seen that powers are attributed to any structure of ideas, and that rules of avoidance make a visible public recognition of its boundaries.... Each culture must have its own notions of dirt and defilement which are contrasted with its notions of the positive structure which must not be negated [10].

People, through prototyping, categorize things and ideas as sacred, profane, or indeterminate. It has nothing to do with any reality but ideology.

Fields of power where agency is contested through the use of ideological narratives exist within, and adjacent to, each other. A person most likely is in

8   Introduction

several at the same moment and in different positions to the individual power locus. Within these fields, people are in-grouped or out-grouped. Using Bourdieu's ideas of distinctions and differences, we can say that distinctions are attributes thought as positive by those in the field close to the power locus and differences are those attributes thought of as negative by those in power in the field. Thus, within a social field, people vie for position through the acclamation and use of what Bourdieu calls capital: social, symbolic, and cultural capital. Examples of capital are higher degrees, luxury items, what Veblen called conspicuous consumption, and skin color or sexual orientation.

For Michel Foucault, the construction of a social field occurs through discourse, and the discourse is defined by the social field, or what Jean-François Lyotard calls the language game. Although some theorists suggest that in all social fields there exists room for resistance, Foucault contends that within the discourse of all social fields is the narrative of resistance. "[I]t is not enough to say that these [acts of resistance] are anti-authority struggles; we must try to define more precisely what they have in common" (*Essential* 129). He goes on to state, "the targets are power effects. [...] They are anarchistic struggles. [...] They are struggles which question the status of the individual. [...] the 'government of individualization' [...] struggles against the privilege of knowledge" (*Essential* 129–130). Since the narrative of resistance is already prescribed within the discourse of any social field, it becomes criterion for out-grouping. This ideology is exclusionary and allows for the physical act of violence as honorable or, as Veblen states, honorific. As this book goes to press, Black people and other minorities have had to take to the streets in protest in what is being called the Black Lives Matter movement. They are protesting not their economic position, although that becomes part of it, but their out-grouping in almost all social fields due to the color of their skin. This collection moves the theories forward and contends that class is an act of separation. For many, class is a violent act and not a position to the means of production at all. It comes into being as social fields come into being, whether ad hoc in a store or a bar, or in official fields created by laws that allow for separation, or communities that turn a blind eye on these acts. The violence in the case of Black people comes in both forms, social and physical violence, in an attempt to out-group them and deny them life chances. Social violence is when, to put it plainly, persons are denied through social means access to life chances by their subordinate position to the power locus of social fields.

Social class inclusion bestows power or appropriates power from those people within a social field by positioning them at some distance, near or far, to a locus of power. Thus the access to life chances, what a Marxist might see as a change in relationship to the means of production, is controlled by social classes distributing agency.

This book has been created after much thought concerning this new understanding of class and class dynamics as social separation by difference and distinction, on the one hand through the use of privilege and on the other through moral/immoral actions. Eric Schocket suggests that the limitation of Weber's critical tradition is that it does not "understand the concept of class as a product of class struggle itself and, therefore, as a signifier with historically heterogeneous meanings" (12). Rather than following Schocket's concept of class as process, which moves away from an understanding of class that is rooted in identity, this book argues that because social class is prevalent within all action within society, all differences must be considered as criteria for class separation, and it must include all markers of separation including race, sex, sexual orientation, and gender. At first, this may seem to downplay the importance of the struggle of people of different races, women, those people of different sexual orientation, and gender. However, to look at class in this light is to put class back into a Marxist configuration, and regulate it to only economics when social class is all-pervasive. We are all in an already existing society. Class, in a sociological configuration, encompasses everything through its action of separation. Thus, we must change our understanding of class from a theoretical grouping of people to the act of separation. In other words, class is separation itself and thus the pervasive social act of a social animal.

All the essays in this book are concerned with class separation and how it is represented in literature. Some essays are concerned with author representation of class separation through the cultural norms such as in "The 'giddy hows-wife' Revealed: Classifying Humor in Sarah Kemble Knight's *The Journal of Madame Knight*" by Teresa M. Coronado. In this essay, Coronado discusses how Knight projects class separation as a cultural norm. "Writing the Spectacle of the Human Zoo: Literary Slumming and the Animalized Other in *Maggie, A Girl of the Streets*" by Kailey Havelock looks at how privilege becomes the transcendental signifier in which, during the second half of the nineteenth century, all other cultures are measured against as deviations of this norm, and while being sympathetic, the authors writing of the "lower classes" are more than just condescending. "Twain's Antithetical Discourses in *Adventures of Huckleberry Finn* and *The Adventures of Tom Sawyer*" discusses both Twain's perpetuation of privileged ideology during most of *The Adventures of Tom Sawyer* to Twain's recantation of this ideology throughout *Adventures of Huckleberry Finn*.

Other essays take a hard look at how class is dealt with within literature. Michael J. Finnegan's essay "Accidents of Birth: A Class Study of Faulkner's Colonel John Satoris, Emily Grierson and Abner Snopes" examines some of Faulkner's dealings with class in a stratified South, which has always been disruptive of the Marxist construction of class. Jason

Marc Harris discusses this same problem in the north in "Haunted Privilege: Uncanny Estates in Flannery O'Connor and Shirley Jackson." Debbie Lelekis's essay "Violence, Labor and Collective Action in William Dean Howells' *A Hazard of New Fortunes*" also takes a look at Howells' complex construction of class reflective of the times, including the Haymarket Massacre through discussion of the different characters' viewpoints concerning the strike mitigated through different class ideologies. This discussion of class ideologies mediating our view of reality is again taken up in "'One had to have castes': Class, Culture and Ideology in *American Tragedy*" by Adam Nemmers through a study of how class plays out within the novel and its reflection on the reality of the times. In "The Sun Also Rises for Some: Hemingway's Exploration of the Ideologies of Social Class in *The Sun Also Rises*," John F. Lavelle and Debbie Lelekis bring to light the working of privilege within a specific social field through competing ideologies and class dynamics of the struggle of power within this field, while Deborah Giggle contends in "Social Radicalism in Sherwood Anderson's *Winesburg, Ohio*" that the condemnation of Anderson's book is due to his approach to class and the representation of class.

True class separation allows for agency/power to be redistributed within the social field. In any class situation, the social field might be constructed in diverse ways and in varying sizes, ideologically incorporating people with differing traits even when those people are not present. In this way, the ideology of privilege is manifest within the field, and the field might incorporate those not even present in in-grouping/out-grouping. This is ideologically how race works. There is no need for the concept of race other than for separation, to deny one group privilege/power while shifting it to another group. The two essays "Losing Control: Contrasting Identity Constructs in Jean Toomer's *Cane*" by Charlene Taylor Evans and "The Root and the Link: Talismans of Class-Consciousness in Douglass' *Narrative* and Ellison's *Invisible Man*" by Mark Henderson deal with this much starker working of class separation, the cultural and legal class separation by skin color or race. The essays go on to elucidate how otherwise out-grouped white males might see themselves as deserving more privilege (due to their skin color) than those of other races.

The mechanisms of class separation exclusion and inclusion encompass all aspects of society and, since humans are social animals, all aspects of social life. While we have been conditioned to see class in a Marxist sense, we have been disallowed a more complex idea of class, not allowing us to see class in all its facets. These facets include separation by race, sex, sexual orientation, ethnicity, and gender. Class is the social act of separation into groups. This separation is the condition that produces the economic situations that have been touted as class. Separation within the fields of power allows for access or denial to life chances that determine economic classes. Class is, as this book contends, all-encompassing in its control of agency/power. Class, as this book also contends, is social separation of people by difference.

Works Cited

Althusser, Louis. *Lenin and Philosophy, and Other Essays.* Trans. Ben Brewster. New York: New York Monthly Review Press, 1972.
Douglas, Mary. *Purity and Danger: An Analysis of the Concepts of Pollution and Taboo.* New York: Routledge, 1984.
_____. "Symbolic Pollution." *Culture and Society: Contemporary Debates.* Eds. Jeffrey C. Alexander and Steven Seidman. New York: Cambridge University Press, 1990. 156–59.
Foucault, Michel. *The Essential Foucault: Selections from the Essential Works of Foucault, 1954–1984.* Eds. Paul Rabinow and Nikolas Rose. New York: The New Press, 2003.
Lawson, Andrew. "Introduction." *Class and the Making of American Literature: Created Unequal.* New York: Routledge, 2014.
Schocket, Eric. *Vanishing Moments: Class and American Literature.* Ann Arbor: University of Michigan Press, 2006.
Somers, Margaret, R. "Narrative Identity, and Social Action: Rethinking English Working-Class Formation." *Social Science History* 16/4 (1992): 591–630.
Veblen, Thorstein. *The Theory of the Leisure Class.* Auckland, New Zealand: The Floating Press, 2009.
Zweig, Michael. *The Working Class Majority: America's Best Kept Secret.* Ithaca, NY: Cornell University Press, 2012.

The "giddy hows-wife" Revealed
Classifying Humor in Sarah Kemble Knight's The Journal of Madame Knight

TERESA M. CORONADO

The ground beneath the feet of Sarah Kemble Knight's horse as she travelled from Boston to New York City was not the only unstable ground Knight traversed. As a woman of some social standing within her community in Boston, Knight walked on shaky ground when she began to take on considerable business duties outside of her roles as a matron and keeper of her household. In *The Journal of Madame Knight*, Sarah Knight writes to confirm her social standing[1] using humor garnered from her travels as a method to bring herself back into the comforting folds of her Bostonian social circle. *The Journal of Madame Knight* (hereafter referred to as the *Journal*) is an example of what Sargent Bush, Jr., calls "an important contribution to the tradition of American humor," in that Sarah Kemble Knight negotiates status differences in the *Journal* through her descriptions of the "dirty" and lower status people whom she meets along the road, in ways that Bush identifies as a "humorous satirical dimension in the work" (70, 76). Differing from Bush, I propose that Knight's use of humor is part of her struggle with her sense of insecurity of her own social standing in colonial New England and that that struggle had everything to do with her place as a woman and a Bostonian merchant.[2] In perceiving in Knight's humor more than just entertainment, I find within the laughter a tension that reflects Knight's concern with her place in Boston's society—a closely-watched social order occupied with status and displays of that status.

My argument works with Pierre Bourdieu's proposal that one's social status is defined by tangible indices, as well as "by a whole set of subsidiary characteristics which may function, in the form of tacit requirements, as real principles of selection or exclusion without ever being formally stated" (102). In this essay, those "tacit requirements" are behavioral and, thus, performative. Knight's *Journal* supports what Daniel T. O'Hara notes in his essay on "Class," "[p]rior to the nineteenth century, the sense of class distinctions appeared embodied in literature via the principle of decorum; how one spoke [and, arguably, how one wrote] marked one's social and even moral status."[3] My essay adds to current Knight scholarship, in that I argue that Knight's journal acts as a form of communication between herself and the community that can work to exclude her for her performance outside of Boston.[4]

My argument depends upon the idea that Knight behaved in ways similar to her peers, but that her behavior was different enough to be at the mercy of a number of social controls, including, for example, gossip. Mary Beth Norton, in *Founding Mothers and Fathers: Gendered Power and the Forming of American Society*, makes a compelling argument that:

> Gossip enables people of similar status to judge one another and to reach collective opinions on crucial questions of credit and trustworthiness. Those who obeyed the rules of community consensus won acceptance and respect; those who violated such rules [...] ran the risk of inciting concerted action against themselves, endangering their reputations and livelihoods, even occasionally their lives.

For Knight, as a merchant woman, gossip, both positive and negative, would affect both her home life and livelihood; Knight's *Journal* performs as an exhibition of Knight's knowledge and practice of acceptable behaviors, especially in comparison to the people she uses as her humorous foils (Norton 276–277).[5]

For a woman like Knight, enterprising and fairly independent, the *Journal* provides context to her life to her peers. Knight's reputation, as both a wife and a merchant, depended on her neighbors understanding her place in her household. Laurel Thatcher Ulrich, in *Good Wives: Image and Reality in the Lives of Women in Northern New England, 1650-1750*, argues that:

> Most occupations were indeed gender-linked, yet colonial Englishmen were far less concerned with abstract notions like "femininity" than with concrete roles like "wife" or "neighbor." Almost any task was suitable for a woman as long as it furthered the good of her family and was acceptable to her husband. This approach was both fluid and fixed. It allowed for varied behaviors without really challenging the patriarchal order of society. There was no proscription against female farming, for example, but there were strong proscriptions toward dutiful wifehood and motherhood. Context was everything [37–38].

For Knight, her actions represent a departure from standard expectations; her behaviors are not wildly outside that norm, in terms of merchant behavior and actions, but just enough outside of the idea of every-day practice in

Boston that her concern for her place in her social circle depends less on her business acumen and more on her performance of a gendered identity. For instance, as Julia Stern hypothesizes, being involved in these "unladylike" exertions is perhaps "why Knight is mistaken for a prostitute at the first inn in which she stops. That a woman of her social rank would be on the road late at night in fine clothes could be understood in no other way in rural Connecticut of 1704" (3). It is because suitability was fluid and fixed that Knight's work shows her vulnerability and nervousness about her position (Norton 253).[6] This essay makes the argument that through the circulation of her *Journal*, Knight uses humor to make her performance and her understanding of her social identity clear to her peers.

Born in 1666, Knight was part of a changing social and economic structure unfolding in New England; however, Knight does not, on the surface, seem to have to be concerned about her place in society. From a good family herself, Knight's marriage to a shipmaster and shipping agent represented a coming together of wealth and status (Martin 51). Perry D. Westbrook remarks that Knight was "addressed as Madame because she was a teacher [of penmanship], was the daughter of a Boston merchant and the wife of a sea captain" (61). Because her husband was frequently away on business, and their capital was mainly invested in the cargo his ships carried, Knight undertook several ventures to supplement their income, including owning an inn and a shop and venturing in Indian trading and farming. Wendy Martin observes, "[Knight's] business acumen was notable as, upon her death in 1727, she left a formidable estate of 1,800 [British Pounds]" (51). Her status was imbued with markers of merchants, but she also worked with, as, and among the lower sort of traders. It is this work, and her journey to New York, that adds to Knight's unease about her place in status laden Boston.

It is already well-known and agreed upon that Sarah Kemble Knight made an incredible journey for a woman of her class—for any woman—in the early eighteenth century. In 1704, Knight traveled alone from Boston to New York, via New Haven Connecticut, a round-trip of five months and two-hundred miles. Except for the occasional friendly companion or paid guide, Knight journeyed alone. This trip is heralded by critics and feminists alike as proof of early American womanly strength, especially, as Wendy Martin notes, "the route itself was [...] difficult and covered somewhat treacherous terrain" (51). The difficulties of that journey and the apparent ease at which she undertook it would have, however, cast doubt on her position because, as Ulrich reminds us, the "gentry were just close enough to the wilderness to flaunt their civilization, yet many were near enough to middle-class (and often Puritan) origins to be anxious about their own gentility" (73). Knight's gentility was at stake, even in, or maybe because of, the amorphous world of status divisions and gossip.

In order to exhibit her performance successfully, Knight needed an audience. However, like many other (secular) early American women writers, Knight's work was not printed for public consumption—the *Journal* was published well after her death. Instead, she circulated her work privately among ladies in a circle of her own rank.[7] Westbrook, in *A Literary History of New England*, argues "Very likely she wrote it for her own and perhaps her family's and friends' amusement. It might, indeed, have been deemed unsuitable for publication in the early eighteenth century, for it conveyed no message, religious or otherwise" (62). Stern supports this when she remarks "Unlike the Puritan women who write about their wilderness trials in the form of the captivity narrative [...] Knight traverses the frontier as an economic agent rather than as a soul driven by divine injunction" (1–2). As a document prepared for private circulation, Knight's *Journal* offers modern readers what Robert F. Sayre, in *American Lives*, calls a "cultural document" from which we can read as much about "the author's assumed audience" as we can learn about Knight herself (13). Her circle of friends was made up of those she could trust with her accounts and to keep them within the circle of the parlor room; these were the men and women who would understand the meanings of her status symbols. In writing a journal teeming with status references, Knight regaled her friends with both adventures from her trip *and* her expertise of the mannerisms that would have been important for her to demonstrate as a good wife and mother.[8]

In literature in which the "other" is usually gendered or racialized, Knight's travel narrative, in particular, points out the *class* "otherness" of people whom she meets on her travels. The laughter and ridicule Knight uses in the *Journal* follow Henri Bergson's theory that "society holds suspended over each individual member, if not the threat of correction, at all events the prospect of a snubbing, which although it is slight, is none the less dreaded. Such must be the function of laughter" (135). In one example in the *Journal*, the incongruities between Knight and the "bumpkins" she sees in New York City become a site of humor for her audience, even today.[9] Robert Micklus, in *Colonial Humor*, notes that, generally, "our earliest humorists were understandably too insecure to enjoy any other than an infrequent laugh at their own expense. By laughing at the manners and beliefs of those who did not meet their standards, they were perhaps able to convince themselves that all was right in their own private worlds or, at least, in their own minds" (152). The most evident illustration of this use of humor in Knight's *Journal* happens when she encounters a particular innkeeper's daughter.

This moment of humor in the text appears in Knight's descriptions of an innkeeper's daughter she meets the first night after she leaves her home in Boston. The innkeeper's daughter "sett herself just before me, showing the way to Reding, that I might see her Ornaments, perhaps to gain the more respect. But her Granam's new Rung sow, had it appeared, would [have] affected me as much." In this brief encounter, Knight reveals that she finds the innkeeper's daughter vulgar. Knight implies that ostentatious displays of wealth, or what one thinks of as wealth, are counter to her rank's sensibilities. Knight conveys her ridicule for this display by giving her audience even more damaging evidence of the innkeeper's daughter's pretension: "Miss star'd awhile, drew a chair, bid me sitt, And then run up stairs and putts on two or three Rings [...] and returning, sett herself before me" (54). Not only is the girl flashy, she is, by Knight's standards, deliberately so.

In this excerpt, Knight takes the opportunity to reify class distinctions by making a mockery of the innkeeper's daughter. Bergson argues, "Laughter is, above all, a corrective. [...] By laughing, society avenges itself for the liberties taken with it. It would fail in its object if it bore the stamp of sympathy or kindness" (197). And there is no sympathy here; instead, the innkeeper's daughter is made to be the comic character in this text—her vulgarity is highlighted by Knight.

Knight suggests that the innkeeper's daughter, besides being offensive, also has little sense of how to entertain guests or visitors of Knight's rank in this situation. She knows, Knight says, to inquire after her journey, but, Knight relates, that she also "asked silly questions, without asking me to sitt down." In fact, the innkeeper's daughter, "[i]nterogate[s]" her in a way that makes Knight stand "aghast." To rebuke her, Knight writes, "I told her shee treated me very Rudely, and I did not think it my duty to answer her unmannerly Questions" (54). Knight puts the girl in her place by instructing her on how to treat a guest, albeit a paying one. In reprimanding the girl, Knight is telling her that there is, in fact, a difference between them. Knight exposes herself here because as a customer she isn't a guest, but a traveler—a mere travelling merchant. In creating a situation in which the innkeeper's daughter is made fun of for her lack of manners—her "silly questions"—Knight can deflect attention from herself. By putting the innkeeper's daughter in her place, Knight is setting a line of demarcation—with Knight firmly established within the confines of her status.

Why does Knight pick on the innkeeper's daughter? Because there is no visible difference between Knight's own method of commerce and the innkeeper's daughter's. Knight herself has owned an inn, so the innkeeper's daughter's wealth and the way in which Knight has earned hers are quite similar. However, Knight comes from a well-known, although not aristocratic, family of some status in Boston circles; thus, she feels herself to be different from the upstart innkeeper's daughter whose apparent lack of manners reveals her lower standing in society. By running upstairs to put her jewelry on, the innkeeper's daughter was obviously trying to convey to Knight that she was not an ordinary girl, but one of some value. For Knight, this gesture only serves to underline the girl's tastelessness.[10] Knight is both criticizing the girl's apparent aspirations of equality to her, a woman of some social standing, and making Knight herself look more genteel.

The performance of Knight's status is also reflected in a sympathetic encounter with a different sort of innkeeper she boards with in Narragansett—an innkeeper who knows her place. Knight makes a point to describe this woman's servility: "I was very civilly Received, and courteously entertained, in a clean comfortable House; and the Good woman was very active in helping off my Riding clothes, and then ask'd what I would eat" (57). As there is no servant, and as Knight does not name her as she does the upper class women with whom she boards, one infers that this innkeeper is of a lower status, like the aforementioned innkeeper's daughter. Knight delivers this particular experience in a simple narrative style, without the jibes at the innkeeper, his home, or his wife, that she delivers in the previous scenario. This episode reveals that Knight is able to write about people of lower status without humor, but only if they show that they know their place and acknowledge hers.

Knight is not always, nor only, critical of the women she meets on her journey, proving to some extent that Knight is not merely being cruel to those of her gender in a pique of female hostility. As she depends on social mores to establish her place in society, she criticizes all lower status people who offer her the opportunity to reestablish herself within her "proper" role. Although Stern writes, "Perhaps uneasy with having ventured out of the purview of female domesticity, Knight refocuses the anxiety she feels for having transgressed eighteenth-century gender codes by projecting hostility back onto the female bodies of unknown others" (6). I agree with Stern that Knight does critique women in her *Journal*, but I depart from Stern's well-established arguments in that I argue that Knight's hostility focuses on working class women *and* men and that Knight's hostility is conducted through humor and performed as corrective for her own benefit. Furthermore, as shown in the example of the "Good woman" of the "neet and handsome" inn, Knight is willing to give praise if this will underscore to her community her understanding of domestic conduct. It is Knight's community that is important to her success within that community and the people who appear in her *Journal* are there as a means to that end.

Knight also shows herself as an expert on civilizing techniques, including on domestic matters in her comments on people she observes in New York. In New York, Knight comments, as both an experienced shopkeeper and a housewife, that she

> Observe[d] here the great necessity and bennifitt both of Education and Conversation; for these people [country folk who have moved to the city] have as Large a portion of mother witt, and sometimes a Larger, than those who have been brought up in Citties; But for want to emprovements, Render themselves almost Ridiculos [...]. I should be glad if they would leave such follies [such as standing speechless in stores in awe] and am sure all that Love Clean Houses (at least) would be glad on't too [66].

Knight postulates that women of her rank, those that "Love Clean Houses," would agree that the education of the lower orders is the only way to make them less "Ridiculos." This education is not for purposes of egalitarianism; rather, it is to improve them—to make them less laughable, but not to make them like Knight. For, of course, as Knight shows in her interaction with the innkeeper's daughter, status *is*, it is not taught.

Critics tend to conscript Knight's work to the realm of humor in American literature because of her wit, but they do this despite her degradation of the lower classes. Scott Michaelson, whose work does investigate the class issues in the text, argues, "linking hatreds and narrative wit, [Knight's *Journal*] quite simply makes class racisms [classism] fun" in a way that seems to be uncomplicated (11). In my argument, however the narrative wit in the text is a method of controlling laughter—the last laugh is the one that gets the upper hand. In Knight's *Journal*, wit is part of the civilizing process[11] in that she uses it (after the fact and for an audience) to punish transgressions of societal boundaries. In creating a space through writing and sharing her *Journal*, a space in which she and her peers can laugh at those under them in the social hierarchy, Knight is reaffirming status distinctions as well as planting herself firmly within the barriers of her rank's behaviors. By creating a place for laughter in the parlors where she shared her manuscript, Knight controls the humor of her journey and shows her social peers that she is a useful part of their society. Knight directs the impulse to laugh *away* from potential ridicule of her *towards* those who violate her rank's codes. A method that Knight uses throughout the *Journal* to point towards her being unaccustomed to being away from home is in the general laying out of how uncomfortable she is travelling.[12] However, much of her presumed discomfort comes back to her actual discomfort at being mistaken for a lesser rank, or being gossiped about her in terms of her gentility.

Throughout Knight's journey she remarks that she has to lie down to "Strech[] my tired Limbs," complains because "my poor bones complained bitterly not being used to such Lodgings" or rests because she is "poor weary" (60, 54, 67, 59). It is not only her bodily pains upon which Knight reflects, but she also writes that she has a delicate stomach. Her delicate stomach does not keep her humor from being biting however. Throughout the *Journal* Knight comments that her meals are poor; in one instance, she and her companion did not eat "our Dinners, wch was only smell." Once, when she is feeling a little ill and wants dinner, she records,

> They had nothing but milk in the house, wch they Boild, and to make it better sweetened wth molasses, which I not knowing or thinking oft till it was down and coming up agen wch it did in so plentifull a manner that my host was soon paid double for his portion, and that in specia.

This last incident took place in a house in which the woman who opened the door to Knight was "a surly old shee Creature, not worthy the name of woman." She stops at this house in "East Chester" on the way to "New Rochell," and Boston (62, 71, 70, 71). The house was not only dirty, but also, in giving her an inedible meal, inhospitable. This anecdote serves Knight well in that it makes her look comparatively delicate. Ostensibly, the poor woman who added molasses to the milk was able to drink this concoction and had found it palatable enough herself to feel comfortable serving it to a guest. For Knight, however, this woman served as a way for Knight to humorously exhibit her own gentility.

Knight also places her suffering in contrast to the men she meets on the road, including one of her first guides, John. John "entertained me with the Adventurs he had passed by late Rideing, and eminent Dangers he had escaped." Later in the evening, "wee come into a thick swamp, wch. by Reason of a great fogg, very much started mee, it being now very Dark. But nothing dismay'd John: Hee had encountered a thousand and a thousand such Swamps." In telling these tales, the guide is trying to scare the lady traveler—and Knight is, given her tone of voice, not afraid as long as she has John, her "Prince disguis'd," to help her (53). Knight contrasts her delicateness to John's "manly" ability to travel at late hours in precarious places. With her sensitive constitution and nervous condition, Knight has proven, superficially at least, that she is a delicate, yet brave, and again, in her coded society, a genteel, woman.

Where Knight leaves off the humorous tone and witty turns of phrase are when she invokes God. Knight does use the idea of Christian virtue to support her account, but combining the two—humor and God—would undermine her performance. Knight is a complex character who realizes her tenuous position in her uncomfortably amorphous world, and she makes sure that her assertion of superiority over other classes is not deemed as a cruel, or, worse, un-Christian-like, attitude. Knight chooses to display her womanly sympathy to a poor family (living near the Paukataug River in Rhode Island)[13] who, despite their poverty, nonetheless exhibits an "Inhabitance" that is "very clean and tydee; to the crossing of the Old Proverb, that bare walls make giddy hows-wifes" (60). Knight praises their cleanliness and shows her charitable side to a family that knows its place and is not rendered ridiculous by untoward behavior or aspirations to a different place in society.

As cleanliness is, of course, next to godliness, Knight values this trait as a marker of being civilized, but, not, again, as equalizing. Notions of cleanliness surface throughout the *Journal*. For instance, in the beginning stages of her journey (when she reaches Kingstown, Rhode Island)[14] Knight states that one of her lodges was "a clean comfortable House." Because of the cleanliness of this house, Knight feels well-disposed to remark that she was quite comfortable in this place, especially as the "Good woman" of the house kept it "neet and handsome." Everyone in that house is "clean," to Knight's "satisfaction" and, thus, Knight writes that she was treated "courteously" and "civilly" (57–58). The women of the house are not her equals, but Knight, again, can praise those who know their place and value domesticity in the same way she does throughout her *Journal*.

It is in this part of Knight's narrative that she also reflects on her own circumstances: "I Blest myselfe that I was not one of this miserable crew." Further, she composes a little poem in which she counts her blessings. In this poem Knight intones that when she thinks about how poor and "Misirable" the people by the river are, "my late fatigues do seem / Only a notion or a forgotten Dream" (60). Knight gives thanks to the God whom she, unlike her literary predecessor Mary Rowlandson, virtually ignores throughout the *Journal*. Knight acknowledges, in giving her thanks to God for her own health and economic status, that she is aware of God's graciousness toward her. Knight's reflection places her closer to the tradition of "divine" travel in the wilderness, again, offering homage to published social norms.

Knight invokes her authorial predecessors and her connection to Puritan Boston throughout the narrative in the segments of the *Journal* when she is alone. In one instance, when Knight is separated from her guides, she describes that she was in "the dolesome woods, my Company next to none, Going I knew not whither, and encompassed wth Terrifying darkness." This she says, "was enough to startle a more Masculine courage." This courage, she writes, is not one with which she is endowed; however, she describes how she was shortly thereafter greeted by "the friendly Appearance of the Kind Conductress of the night" (56). The light of the moon, Knight notes, gave her the courage to continue on her journey. The descriptions of this particular experience are effective in two distinct ways. First, Knight makes the obvious connections to being lost in the wilderness and being a sinner on a dark path that only God's grace can illuminate. This is yet another way that Knight links herself to her journaling female predecessors. The second connection she calls attention to a little later, when she writes that the moon "fill's" her imagination.

For Knight, the moon, "especially wn the moon glar'd light through the branches, fill'd my Imagination wth the pleasant delusion of a Sumpteous city, fill'd wth famous Buildings and churches, wth their spiring steeples, Balconies, Galleries and I know not what." These inspiring thoughts, which entertained her "agreeably [...] without a thou't of any thing but thoughts themselves" also place her firmly back into polite society (57). By comparing the city with the forest, Knight is carrying the city with her and, thus, bringing the marks of her city gentility with her, into said forest. The country folk she sees in New York City carry the country into the city with them—a mark of a lack of being touched by the civilizing process. Although she is traveling in the wilderness, Knight asserts that she belongs in a higher society and culture. Knight does not belong among the poorer, dirtier, or uneducated classes who live in the woods or even those who are "backwoods" within the confines of the city. Her sensibilities, as *she* avers in the *Journal*, are not on the edge, but firmly grounded in her status-laden culture. Knight, a woman of class and some housewifery, establishes herself in the respectability of the city and the safe-sphere of home and domesticity, and, thus, a part of a civilizing influence within her rank.

Knight was part of a culture of an increased capitalist ethic that influenced the small neighborhoods and growing cities of New England. At the same time this ethic was increasing, the populations of New England grew and people began to move west, creating a complex social and economic network outside of the central city of Boston (Greene 79). Thus, even though ministers such as Cotton Mather were still an integral part of the religious and governmental systems of New England, these systems had less influence on outlying communities. With a growing population within the cities themselves, the clergy even struggled to maintain its control within city limits. And, as Puritan control waned, the Puritan social structure also diminished. Other arrangements formed to take the place of the religious one—particularly a secular social system founded on wealth, manners, and education. In being a member of a large, and layered, merchant class, Knight had to contend with somewhat amorphous rules—because the rules of status do change. In his discussion of the conflict between court aristocracy and a rising bourgeois strata, Norbert Elias states, "the constant pressure from below and the fear it induces above are, in short, one of the strongest driving forces—though not the only one—of that specifically civilized refinement which distinguishes the people of this upper class from others and finally becomes second nature to them" (424). Simply put, those people who wished to be distinguished from the lower orders, and even those of lower status within the merchant class itself, had to define themselves through a strict self-control of mores, such as manners.

As Knight's incident with the innkeeper's daughter shows us, this refinement may be the only tangible dissimilarity available to that rank to differentiate themselves from those they see as belonging to a lower sphere. David Freeman Hawke notes that "Old [European] attitudes toward social status remained intact, but in economic terms the distance between the bottom and the top of society was relatively slight" (2). With the spread of a capitalist market economy and increased mobility, more people like the innkeeper's daughter would attempt to "pass" in the culture guarded by people like Sarah Kemble Knight. The humorous situations and language Knight uses to describe those situations in her *Journal* reflect her particular method of distinguishing her status—with herself, of course, deeply embedded within it—from the people she encounters on the road.

While Michaelson finds that most scholarship on Knight's *Journal* "concerns the triumph of a funny, early modern woman (a business-woman—as shop owner, trader, and expert on estates) exceeding the religious, pietistic, and gender boundaries that ensnared many other Puritan women," Knight is a woman very much "ensnared" in the ideological rules guiding the boundaries that held her contemporaries (2). Knight is not simply or steadily within those boundaries: she is desperately fighting to keep herself within them. In her *Journal*, Knight rewrites herself into a socially controlled definition of gentility extolled by the gentry and takes her place in the hegemonic structure of eighteenth-century colonial America. Through the hard work of her performative journal, Knight labors to properly situate herself within the status-laden realm of a developing class-based American society.

Notes

1. I will be using the terms rank and status in the essay, following Mary Beth Norton's argument in *Founding Mother and Fathers: Gendered Power and the Forming of American Society*, that "The only contemporary term used to describe the elements of England's all-encompassing social and political hierarchy was rank, employed in English as early as the late sixteenth century to mean 'one's social position or standing.' Other roughly comparable words, like status or class came into use later, primarily in the eighteenth and nineteenth centuries" (18). One of the ways in which I am addressing the issue of rank and status in this essay, being well aware that there is a gulf between today's understanding and how class was enacted and defined in the eighteenth century, is best summed up by Cornelia Hughes Dayton in *Women Before the Bar: Gender, Law, and Society in Connecticut, 1639-1789*: "Although there has been much hesitation over applying the language of class to early America before wage dependency was extensive, as social structure and a set of practices later identified as middle-class were emerging in the eighteenth-century. [...] The signs of interest in acquiring the badges of cultivation appeared as early as the 1690s" (12).

2. Knight's *Journal* offers modern readers a revelation of what life for a woman of "middling economic and social standing" was like during her time (Bush, introduction, 72). In the colonies, according to Edwin T. Perkins, "given the absence of factory work in the colonial

era, urban areas were commercial and handicraft centers populated by merchants, artisans, mariners, and common laborers. The term 'merchant' was loosely applied to persons ranging from poor storekeepers on the frontier to wealthy shipowners in the major ports" (Perkins 115). Knight's merchant title allowed her to be a part of the merchant elite, but also made her part of a loose collection of other types of merchants, which made her susceptible to status confusion in the New England colonies. Laurel Thatcher Ulrich, in *Good Wives*, argues that "The premodern world did allow for greater fluidity of role behavior than in nineteenth-century America, but colonial women were by definition basically domestic" (36). Thus, "As long as independent female trade remained a minor theme within a larger communal ethic, it did not threaten either male supremacy or the economic unity of the family" (Ulrich 46–47). Knight's problem is the informality of rank and status, as Norton points out: "The *community* or *informal* public [...] had no such formalized regulatory role to perform, but it contributed to the formation and perpetuation of social order nonetheless. Roughly, it consisted of peers: of heads of households and their dependents who saw one another frequently and commented on one another's doings. [...] A seventeenth-century colonist ignored the judgment of the community at his or her peril" (Norton 19–20), which means that Knight had to face the instability of the social system, adding her narrative to "The story of female experience in America [which] is not to be found in a linear progression from darkness to light, from constricted to expanding opportunities, from negative to positive valuation (or vice versa), but in a convoluted and sometimes tangled embroidery of loss and gain, accommodation and resistance" (Ulrich 240–41).

3. Daniel T. O'Hara, "Class," in *Critical Terms for Literary Study*, ed. Frank Lentricchia and Thomas McLaughlin (Chicago: University of Chicago Press, 1995), 407 fn1. Through her *Journal*, Knight shows that despite this transgression, she is aware of that transgression and quite knowledgeable of the expected social codes in her description of, for instance, manners and cleanliness, signs of being "civilized." However, to avoid censure, Knight cannot merely be civil; she must show that she is part of the civilizing community. Thus, Knight was required to prove herself to her social peers using her knowledge of these nuanced rules. Scott Michaelson, in "Narrative and Class in a Culture of Consumption: The Significance of Stories in Sarah Kemble Knight's *Journal*," has done excellent work concerning class in Knight's *Journal* and I am indebted to his argument. My argument furthers his work by exploring the context of Knight's gender in the class structures Michelson examines. As well, I explore humor in the *Journal* in regards to Knight's interactions and observations rather than on the idea of taste, stories, and entertainment, as Michaelson does. Further, Michaelson begins his article with the idea that Knight's text works with an understanding that "classes are figured in the middle-class imagination as natural formations, with certain classes inherently inferior to others" (2), while my argument makes the case for Knight's class awareness coming from the idea that Knight is uncomfortably aware that the "natural formations" are always in question. Michaelson argues that Knight "uses her sense of good conversation or entertainment in order to distinguish herself from others, in a way increasingly prevalent in the eighteenth-century colonies" (5). Again, differing from Michaelson, I would argue that she uses it in order to reinscribe herself into her community and, in the *Journal* more specifically, as a corrective.

4. Through her reinforcement of normative behavior for her rank in her *Journal*, Knight reinscribes herself into Boston's genteel set. In her *Journal*, Knight contrasts manners of others with her own familiarity of her rank's behaviors to draw attention to her knowledge of their rules. Richard Slotkin argues in *Regeneration Through Violence* that "In societies that are still in the process of achieving a sense of identity, the establishment of a nominative, characteristic image of the group's character is a psychological necessity; and the simplest means of defining or expressing the sense of such a norm is by rejecting some other group whose character is deemed to be the opposite" (68). If Knight had failed to show her knowledge of status symbols, genteel Boston would have rejected her much as she rejects the lower ranked women in her *Journal*.

5. Gossip, among other things, served as a form of social control and was based on standards that were ever-changing. Laura Thatcher Ulrich, in *Good Wives: Image and Reality in the Lives of Women in Northern New England, 1650–1750*, argues that: "casual watching-and-warding by neighbors was far more significant to most women than the power

of magistrates." Ulrich states further that "For colonial women, having the 'character' of a good wife was as valuable as having a good lawyer might be today" (59-60).

6. Ulrich also argues that "There can be no simple explanation of female status because that status is in itself so complex. To enlarge the role of deputy husband might mean to contract the often highly cherished roles of housekeeper and mother. To enhance the domestic might mean to neglect the communal, to control reproduction to lose one's sexual nature, to adjure violence to abandon the right to resist" (241).

7. Scott Michaelson, "Narrative and Class in a Culture of Consumption: The Significance of Stories in Sarah Kemble Knight's *Journal*," *College Literature* 21.2 (1994): 1-16, EBSCOhost (accessed March 4, 2011), fn21.

8. Ulrich, in *Good Wives*, argues that "The value of any activity is determined by its meaning to the participant, not to the observer. In early America, position was always more important than task. Colonial women might appear to be independent, even aggressive, by modern standards, yet still have derived their status primarily from their relationship to their husbands" (42).

9. To support my argument that Knight's *Journal* is humorous, Robert F. Sayre argues that Knight's *Journal* is "an early illustration of one of the most basic types of American humor, in which a cultivated outsider ridicules the grossness of country bumpkins. For a New England woman, perhaps for any New Englander, this is both a new self and a new way of expressing it. It is secular, partially comic, sophisticated, and dramatic" and, in my argument, has everything to do with status insecurities (Sayre 70).

10. Norton, in *Founding Mothers & Fathers*, argues that "in the seventeenth century clothing was a crucial identifier of persons. Not only did males and females wear very different garb, but persons of different ranks were also expected to reveal their social status on their dress. In short, one was supposed to display visually ones sex and rank to everyone else in society. Thus, ideally, new acquaintances would know how to categorize each other even before exchanging a word of greeting" (190).

11. Norbert Elias discusses the conflict between court aristocracy and a rising bourgeois strata in his argument: "inner tension [...] constitute[d] one of the most powerful driving forces of [...] social control that every member [of a particular class] exert[ed] over himself and other people in his circle" (Elias 424). Elias continues, "the constant pressure from below and the fear it induces above are, in short, one of the strongest driving forces—though not the only one—of that specifically civilized refinement which distinguishes the people of this upper class from others and finally becomes second nature to them" (Elias 424).

12. Stern explains "[Knight's] account vividly catalogues every ache, pain, chill, bad meal, and sleepless night of her own suffered on the road. Such a litany testifies to the difficulty of the journey and suggests by contrast that Knight is not accustomed to the physical strain of the traveler's life, that she is, under ordinary circumstances, sedentary, domestic, and the frequent object of attentive service." ("To Relish and to Spew," 3)

13. Bush, introduction, 97, Figure 2.4.

14. Bush, introduction, 94 fn 22.

Works Cited

Bergson, Henri. *Laughter: An Essay on the Meaning of the Comic*. Trans. by Cloudesley Brereton and Fred Rothwell. London: Macmillan, 1911.

Bourdieu, Pierre. *Distinction: A Social Critique of the Judgment of Taste*. Trans. Richard Nice. Cambridge, MA: Harvard University Press, 1984.

Brown, Richard D. *Knowledge is Power: The Diffusion of Information in Early American, 1700-1865*. Oxford: Oxford University Press, 1989.

Bush, Jr., Sargent. Introduction. *The Journal of Madame Knight*. By Sarah Kemble Knight. *Journeys in New Worlds: Early American Women's Narratives*. Ed. William L. Andrews. Madison: University of Wisconsin Press, 1990. 69-83.

"Class." *Oxford English Dictionary*. 27 Feb. 2006 <oed.com>.

Dayton, Cornelia Hughes. *Women Before the Bar: Gender, Law, and Society in Connecticut*,

1639-1789. Institute of Early American History and Culture. Chapel Hill: University of North Carolina Press, 1995.
Dietrich, Deborah. "Sarah Kemble Knight." *Dictionary of Literary Biography*. Vol. 200 *American Women Prose Writers to 1820*. Ed. Carla Mulford et al. Detroit: Gale, 1999. 221–27.
Elias, Norbert. *The Civilizing Process: Sociogenetic and Psychogenetic Investigations*. Trans. Edmund Jephcott. Rev. ed. Malden, MA: Blackwell, 2000.
Greene, Jack P. *Imperatives, Behaviors, and Identities: Essays in Early American Cultural History*. Charlottesville: University Press of Virginia, 1992.
Hawke, David Freeman. *Everyday Life in Early America*. The Everyday Life in America Series. Ed. Richard Balkin. New York: Perennial, 1988.
King, Kathryn R. "Elizabeth Singer Rowe's Tactical Use of Print." *Women's Writing and the Circulation of Ideas: Manuscript Publication in England, 1550–1800*. Eds. George L. Justice and Nathan Tinker. New York: Cambridge University Press, 2002. 158–81.
Knight, Sarah Kemble. "The Journal of Madam Knight." *Colonial American Travel Narratives*. Ed. Wendy Martin. New York: Penguin, 1994. 52–75.
Koehler, Lyle. *A Search for Power: The "Weaker Sex" in Seventeenth-Century New England*. Champaign: University of Illinois Press, 1980.
Martin, Wendy. Introduction. *The Journal of Madame Knight*. By Sarah Kemble Knight. *Colonial American Travel Narratives*. Ed. Wendy Martin. New York: Penguin, 1994. 49–52.
Michaelson, Scott. "Narrative and Class in a Culture of Consumption: The Significance of Stories in Sarah Kemble Knight's *Journal*." *College Literature* 21.2 (1994): 1–16. March 4, 2011. EBSCOhost. Online.
Micklus, Robert. "Colonial Humor: Beginning with the Butt." *Critical Essays on American Humor*. Eds. William Bedford Clark and W. Craig Turner. Boston: G.K. Hall, 1984. 139–55.
Nash, Gary B. "Poverty and Politics in Early American History." *Down and Out in Early America*. Ed. Billy G. Smith. University Park: Pennsylvania State University Press, 2004. 1–37.
Norton, Mary Beth. *Founding Mothers & Fathers: Gendered Power and the Forming of American Society*. New York: Knopf, 1996.
O'Dair, Sharon. *Class, Critics, and Shakespeare: Bottom Lines on the Culture Wars*. Ann Arbor: Michigan University Press, 2000.
_____. "Class Matters: Symbolic Boundaries and Cultural Exclusion." *This Fine Place So Far From Home: Voices of Academics in the Working Class*. Eds. C.L. Barney Dews and Carolyn Leste Maw. Philadelphia: Temple University Press, 1995.
O'Hara, Daniel T. "Class." *Critical Terms for Literary Study*. Eds. Frank Lentricchia and Thomas McLaughlin. Chicago: University of Chicago Press, 1995. 406–29.
Oring, Elliott. *Engaging Humor*. Champaign: University of Illinois Press, 2003.
Ousterhout, Anne M. *The Most Learned Woman in America: A Life of Elizabeth Graeme Ferguson*. University Park: Pennsylvania State University Press, 2004.
Perkins, Edwin J. *The Economy of Colonial America*. 2nd ed. New York: Columbia University Press, 1988.
Sayre, Robert F., ed. *American Lives: An Anthology of Autobiographical Writing*. Madison: University of Wisconsin Press, 1994.
Slotkin, Richard. *Regeneration Through Violence: The Mythology of the American Frontier, 1600–1860*. Middletown, CT: Wesleyan University Press, 1973.
Smith, Billy G. Introduction. *Down and Out in Early America*. Ed. Billy G. Smith. University Park: Pennsylvania State University Press, 2004. xi–xx.
Stern, Julia. "To Relish and to Spew: Disgust as Cultural Critique in *The Journal of Madame Knight*." *Legacy* 14.1 (1997): 1–12.
Ulrich, Laurel Thatcher. *Good Wives: Image and Reality in the Lives of Women in Northern New England, 1650–1750*. New York: Knopf, 1982.
Westbrook, Perry D. *A Literary History of New England*. Bethlehem, PA: LeHigh University Press, 1988.
_____. "The Qualities and Origins of New England Humor." *American Humor* 4.1 (1977): 5–7.
Williams, Raymond. "Class." *Keywords: A Vocabulary of Culture and Society*. Rev. ed. New York: Oxford University Press, 1983. 60–69.

Wish, Harvey. *Society and Thought in Early America: A Social and Intellectual History of the American People Through 1865.* Vol. 1. New York: David McKay, 1950.

Wulf, Karin A. "Milcah Martha Moore's Book: Documenting Culture and Connection in the Revolutionary Era." *Micah Martha Moore's Book: A Commonplace Book from Revolutionary America.* Eds. Catherine LaCourreye Bledui and Karin A. Wulf. University Park: Pennsylvania State University Press, 1997. 1–57.

Twain's Antithetical Discourses in *Adventures of Huckleberry Finn* and *The Adventures of Tom Sawyer*

JOHN F. LAVELLE

Reading Tom as a precocious boy in *Adventures of Huckleberry Finn* is a misreading, as his actions in the "evasion" section show. This reading is a standard one, though, as most readings of *The Adventures of Tom Sawyer* are misreadings. Because *Huck Finn* carries Mark Twain's main theme and purpose from *Tom Sawyer*, that of working out, through Huck, the existence of two antithetical ideologies that existed in America during Twain's time and are very much prevalent today. To truly understand the beginning "book" of this diptych, *Tom Sawyer* must be read against a reading of *Huck Finn*, the character of Tom, in the latter, informing the reading of the character of Tom in the former.

In my reading of these two books, *Tom Sawyer*, now only one half of the story, becomes the story of a boy's quest to establish himself within the power network of the social field of St. Petersburg through the exercise of will-to-power, the understanding, employment, and manipulation of the discourses of a privileged ideology. This reading, then, allows not only both parts of *Huck Finn* to cohere, but *Tom Sawyer* to fit together with *Huck Finn* as one novel with one unified theme.

The "evasion" section, the ending of *Huck Finn*, has been sometimes seen as an unneeded add-on or as Twain's inability to find a decisive ending to the story. This section has also generated myriad readings attempting to read it back into the rest of the story to make the entire story cohere, or it has been ignored altogether. Most critics, undecided on Twain's intent concerning the ending, emphasize the novel's critique of the legal and moral aspects of slavery, and the discrimination and segregation of black Americans after slavery, contending that "unlike many of his historical contemporaries, Mark Twain repeatedly explored the race question after the Civil War" (Sloan 159).

Within many of those readings proposing that *Huck Finn* is a comment on the condition of post Civil War Blacks, the authors attempt to construct the character of Tom in this novel with the same supposed childhood innocence of the Tom in *Tom Sawyer*, even though he is the perpetrator of the cruel tricks and jokes of the evasion section putting Jim, himself, and Huck at mortal risk and concocting a rather nasty sexual innuendo disparaging Aunt Sally. This defense of the character of Tom, as portrayed in *Huck Finn*, might be prompted by having first read *Tom Sawyer*, a normal approach to both books since *Tom Sawyer* comes before *Huck Finn* chronologically in both their writing and the playing out of the plots. Tom, as the protagonist of Twain's "boys' book," is normally seen as the hero of his story, saving both Muff Potter and Becky Thatcher and acquiring a large sum of money, and although not the protagonist of *Huck Finn*, Tom takes his place as a main character of the latter part of Huck's story (his characterization recalled from *Tom Sawyer*), seeing Huck stepping away from the story's center.

As stated previously, reading Tom as a precocious boy in *Huck Finn* is a misreading. A correct reading *of Tom Sawyer* is dependent on the construction of the character of Tom Sawyer in *Huck Finn*, not the other way around. To understand the ending of *Huck Finn* where Tom reappears in his true form, both stories need to be seen as two parts of one novel, so that *Tom Sawyer*, the first "book" of the novel might be read against a reading of *Huck Finn*, the second "book" and ending of the novel where the themes and meanings cohere, rather than the standard readings of *Huck Finn* against *Tom Sawyer*.

Huck Finn carries Twain's main theme and purpose from *Tom Sawyer*: that of working out, through Huck, the existence of two antithetical ideologies that existed in America during Twain's time and are very much prevalent today; the evasion section being what Paul Lynch, in a Bakhtinian reading of the story, believes is, "the final confrontation between the authoritative word and the internally-persuasive word" or what might be called discourses and ideologies (183). To truly understand the beginning "book" of this diptych, the second "book" must be read. By reading *Tom Sawyer* against a reading of *Huck Finn*, the character of Tom, in the latter, informs the reading of the character of Tom in the former. *Tom Sawyer*, now only one half of the story, becomes the story of a boy's quest to establish himself within the power network of the social field of St. Petersburg through the exercise of will-to-power through what Jean-Francois Lyotard names performance: the understanding, employment, and manipulation of the discourses of the privileged ideology. Although Tom is still the protagonist of his story, he is less than a hero, at best an antihero, at worst a villain. This reading, then, allows not only both parts of *Huck Finn* to cohere, but *Tom Sawyer* to fit together with *Huck Finn* as one novel with one unified theme.

To read *Huck Finn* outside the intertextuality it suggests with *Tom Sawyer* is a rather difficult task. Very few people in the Western World do not know the story of Tom Sawyer and usually come to either book with preconceived notions of plot and character. More than several movies and television shows have been made of the boy growing up in St. Petersburg. Almost all were constructing the character of Tom as a precocious and innocent boy existing in a bucolic world. There is the threat of Injun Joe, but it never comes to fruition. The first time Tom is mentioned in *Huck Finn* is in reference to the ending of *Tom Sawyer*, specifically the incident in which Tom hunts Huck down and coerces him into returning to "civilization" in the semblance of the Widow Douglas.

This passage, then, demands intertextuality; however, this passage, as much as any other in *Tom Sawyer,* needs to be read from the vantage point of knowing the self-serving young adult Tom is at the end of *Huck Finn*. In *Huck Finn* will-to-power through "cruelty is the sole motivation behind Tom's joke[s]," will-to-power being "the cardinal concept of [Nietzsche's] only systematic venture.... The will to power is the agency where by man ... becomes master of the earth" (Fetterly 69, Stern 80). Christine Daigle states of will-to-power,

> Nietzsche is clear: "What is happiness?—The feeling that power *increases*—that a resistance is overcome." Happiness comes upon the exercise of will to power, when one's own self is the expression of this will to power. [Yet] this assertion of power is in no way the same as the contemplative life advocated by Aristotle [3].

Thus Tom, exercising his will-to-power, threatens Huck with what sociologists call out-grouping, an act of social categorizing producing

> distinct and polarized ingroup—and outgroup—defining prototypes that assimilate relevant group members ... when applied to self (i.e., self-categorization), transforms one's self-representation, perceptions, cognitions, feelings, and behavior so that they are governed by the ingroup prototype [Hogg and Abrams 1–25].

Huck returning to the Widow Douglas's house is, for Tom, Twain, and readers, a reaffirming of in-group prototypes and justification of their ideological point of view, which states that living within the in-group of a social field of St. Petersburg constructed through dominant discourses of the social field, the authoritative word, is superior to living within the social field as a member of an out-group.

Although Alan Goldman in "Huckleberry Finn and Moral Motivation" uses *Huck Finn* to argue, "rational agents [may not] be motivated to act on their moral judgments or must be concerned for the interest of others" arguing against the assumption Huck does not act rationally in his decision to help Jim, he seems to assume Huck reasons without precepts (1). Goldman assumes humans have an instinctual understanding of right and wrong while Lynch, reading the stories as a struggle between the authoritative word and the internally-persuasive word, suggests "the distinction between the authoritative and internally-persuasive word can ... distinguish the central differences between *Adventures of Huckleberry Finn* and *The Adventures of Tom Sawyer*" assuming humans do not have an instinctual understanding of right and wrong but that there exist precepts for Huck to draw upon, although Lynch does not extrapolate as to where the authoritative word and the internally-persuasive word originate (173). The authoritative word, the set of discourses of which Huck must decide against, and the internally-persuasive word exist within the available metanarratives within the ideologies, permeating his reality, the internally-persuasive word having been subordinated to the authoritative word or the privileged discourse. Thus in *Huck Finn* Twain presents two preexisting core ideologies antithetical to each other, constructed from differing metanarratives, and it is between these two ideologies Huck struggles, the dominant, privileged or authoritarian ideology of *Tom Sawyer* and a subordinated equalitarian ideology of *Huck Finn*.

Coincidently, Nietzsche is contemplating these same ideologies around the same time Twain is working through them in *Huck Finn*. Although it is doubtful either author read the other, both seem to have observed these antithetical ideologies within contemporary society. However, these authors come to opposite conclusions. This might be because Twain was exposed to the aftermath of slavery, segregation, and the subjugation of the working class in a country whose major metanarrative constructs that country as a classless society in its belief in equality for all humans, while Nietzsche lived in a society that prided itself on its class structure and where slavery had been abolished long before his birth.

Nietzsche proposed a concept of two antithetical ideologies when he proposed there existed two core moralities: master/noble and slave in *Beyond Good and Evil*. According to Mark Warren, "Although Nietzsche did not use the term 'ideology' ... he did write of the way culture is made up of ideals, idols, illusions and falsehoods" (543). Derrida and other poststructuralists allude tangentially to these same ideologies in the discussion of the existence of a transcendental signifier. Although they contest the existence of a transcendental signifier where all meaning arrives, this does not disallow the belief in such logocentrism. The difference within the two core ideologies in the Western World centers on the placement of this transcendental signifier. Simply put, the locus of meaning, or the transcendental signifier, and thus morality, is ideological. This signifier exists either internal to the person or external of the person, as Nietzsche suggests in his two moralities, also suggesting no natural or genetically inherited moral core exists such as Lynch's internally-persuasive word or Goldman's instinctual understanding of right and wrong. Tom certainly does not have it in *Huck Finn*.

Twain begins *Tom Sawyer* constructing the reality of the social field of St. Petersburg from narratives given to him through the discourses of the dominant hegemony of the community of Hannibal, Missouri[1] not questioning the "truths" he is perpetuating throughout the story. As he states,

> MOST of the adventures recorded in this book really occurred; one or two were experiences of my own, the rest those of boys who were schoolmates of mine. Huck Finn [*The Adventures of Tom Sawyer* Huck Finn] is drawn from real life; Tom Sawyer also, but not from an individual [2].

Twain is, then, reconstructing the social fields and the discourses of Hannibal, Missouri, and much of the United States from the privileged dominant discourses he's grown up with re-inscribing the positionalities within the social fields as prescribed by the dominant discourses themselves. Chantal Mouffe states, "Within every society, each social agent is inscribed in a multiplicity of social relations.... All these social positions determine positionalities or subject positions and every social agent is therefore the locus of many subject positions" (90). These discourses of each social field allow for subjugation of persons as specific subjects with specific positions within the field. "The individual is interpellated as a (free) subject in order that he shall submit freely to the commandments of the Subject ... in order that he shall (freely) accept his subjection ... in order that he shall make the gestures and actions of his subjection 'all by himself'" (Althusser 123).

Perpetuated by the social field of St. Petersburg are discourses allowing for a position of privilege by certain individuals over other individuals, allowing for unequal treatment of others including the enslavement of certain peoples, and yet this same ideology perpetuates a discourse of civility, Christian purpose, and equality, its antithetical ideology. While Marx saw within capitalism the seeds of its own destruction, that of competition, over production, and the development of the proletariat, Gramsci complicated this notion by insisting that revolution would be fought, not with guns, but with ideas, a dominant hegemony attempting to defend its discourses against those discourses of subordinate hegemonies who wished to displace the dominant ideology and its discourses. Marx's paradox still exists in Gramsci's configuration. The dominant privileged ideology must disseminate an ideology antithetical to it, which critiques the tenets of this same privileged ideology as morally reprehensible in order to maintain its exclusiveness and thus power. The reason for this paradox is simple. A constant struggle exists to create, maintain, and exercise agency within the social field through exclusion and inclusion to gain and control power (agency) in its real sense, which "is neither given nor exchanged, nor recovered, but rather exercised, and it only exists in action" (Foucault, "Body/Power" 89). The majority of people must be excluded while a select minority included. *Tom Sawyer* is thus a story about one boy's quest for power through performance within the social field by the control, understanding, and manipulation of the dominant discourses, which is performance. According to Lyotard, performance is the ability to generate proofs of "a unitary and totalizing truth" (12). It is "designed to win agreement for the addressees ... [while] increase[ing] the ability to produce proof, it also increases the ability to be right" (Lyotard 46). Tom is in-grouped and Huck is out-grouped because a power network gains its power through inclusion through performance, something Tom is adept at, and exclusion or out-grouping those who manifest alternate discourses.

For Tom, in both stories, the transcendental signifier exists within himself. Right and wrong depend on how the situation affects his well-being. This self-centered ideology is not unusual for a small boy. However, rather than grow out of it, this self-centeredness intensifies as Tom matures, and as he gains more power, he feels less guilt until, in *Huck Finn*, he is incapable of feeling guilt at all. *Tom Sawyer* begins with Tom hiding in the closet to avoid Aunt Polly's wrath. Although he is found out, he still gets away. The next day he plays hooky and lies about it, and when his brother notices his shirt button is sewed with the wrong colored thread, Tom vows revenge on his brother rather than feeling guilty for lying or playing hooky. Tom attacks a new boy in town, reasserting his dominance, his position of authority, and reasserting the discourse of the social field of the "schoolyard" disallowing the language of clothing to be introduced into the discourse. There is the famous fence whitewash "fraud," and just after that he gets his revenge on Sid. Instead of learning Bible verses and receiving tickets, he buys tickets from other children with the capital he has acquired through his whitewash scam. Tom runs away to Jackson Island and returns on the day of his funeral, purposely orchestrated to take full advantage of the situation. Tom then attempts to pass himself off as a profit, one of the few times he feels guilty for hurting his aunt. He drops Amy Lawrence when he sees Becky Thatcher and sets his sights on Becky after working for several months to acquire Amy Lawrence's unconditional vow of love. Two times he allows himself to be punished to get into the good graces of Becky. While these last actions seem romantic, his motives might be questioned, especially when he takes the blame for her tearing a page in the teacher's book. The underlying purposes of Tom's actions question the very idea of what Becky means when she asks "Tom, how *could* you be so noble?" unless Twain was taking an ironic poke at Nietzsche, since Tom's motive is to gain access to Becky and her father, a less than noble act (*Tom Sawyer* 132). Again, Judge Thatcher, after informed Tom has lied to save Becky from a whipping, calls the lie "noble, a generous, a magnanimous lie—a lie that was worthy to hold up its head and march down through history breast to breast with George Washington's lauded Truth about the hatchet" (211). Twain here may just be poking fun at the absurdity of discourses which justify their means by their ends. These transgressions are overlooked by most readers and, in fact, are not considered transgressions at all and chalked up to a (white middle-class) boys-will-be-boys explanation. Neither a Black child nor a child from Huck's class would be treated so magnanimously for those same transgressions.

Huck has been out-grouped by the discourses of the social field of St. Petersburg. Huck is "the juvenile pariah of the village.... Huckleberry was cordially hated and dreaded by all the mothers in town" (46). Huck's greatest threat to the discourses is his defiance of the major narratives within the dominant discourse. "Huckleberry came and went at his own free will.... He did not have to go to school or to church or call any being master or obey anybody" (*Tom Sawyer* 47). Huck's threat to the privileged discourses is brought to the reader's attention when Tom uses Huck's designation as one of the out-group to get access to Becky, admitting to being with Huck so that he might be punished and sent to sit with the "girls."

While Tom seems to defy the narrative of the dominant ideology of St. Petersburg, he does so in a prescribed way bringing to himself a sort of honorific attention by demonstrating his ability to manipulate these same discourses. Importantly almost all Tom's transgressions seem to result in positive deeds for, at least, the "right" and "good" people of the town, allowing for a reaffirming of Twain's and the readers' discourse. After all, everything comes out all right in the end for the right people. That others suffer for Tom's actions seems to go unnoticed or given short shrift.

At the beginning of *Tom Sawyer*, Tom has already positioned himself within a power network within a sub-field of the social field of St. Petersburg, that of the male children. Tom's authority to control the discourse of this social field comes partially from his willingness and ability to physically injure other children. Twain writes of the attempt of "one poor chap" to use Tom's supposed death as social capital "who had no other grandeur to offer said … 'Well, Tom Sawyer he licked me once.' But that bid for glory was a failure. Most of the boys could say that" (115). These acts of aggression, whether physical or emotional, are seen by Twain, readers, and the community of St. Petersburg as honorific acts. In fact, Tom's quest to acquire a position of influence through becoming aligned with the adult power network is nothing more than a series of honorific acts as a show of performance.

His ability to injure children, to place himself in a position of authority, gives him control of the language game, "various categories of utterance[s] [which] can be defined in terms of the rules ... determining their properties" (Lyotard 10).

His authority concerning his right to manipulate the rules to the language game is never challenged except once by Joe Harper who is also a member of the in group. Tom seems to have an intimate understanding of the rules of the language game and thus an ability to manipulate these rules. The other children follow because "it is part of our language game ... that a speaker may, without ultimately giving any justification, follow his own confident inclination that this way ... is the right way to respond rather than another way" (Kripke 87–88).

In both novels, Tom "insists" on playing games that allow him to be placed into a position of authority, allowing him to control the rules of the game. Although many of the games are make believe, boy-play in *Tom Sawyer*, this taking a position of authority is practice for adulthood and is practice for Tom to manipulate the rules of the language games of the ideologies within the social field of St. Petersburg as Judge Thatcher does, as is evident in the evasion section of *Huck Finn*. When Tom is tasked with whitewashing Aunt Polly's fence, Tom redefines the discourse's definition of work, thus redefining his position within the social field of the young boys in the community. Whitewashing a fence is no longer work, but a rare opportunity only allowed to those few who are "capable." This new narrative out-groups Ben Rogers who instinctively understands this out-grouping to be a bad thing for him. The act of whitewashing the fence becomes symbolic capital for Ben Rogers and social capital for the other boys. Having succeeded with Ben, Tom "planned the slaughter of more innocents" (20). By changing the discourse, Tom exchanges this capital for other types of capital capable of being used later in exchange for tickets for a Bible to use as influence, symbolic capital, to impress Becky Thatcher, and importantly her father and uncle, the judge and lawyer.

The next instance involves Tom and his "bosom" friend Joe Harper.[2] Both Tom and Joe take on the authoritarian position of generals conducting the battle but not bothering to fight the war themselves, "conduct[ing] the field operations by orders delivered by aide-de-camp" (23). When Joe and Tom play fantasy games learned from books, such as *Robin Hood*, sanctioned by the social field of school,[3] and the discourse of the adults, Tom insists that the game proceed as the book states, that, in fact, Joe must "die" since Tom is Robin Hood who cannot die. Finally Tom and Joe, having been usurped from their authoritarian positions and blaming everyone else for their misfortune, decide to lead a life of crime by running away to Jackson Island and becoming pirates culminating in their advantageous reappearance at their own funerals not only regaining their authority over the children but gaining authority within the adult power network.

Tom also plays games in *Huck Finn*. However, there is a difference in how the games are played. The stakes and rewards are different, although the "games" are the same "play." These games lack the innocence and naivety of the games in *Tom Sawyer*. In *Tom Sawyer*, Tom still has the immaturity to almost believe he is a pirate, although he is also playing a game of dominance within this game over both Joe and Huck.

The adventure on Jackson Island seems innocent enough, Huck being the more mature of the players at least at living on his own. Although both Joe and Tom become homesick and guilt-ridden, Tom overcomes these altruistic feelings to orchestrate a return, or as Harold Aspiz contends, "Tom cannot resist climaxing this game of death with the spectacle of his own resurrection," a resurrection that will allow him to manipulate the social field through the use of the discourses of sorrow and the honorific position of the young dead (145). In accomplishing this feat of deception, Tom has not only made a move within the social field of the town, but he has also learned that in certain circumstances you can get away with certain acts if the results are in some way honorific, recognizing the importance of honorific acts within the ideology of the privileged group of the social field of St. Petersburg. He recognizes not only the esteem such an act brings, but the power he gains through his exercise of will-to-power. As the narrator states, from this moment on, Tom "would live for glory" (121). Tom has been resurrected, but not as the child he was before. This act is Tom's first community-wide public act gaining a type of honor within the community, incidentally anchored in a type of cruelty through taking advantage of the suffering of those who loved him and the relief when he is found alive.

In *Tom Sawyer*, Tom is being groomed to take his place within the power network of the social field. All that is left to decide is how close to the power locus he will be situated. This is reflected in his punishments, when and why punished, and the attitude toward Tom and his wrongdoings. The sadistic characterization of the teacher aside, Tom's harshest punishments are accrued for acts of laziness and most duplicitous acts are left unpunished (thus in a way rewarded) or given civil punishments. When he does not immediately begin to whitewash the fence, Aunt Polly whips him. "In another moment he was flying down the street with his pail and a tingling rear" (18).

A major plot point in Twain's novel is Tom's quest to win Becky Thatcher. Although Twain disguises Tom's motives as romantic, Twain still suggests Tom's desire for Becky is at least a reification of her to her status.

As Robert E. Mackay argues, "Tom will avoid punishment if he can, except when being punished serves some ulterior motive," specifically the two instances when he allows himself to be punished, one to acquire the seat next to Becky and the other to impress Becky and to put her into emotional and physical debt to him (78).

Acquiring Becky and her status will allow him to secure a power position within the adult power network. As Tom passes the home of Jeff Thatcher, he spies "a new girl in the garden—a lovely little blue-eyed creature with yellow hair plaited into two long tails, white summer frock and embroidered pantalettes" (24). Twain writes the Thatchers as major players within the power locus of St. Petersburg, Jeff Thatcher's father a lawyer, Becky's father a judge. She, then, is the catch of the town among all the young girls, beautiful, and associated with the power locus or what is called today being well connected. She is solidly of the privileged class and, of course, the correct "woman" for the hero of the novel to acquire, reaffirming the in-group/out-group discourse of the readers, a type of Weberian class bigotry. Although readers would deny Tom is making the same observation, only a week before Tom had gotten Amy Lawrence to confess her love for him. "He had been months winning her" and suddenly he is no longer in love with Amy. Tom's fickleness questions whether he is even capable of understanding the emotion of love for another person. Rather he is only capable of understanding love for himself.

Tom sets about winning Becky, unable to acquire her until he takes the punishment for Becky tearing the page of the teacher's anatomy book. Although Twain seems to construct an innocent enough scenario of two young adolescents developing mutual crushes on one another, the innocence is less than innocent as Becky's appearance to Little Eva in *Uncle Tom's Cabin*, the consummate angel of the house destined to die before she could obtain puberty, becomes ironic when Twain has this "Little Eva" searching out a naked picture of a male. The "noble act" of Tom taking the punishment for Becky is certainly less than noble since it has ulterior motives, that of acquiring Becky's emotional debt, thus her "love." Becky's love is, for Tom, social and symbolic capital, "the degree of accumulated prestige, celebrity, consecration or honour and is founded on a dialectic of knowledge (*connaissance*) and recognition (*reconnaissance*)" (Johnson 7). Tom, however, is not just acquiring Becky as a trophy, as Veblen contends, suggesting civilization pivoted on the idea of honorific acts, of seeking trophies, symbolic capital, as proof of these acts, one of the first trophies being the acquisition of women. Becky is also Tom's entrance into the adult power network of St. Petersburg.

When Tom and Huck witness Injun Joe discovering the "treasure," Tom has an understanding of his position within the privileged class of

St. Petersburg and knows, by being a member of the in-group, he might steal Injun Joe's treasure with social impunity since Injun Joe is one of the marginalized out-group. Whether Twain was tweaking the reader's nose is doubtful, but, although Joe did have in his possession ill-gotten goods, neither he nor his partner stole the treasure but found it. Thus Joe has rights to the treasure, but as Twain writes it, Joe has forfeited his rights to anything by his heinous acts, and Tom is the paragon of innocence, allowing the reader to accept Tom's larcenous plans. Carter Revard contends the characterization of Injun Joe, even his derogatory name, is a reflection of Twain's hatred for Native Americans "and he expressed this hatred quite viciously" (643). Joe's murder of Dr. Robinson is not the impetus that allows readers to accept Tom's planned theft of the gold, but Tom's location versus Joe's position in the social field, the discourse allowing the reader to out-group Joe. Tom, the reader, and maybe Twain see the theft and ownership of the treasure as Tom's right or to say his privileged (noble) ideology places him in a position giving him the right to take it from its rightful owner, more rightful than Tom or Huck who end up with the loot.

Tom's final move for Twain is to take Becky to the cave. By this time, though, the reader has bought into the prepubescent purity of both Tom and Becky—an idea Twain subverts since neither Tom nor Becky are that innocent. Tom has no difficulty taking advantage of any situation which is advantageous to him, thus being worldly enough to recognize an advantageous situation when it presents itself. Becky tears the page in the anatomy book because she wants to view a picture of the male body. This might be chalked up to childhood curiosity, but it also points to her knowledge of the differences between man and woman and why.

Revard states, "Twain's attempt to make a stageable drama of *Tom Sawyer*, which presents Tom—once he has heroically outwitted Injun Joe in the cave, and gotten Becky and himself out of it—as telling his Aunt Polly that he and Becky were 'married' in the cave" alluding to Tom and Becky doing more in the cave than just searching for a way out (659). This seems a bit of a stretch, less, though, if Tom is aggressively attempting to acquire Becky and the blatant sexual innuendo toward Aunt Sally suggests Tom has acquired sexual knowledge at some time either before the ending of *Tom Sawyer* or during Huck's separation from St. Petersburg in *Huck Finn*. There is no doubt, though, Tom is attempting to isolate Becky physically and emotionally. He is not only physically acquiring Becky, but by "saving her," (he, of course, put her in danger in the first place), he acquires Judge Thatcher and the goal of his quest. He has become the hero within the social field of St. Petersburg, acquiring a position within the adult power network in that social field and now able to define the discourses within the field.

By first constructing the character of Tom through Twain's characterization of him in *Huck Finn*, the character of Tom in *Tom Sawyer* becomes much less naïve. He is inculcated within the privileged group of the social field and chooses and adheres to a privileged ideology that allows him a space to exercise his will-to-power. This change, then, from Tom of *Tom Sawyer* to Tom in *Huck Finn* is really not change at all but a continuation of Tom's exercise of his will-to-power, usually accepted by readers at an ideological level, accepting Tom as Twain constructed him on a surface level in *Tom Sawyer*, as, if not the precocious boy, then the upstanding young adult of St. Petersburg and not as the heartless young man he is in *Huck Finn*.

In *Huck Finn* dominance, through applied cruelty, is the only reason and goal of Tom's games. He is now consciously exercising his will-to-power. One of Twain's more brutal yet subtle critiques of Tom and his privileged ideology in *Huck Finn* is when he alludes to Tom as Don Quixote. Although allowing Tom his position of authority, Huck now doubts the veracity of what Tom proposes as truths. Tom, assured in his authority and the narratives he has come to understand are truths, ridicules Huck calling him a "numbskull" and refers to *Don Quixote* as proof of his authority and the truth of his narrative (*Huck Finn* 21). Twain is alluding to the tentative grasp on reality of Alonso Quijano. He thus positions Tom as Don Quixote and Huck as Sancho Pansa who sees the world as it is. Twain continues this satirical critique of the metanarratives of this ideology in the Grangerfords and Shepherdsons episode, critiquing several different aspects of his contemporary culture, including romantic, sentimental, and gothic literature. Twain, like Cervantes, spoofs the chivalric romances of his day. Emmeline Grangerford also echoes what Twain thought to be the overly romanticized ideology of the South in its construction of itself as a planter society reminiscent of the romanticized ideal of the feudal society of Europe in such works as *Le Morte d'Arthur* and works of Scott and the representations of plantation fiction after the war, a nostalgic recreation of the antebellum South having only a slim resemblance to the actual South.

Although the ideology of the Grangerfords and Shepherdsons would seem different than Tom's privileged ideology, it has the same basic tenets. There is a quixotic aspect to the episode. Col. Grangerford's physical resemblance to Don Quixote is telling. "He was well born, as the saying is, and that's worth as much in a man as it is in a horse … very tall and very slim and had a darkish-paly complexion" (112). Like Quixote's ideology, the Grangerfords' and Shepherdsons' ideology demands honorific acts and thus the feud. Buck, the thirteen-year-old son of Col. Grangerford, berates Huck when he suggests that Baldy Shepherdson was a coward for killing Bud, an unarmed fourteen-year-old Grangerford. To Buck the killing was worthy of honor as was the dying. Veblen states of this "noble" class, "there is no point in cultural evolution prior to which fighting does not occur. But the point in question is not as to the occurrence of combat, [but] to an habitual bellicose frame of mind—a prevalent habit of judging facts and events from the point of view of the fight" (Veblen 12). It is "when the predatory attitude has become the habitual and accredited spiritual attitude for the members of the group" when the fight has become the dominant note in the current theory of life (12).

The narratives they use to construct their reality come from a privileged discourse, Nietzsche's noble morality. Mark Migotti states, "in two salient respects Nietzsche's primitive masters resemble to the point of indiscernibility Veblen's leisured classes ... in their orientation toward intrinsic value, with disdain for goods of mere survival and comfort, and their predilection for boisterous mayhem" (745–79). Veblen's leisure class begins as a violent class and changes little throughout history other than their "acts" of violence. Their acts are not honorable deeds for the most part but deeds to gain public honor, honorific. Like Tom, they act in a way to gain glory and avoid disprase. However, as Veblen states, an "honorific act is in the last analysis little if anything else than a recognized successful act of aggression" (11). Tom's statement that he would "live for glory" is echoed in *Huck Finn* when Tom confesses to Aunt Polly, "I wanted the adventure of it; and I'd 'a' waded neck deep in blood" (294).

The Tom in *Huck Finn* is worldly and capable of purposeful cruelty and now considers others as pawns in his games, including Huck and especially Jim. Once Huck explains his plan to steal Jim, Tom immediately goes about insulting it and Huck, reestablishing himself as authority, and stating, "It wouldn't make no more talk than breaking up a soap factory" (238). Tom then comes up with a plan of his own—wanting it to be an honorific act bringing glory to himself. He begins the plan by first usurping Aunt Sally and her husband's position of authority through masquerading as "William Thompson," a stranger from Hicksville, Ohio. Tom kisses Aunt Sally stating afterward, "they all said kiss her; and said she'd like it. They all said it—every one of them" (234). It is a cruel innuendo accusing Aunt Sally of a lack of propriety if not something much worse, a grave insult and importantly a sexually oriented one. The innuendo is purposely worded in such a way that once Tom says he is Sid Sawyer (another lie) the innuendo must be reinterpreted and Tom, who once seemed to be the perpetrator of a grave insult, looks to be a victim of a gross misunderstanding gaining capital within the family and relegating Aunt Sally and her husband to a subordinate position.

The character of Tom, then, in *Tom Sawyer* is congruent with the character of Tom in *Huck Finn*, except now he is lacking the sympathy or empathy Huck seems to have in abundance. Twain seems to see Tom's hard-heartedness and Huck's open-heartedness as not some inherited propensity but due to their upbringing and their station in life or to say their position in the social field and their habitus. Habitus, according to Bourdieu, is the

> generative principles of distinct and distinctive practices. [...] But habitus are also classificatory schemes, principles of classification, principles of vision and divisions, different tastes. They make distinctions between what is good and what is bad [...] right and wrong [...] distinguished and what is vulgar [...] but the divisions are not identical. [...] Some behavior or even the same good can appear distinguished to one person and pretentious to someone else, cheap or showy to another [8].

This is, then, the core of what Twain is attempting to work through in *Huck Finn*, the existence of two antithetical core ideologies existing in America allowing for slavery, classism, the continued discrimination of black people, including segregation, and a myriad of other bigoted acts while purporting to be humanist, Christian, and democratic.

The first part of *Huck Finn* concerns itself with Huck's realization of these two antithetical ideologies, the dominant or privileged one whose discourse, through its position of authority, narrates the precepts of the morality of the social field, and the subordinate ideology that contends a person's deeds or actions toward others defines that person rather than the position the person occupies within the social field, an equalitarian ideology.

Twain, from the beginning of *Huck Finn*, critiques the tenets of the privileged discourse. At the end of *Tom Sawyer*, and the beginning of *Huck Finn*, Huck runs away from the Widow Douglas who feels indebted to him for helping to save her life and wants to civilize him, to teach him to be an acceptable member of St. Petersburg, taking a position nearer to the power network within the social field. Tom convinces Huck to go back to the widow with a veiled threat of out-grouping. "But Huck we can't let you into the gang if you ain't respectable, you know ... a robber is more high-toned than what a pirate is—as a general thing. In most countries they're awful high up in the nobility—dukes and such" (*Tom Sawyer* 213). Beverly Skeggs asserts,

> Appearance has always mattered. It is the means by which others are recognized and it is a part of the way we want ourselves to be recognized. But this is not just a matter of interpersonal, or even dialogical construction of subjectivity; it is a matter of how symbolic violence may or may not occur [129].

Huck's reply to Tom's threat is, "You wouldn't shet me out would you, Tom?" (*Tom Sawyer* 213). Huck attempts to become civilized to keep the only friend he seems to have in the world, but he sees in Tom Sawyer and others the contradictions inherent within the discourses, seeing morality as "a product of social development; there is nothing immutable about it; it serves social interests; these interests are contradictory; morality more than any other form of ideology has a class character" (Trotsky 21). Huck's comment on the widow's refusal to allow him to smoke when she took snuff is Twain's comment on the existence of contradictory narratives within the discourse. "Of course that was all right, because she done it herself" (*Huck Finn* 10).

Miss Watson, in an attempt to civilize Huck to not "put your feet up there ... scrunch up like that ... gap and stretch like that, Huckleberry—why don't you try to behave," informs the boy of Hell, although these acts would not get him into Hell but would out-group him in the social field of St. Petersburg (11). Huck doesn't seem to think Hell all that bad. Obviously Huck does not have a good grasp on the idea of eternal punishment, but Twain is actually commenting on Huck's lack of understanding of social, symbolic, and cultural capital. Having been indoctrinated in Puritan values, Miss Watson strives to be one of the elect. "She was going to live so as to go to the good place" (*Huck Finn* 11). Yet she owns slaves, which, in her privileged ideology, is morally correct and her "morality" is more in line with guaranteeing her a place within the privileged group of St. Petersburg than a place in Heaven.

As Tom was a tourist in Huck's world, Twain shows Huck to be a transient in Tom's. While Huck for the first time consciously separates himself from Tom's discourse, thinking "that stuff was only just one of Tom Sawyer's lies…. It had all the marks of Sunday school," Huck becomes accustomed to other discourses of the social field (*Huck Finn* 22). "So the longer I went to school the easier it got to be. I was sort of getting used to the widow's ways, too, and they warn't so raspy on me" (23). However, Huck is quick to recognize his true position to the power locus, understanding the protections afforded to Tom by the social field will do little to protect him from his own father. He offers Judge Thatcher all his money almost immediately after recognizing his father's boot print, understanding the reality of the situation, that his life is in danger.

In the social field in which Pap resides, and thus Huck, wealth is a detriment and may be the reason Pap is killed. The physical brutality of Pap's ideology is the physical resistance to the out-grouping of the privileged ideology of those people no more brutal than Tom, but with less ability to be manipulative, marginalized from access to social power, acting out their will-to-power with physical brutality. According to Foucault, "The targets [of resistance] are power effects…. They are anarchistic struggles…. They are struggles which question the status of the individual ... the 'government of individualization' ... struggles against the privilege of knowledge" (129–30).

The king and duke are Twain's most ardent condemnation of privileged ideology. Both the king and duke are capable of perpetrating any act to gain wealth and power. Daniel Hoffman contends

> [It] is curious how closely the King and Duke's stock-in-trade of shifty disguises parallels Tom's dreams of glory memorized from old romances. Tom was always concerning himself about captive or outcast nobles; they turn up as the dispossessed Duke of Bilgewater and the lamented Dauphin of France [328].

They are actors in the truest sense as Tom is, capable of taking on any part or saying anything to gain an advantage within a social field. While the Grangerfords and the Shepherdsons are Twain's critique of misplaced chivalry, the king and the duke are Twain's critique of the historic violent class, the royalty of old and the robber barons of his day. The king and duke, like Tom, recite from canonized literary texts. These are "narratives of origins, which make up much of the core of western thought" (Strozier 21). Derek Hook believes "the 'top heaviness' of primary texts [assure] they will remain permanent" that their usefulness in generating discourses allowing one group to gain and maintain power over others assures the texts' survival (107).

The episode of the king and duke is split by the killing of old Boggs by Colonel Sherburn. Twain describes Sherburn as "a proud-looking man about fifty-five—and he was a heap the best dressed man in town" (*Huck Finn* 149). Again Twain starts this episode with a comical rendition of the town and the people in it. The town seems to be ramshackle and the people are described as loafers except those who'd gone to the revival meeting. However, the scene turns tragic as Sherburn guns down Boggs in the street. Twain seeing Sherburn's killing of Boggs as an honorable act is doubtful. Neither was it an honorific act. Besides it being Twain's condemnation of the mobs of the South and of the South after the Civil War, reminiscent of William Faulkner's *As I Lay Dying* and *Light in August*, the incident was a condemnation of the discourses which allowed dishonorable deeds to be seen as honorable, referring back to the discourses and acts of the duke and king. This section specifically targets lynching alluding to the shocking attempt by Tom to symbolically lynch Jim at the beginning of *Huck Finn*.

What Paul Lynch sees as a rejection of the authoritative word for the internally-persuasive word is actually Huck's rejection of the discourses of a privileged ideology for those of an equalitarian ideology. This moment of Huck's change, seen as an epiphany of Jim's humanity, is actually a two-step process. It starts when the duke and king attempt to cheat the Wilkes daughters out of their late father's fortune. Anna Mary Wells argues that "Huck has always accepted humbly and unquestionably the view that society is right and he is wrong," believing, more than once, he did not fit within the "truths" of the social fields (1131).

Huck is beginning to doubt the discourse's position of authority when he makes up his mind to help the Wilkes. The Wilkes sisters are the first white people Huck meets who put into practice the discourses of the equalitarian ideology as the older Wilkes sister explains, "it don't make no difference what he said—that ain't the thing. The thing is for you to treat him kind" (*Huck Finn* 181). Their ideology insists they define themselves as good or evil through how their actions affect others. They are kind to Huck even though several of them are sure he's been lying. Their ideology is much closer to his own ideology, that of the slaves who fed him when he was hungry in *Tom Sawyer* and Jim in *Huck Finn*. It gives Huck the courage to act on his own beliefs, stealing back the Wilkes girls' money and exposing the duke and king as frauds who he says "was enough to make a body ashamed of the human race" (169).

Craig Taylor argues that "Huck is conflicted; on the one hand there are the demands of a conscience distorted by racism, on the other there is his compassionate response to Jim," the same response of the Wilkes toward him (61). The incidents concerning the Wilkes sisters have also given Huck the courage to question the privileged ideology itself and its right to its dominant position. It becomes the turning point for Huck. He decides to go against these established discourses and their truths. He is unable to rationalize against the ideology being the truth, but comes to the conclusion that he will live by the other set of discourses he has been given when he decides to help Jim, stating, "all right, then, I'll go to hell" (220).

Finally, Huck only capitulates to Tom at the Phelp's farm because Tom seems to be going along with Huck's idea to steal Jim out of slavery, Huck mistaking his motives. This allows Tom to again gain authority over Huck and the situation. At the end, though, Huck, unable to completely reject the narratives of the dominant discourse, and he decides to "light out for the territory ahead of the rest because Aunt Sally she's going to adopt me and sivilize me and I can't stand it. I been there before" (298). Huck's last encounter with Tom "is not just the uncomfortable encounter of the grown-up adolescent with the still-childish one ... what Huck finally sees in Tom is unendurable" (Wells 1131). This is his and thus Twain's condemnation of what Huck sees as the "sivilized" discourse, which allows people like Tom to subordinate others to their will.

Twain was a humanist and a contemporary of Nietzsche. Twain and Nietzsche observed these two antithetical ideologies (moralities) within their societies: privileged (noble/master) and equalitarian (slave). Twain's reaction to the two core ideologies of the Western world was polar opposite to Nietzsche's seeing the privileged ideology as inhumane and the cause of most of the suffering in the world, while seeing the equalitarian ideology as altruistic and actually noble.

These two books, then, cohere into one novel, as do the two major sections of *Huck Finn*, as critiques of a privileged ideology, the dominant ideology within most social fields in America during Twain's lifetime and the present time. Although a prequel is usually written after the main story, because *Huck Finn* is a major work of American literature and the major work of the two novels, the book *Tom Sawyer* becomes a prequel to *Huck Finn*, because *Tom Sawyer* must be read in light of *Huck Finn* so that *Huck Finn* might explain the true character of Tom within *Tom Sawyer* and the true relationship of the novels: how a child might be inculcated into the privileged discourses of a dominant ideology of a social field that allows for unequal treatment of humans by others, and how that boy might grow from a precocious child to a cruel and inhumane self-serving adult. The main thrust, then, of *Huck Finn* is to expose the paradoxes within the dominant ideology in America at the time and to suggest that a better ideology for America would be an equalitarian ideology now subordinated to the self-serving privileged ideology.

Notes

1. Hannibal, MO, or St Petersburg, according to Bourdieu, designates a social space or field, "a structure of objective relations which determines the possible form of interactions and of the representations the interactors can have in them." Social spaces or fields "are also strategic emplacements, fortresses to be defended and captured in a field of struggles" (*Distinctions* 244).
2. Notably, Huck is not, nor is ever, Tom's bosom friend. Tom "did not care to have Huck's company in public places" (*Tom Sawyer* 166).
3. For Althusser, the state educational system, by this time, has replaced organized religion as the major ideological state apparatus.

Works Cited

Althusser, Louis. *Lenin and Philosophy, and Other Essays*. Trans. by Ben Brewster. New York: New York Monthly Review Press, 1972.
Aspiz, Harold. "Tom Sawyer's Games of Death." *Studies in the Novel* 27.2 (1995): 141–53.
Bourdieu, Pierre. *Practical Reason*. Translated by Richard Nice. 1994. Stanford: Stanford University Press, 1998.
Daigle, Christine. "Nietzsche: Virtue Ethics ... Virtue Politics." *Journal of Nietzsche Studies* 32 (2006): 1–21.
Fetterly, Judith. "Disinchantment: Tom Sawyer in *Huckleberry Finn*." *PLMA* 87.1 (1972): 69–75.
Foucault, Michel. "Body/Power." *Power/Knowledge: Selected Interviews and Other Writings 1972–1977*. Ed. Colin Gordon. New York: Pantheon Books, 1980.
_____. *The Essential Foucault*. Ed. Paul Rabinow and Nikolas Rose. New York: The New Press, 2003.
Goldman, Alan. "Huckleberry Finn and Moral Motivation." *Philosophy and Literature* 34.1 (2010): 1–16.
Hoffman, Daniel. *Form and Fable in American Fiction*. Charlottesville: Virginia University Press, 1994.
Hogg, Michael, and Dominic Abrams. "Social Identity and Social Cognition: Historical

Background and Current Trends." *Social Identity and Social Cognition*. Eds. Dominic Abrams and Michael A. Hogg. Oxford: Blackwell, 1999. 1–25.
Hook, Derek. *Foucault, Psychology and the Analytics of Power*. New York: Palgrave MacMillan, 2007.
Johnson, Randal. Introduction to Bourdieu, Pierre. *The Field of Cultural Production*. Ed. Randal Johnson. New York: Columbia University Press. 1993.
Kripke, Saul, A. *Wittgenstein on Rules and Private Language: an Elementary Exposition*. Cambridge, MA: Harvard University Press, 1982.
Lynch, Paul. "Not Trying to Talk Alike and Succeeding: The Authoritative Word and Internally Persuasive Word in *Tom Sawyer* and *Huckleberry Finn*." *Studies in the Novel* 38.2 (2006): 172–86.
Lyotard, Jean-François. *The Postmodern Condition: A Report on Knowledge*. Translated by Geoff Bennington and Brian Massumi. Minneapolis: University of Minnesota Press, 1984.
Mackay, Robert, E. "Noble Delinquence and Kind Complicity: Themes in Restorative Justice for Juveniles from Twain's *Tom Sawyer* and Chopin's 'A Night in Acadie.'" *British Journal of Community Justice* 2.2 (2003): 67–80.
Migotti, Mark. "Slave Morality, Socrates, and the Bushmen: A Reading of the First Essay of *On the Genealogy of Morals*." *Philosophy and Phenomenological Research* 58.4 (1998): 745–79.
Mouffe, Chantal. "Hegemony and New Political Subjects: Toward a New Concept of Democracy." *Marxism and the Interpretation of Culture*. Eds. Cary Nelson and Lawrence Grossberg. Champaign: University of Illinois Press, 1988. 89–104.
Revard, Carter. "Why Mark Twain Murdered Injun Joe—And Will Never Be Indicted." *The Massachusetts Review* 4.4 (1999/2000): 643–70.
Skeggs, Beverley. "The Appearance of Class: Challenges in Gay Space." *Cultural Studies and the Working Class: Subject to Change*. Ed. Sally Munt. London: Cassell, 2000. 129–50.
Sloan, Karen. "Twain's Adventures of Huckleberry Finn." *The Explicator* 63.3 (2005): 159–63.
Stern, J.P. *Nietzsche*. Fontana: William Collins Sons and Co. Ltd. 1981.
Strozier, Robert, M. *Foucault, Subjectivity, and Identity: Historical Constructions of Subject and Self*. Detroit: Wayne State University Press, 2002.
Taylor, Craig. "Moral Incapacity and Huckleberry Finn." *Ratio* 14.1 (2001): 56–67.
Trotsky, Leon. *Their Morals and Ours*. New York: Pathfinder, 1969.
Twain, Mark. "Adventures of Huckleberry Finn." *The Adventures of Tom Sawyer and Adventures of Huckleberry Finn*. Ed. Shelley Fisher Fishkin. New York: Penguin Signet Classic, 2002.
_____. "The Adventures of Tom Sawyer." *The Adventures of Tom Sawyer and Adventures of Huckleberry Finn*. Ed. Shelley Fisher Fishkin. New York: Penguin Signet Classic, 2002.
Veblen, Thorstein. *The Theory of the Leisure Class*. New York: Dover Publications, Inc. 1994.
Warren, Mark. "Nietzsche's Concept of Ideology." *Theory and Society* 13.4 (1984): 541–65.
Wells, Anna, Mary. "Huck Finn, Tom Sawyer, and Samuel Clemens." *PMLA* 87.5 (1972): 1130–31.

Violence, Labor and Collective Action in William Dean Howells' *A Hazard of New Fortunes*

Debbie Lelekis

The title of William Dean Howells' novel *A Hazard of New Fortunes* (1890) is an allusion to William Shakespeare's play *King John*, in which English invaders of France "wager with fortune" in a state of uncertainty and endless change, or what Gib Prettyman calls a spirit of "abrupt relocation, disputed territory, and imminent violence" (437). Howells' characters circulate in a similarly tumultuous era, the late 1880s of New York City. The urban environment that Basil March enters into encompasses the harshly commercial literary marketplace (in the form of the new literary magazine, *Every Other Week*, of which he becomes editor), as well as a labor strike and its resulting violence. Densely populated urban areas, which contained much of the working population, were, as Michael Spindler argues, the "centre of gravity of American social life" in the late nineteenth century (2).

Hazard is a prime example of Howells' attempt, through literary realism, to examine the conflicts in American society during the nineteenth century over the core tenets of democracy. In my book *American Literature, Lynching, and the Spectator in the Crowd: Spectacular Violence* (2015), I examine texts by Theodore Dreiser, Miriam Michelson, Irvin S. Cobb, and Paul Laurence Dunbar that expose these conflicts as the constant struggle for balance between the rights of the individual and the demands of the community. In those texts, that tension plays out in the form of racial violence in lynch mob scenes, but in Howells' novel it can be seen most prominently in the crowd scene depicting labor and economic unrest; Howells uses the character of Basil March as a spectator figure to respond to and address this friction.[1] March begins as a traditional spectator who initially travels aimlessly through the city and observes, but he evolves into a more active figure after his interactions with the crowd. Due to this contact with the crowd, the strongest social commentary of the novel arises, revealing the author's sympathies for the labor movement and the working class. Howells is forcing his reader's gaze towards the unpleasant and uncomfortable in the way that the character Conrad Dryfoos suggests when he says to March, "If you can make the comfortable people understand how the uncomfortable people live, it will be a very good thing" (132).

In a significant section of the novel, a transit strike literally stops or changes the movement of the characters, causing them to pause and consider the effects of the events. The newspapers also play a significant role in directing the movement of the spectators of these events and their understanding of the strike situation. Initially the strike in *Hazard* "seemed a very far-off thing" to March and his colleagues, despite the newspaper being "full of noisy typography about yesterday's troubles on the surface lines," and there seems to be "not much thinking, about the six thousand men who had taken such chances in their attempt to better their condition" (376). The use of the word typography is especially pertinent because it connotes the practice of using typographical elements to evoke certain effects in the readers (often dramatic) and to guide the reader's gaze as they navigate their way through the print. The significant role of print media is further emphasized by the description of the typography as "noisy," which both attributes a "voice" for something that is by nature a visual (words on a page) and also evokes the physical clashing itself between potential strikers, police officers, and scabs in the streets. The newspapers alert the main characters in the novel of the strike whether they choose to ignore it or confront it. People like Jacob Dryfoos dismiss the seriousness of the situation until they are literally prevented from moving freely through the city due to the strike. It is Basil March, however, who becomes the most significant spectator of the strike in *Hazard*. Although he is vaguely aware of the troubles with the surface lines, thanks to the newspaper reports, he doesn't show much thought about its implications before witnessing it firsthand. After learning of the strike through the newspapers, Basil is ultimately led into direct involvement with the situation.

March begins as a flâneur-type character who struggles to find a way to engage actively in the scenes he observes early in the novel. In terms of class, the flâneur is associated with leisure, and by nature is described as detached and passive, watching and collecting sketches of urban life "from the perspective of a strolling or panoramically situated observer" (Brand 6).[2] Within this context, March and his wife witness a street of tenement housing, which makes them more aware of the lives of the poor, but they do not act in any way to address their plight. March comments that it makes them "feel rather small and otherwise unworthy when [they] see the kind of street these fellow beings of [theirs] live in," yet they justify their selfishness and dismiss class tensions by oddly concluding that it would do no good if they shared their wealth and they are not "humbled in the least by what [they] had seen" (56).

The randomness of the scenes they encounter is viewed like a performance to be watched. The flâneur's function within such a scene is to "read" the crowd as if it was a text requiring interpretation and classification of its components (Brand 6). In the street scenes that the Marches experience, the word "picturesque" is used as a descriptive term and its use emphasizes how March's role as a flâneur-spectator initially allows him to distance himself. Carrie Tirado Bramen defines the picturesque as having the qualities of "roughness and contrast" and locates it within "small and often crowded spaces" (86). This description can be applied effectively to the scenes the Marches observe in the tenement streets and crowds. They are visually entertained by the scenes they witness without being especially troubled by the poverty or compelled to action.

As Bramen asserts, the term picturesque "provided a much-needed vocabulary for middle-class inhabitants of the city [and] offered a discourse of color and variety with which urban dwellers could visually transform the rubbish, congestion, and misery of the city into a source of rough and rugged pleasure" (87). Amy Kaplan argues that the picturesque also allows the Marches to feel familiarity when viewing the scene because it reminds them of their European travels. This sense of familiarity permits them to distance themselves from the poverty. Furthermore, the picturesque allows people to make "otherness" less strange and tames anxiety about the city by making it recognizable and more comfortable (Bramen 88). In a larger context, the flâneur "reduces the city to a panorama ... transform[ing] [it] into a legible, accessible, and nonthreatening version of itself"; by doing so, the flâneur could "impose order upon the potentially disorienting diversity of the city, reducing it to accessible images that could be collected and consumed" (Brand 7).

It's out of this sense of detached aestheticism that March comes up with the idea to write sketches of the city based on his spectatorship of urban scenes. While March is struck by the visual aspect that his sketches might evoke, Conrad Dryfoos urges him to incorporate a moral aspect to the sketches that would make the wealthy better understand the plight of the poor and working classes. Bramen argues that Howells uses the picturesque and the contrast between March's and Conrad's perspectives as an "opportunity to go deeper, to consider the material conditions of urban diversity" (90). Although March never manages to produce his sketches, his role as spectator becomes more complicated as he becomes more aware of the circumstances of the poor (through Lindau and Conrad) and as he becomes a more active witness. As Bramen describes, "The danger of walking in New York, [of being a spectator], then, is that it threatens to collapse the distance between the picturesque traveller and the object of his gaze, converting the delightful into the terrible and the charming into the wretched" (92). The picturesque requires distance and the safety this detachment offers is appealing to March but initially limits his effectiveness as a spectator. However, once March's proximity to the events of the strike increases, he can no longer remain a detached observer; instead, he takes on a spectator role that fits within Dennis Kennedy's sense of the term as an active participant and one that does not merely consume what he witnesses in a passive way.[3]

Notably, March gains a "sense of complicity … a sense of the striving and the suffering deeply possessed him, and this grew the more intense as he gained some knowledge of the forces at work—forces of pity, of destruction, of perdition, of salvation" (276–77). The Marches' life before had been what he calls "death in life"—a time when they were blissfully ignorant and unaware. While March is still in the transitional stage as a flâneur-spectator, he has a moment of connection with the strikers when he "began to feel like populace" but then he relapses when he "regained his character of [the] philosophical observer," distancing himself once again from their situation (374).

Brand suggests that urban spectatorship and the figure of the flâneur, "in spite of its detachment, is capable of stimulating a socially constructive interest in the diversity of the urban population" (194). March's ambiguous relationship with the crowd at this point in the novel can actually be seen as a productive stage in his growth as a spectator. Brand contends that within a highly populated space like the nineteenth century New York City that March experienced, we need the "more abstract understanding of community and moral obligation" that urban spectatorship fosters with its "experience of seeing and watching" rather than an avoidance of the sight of strangers (194).

Although the flâneur is often portrayed as superficial, and March certainly fits this description early in the novel, he offers the possibility of a "posture of curiosity and tolerance that, even if it was merely spectatorial, was nevertheless superior, as a constructive social attitude," to the demonization of the other and the stereotypical presentation of the wickedness of the metropolis (Brand 195). In the flâneur stage, March was not prepared to consider the magnitude and implications of what he observed, but the flâneur's "benign tolerance," as Brand calls it, at least acknowledged the legitimacy of the scenes and people he witnessed. This stage in March's development, although shallow and limited at times, establishes his eventual growth as a spectator whose new sense of social consciousness allows him to reconsider the circumstances of the people he observes.

Howells himself shares undeniable similarities with his main character, which further underscores his own participation in the experience of spectatorship and the development of social consciousness. His emphasis on discomfort, pain, fear, and even physical proximity to danger supports the necessity of being an active spectator, rather than a passive observer. The strike scene in *Hazard* was heavily influenced by Howells' feelings about the trial, conviction, and execution of the "anarchists" charged in the Haymarket Square bombing in Chicago in May of 1886.[4] What began as a strike and rally ended in a riot with several deaths and casualties after police started firing into the crowd following the explosion of a bomb. Howells was profoundly affected by this event and its aftermath, protesting the conviction of the men who he believed were tried "for socialism and not for murder" (Howells, *Selected Letters*, Vol. 3, 193).

The crowd scene in the novel not only provides a climax for the story, but as Nicolaus Mills argues, it "forever changes the personal and political lives of all the main characters" (81). Furthermore, Stephanie Palmer describes this as an expansion of their "horizon of consciousness" and suggests that the incident "provide[s] a space for the characters to hesitate, re-think, and make decisions" (234). Other scholars of depictions of labor in fiction, such as Laura Hapke, contend that most American fiction has "demonstrated a curious resistance to proletarian art" and she further argues that "even in novelists with liberal sympathies, anxious fantasies of worker upheaval generate, almost ritualistically, literary defenses of individualism, both economic and personal" (*Labor's Text* 11). John Lavelle pushes back against Marxist readings like this in his book *Blue Collar, Theoretically* (2011) where he sees Hapke's approach as a limiting discourse "demanding an interpretation of the text through exploitation, victimization, and struggle against capitalism, marginalizing other aesthetic attributes and deeper readings of more universal struggles" (103). Additionally, William Scott's book *Troublemakers: Power, Representation, and the Fiction of the Mass Worker* (2011) explores how the notion of working-class power influenced fictional portrayals in the early twentieth century. He focuses on workers in novels such as Upton Sinclair's *The Jungle* and Jack London's *The Iron Heel*. Michèle Lamont examines another aspect of labor fiction when she describes the workers' collective identity as reinforced by the way that mass media often represents them as a cultural unit (11). She looks at the moral standards that workers use to define who they are and to delineate an imagined community of people who share the same values; notably, these communities "may overlap with, or cut across, class and racial lines" (2–3).[5]

Howells' novel is a good example of a text that challenges the general ambivalent attitude towards the working class that Hapke describes in her book *Labor's Text* (2001).⁶ Key to March's experiences as a spectator is his direct contact with and nearness to the peril and terror caused by the violence of the crowd, which demands that he become an active spectator rather than a passive observer. Hapke is critical of authors like Howells who she sees as part of the group of writers who were "slum tellers" of the 1890s because she sees them as mostly ambitious journalists with genteel credentials. She asserts that Howells "buried the labor action in the narrative as a curiosity of slum life, against the contrasting normality of the middle-class city dweller" (96). I disagree with her assessment and contend that the labor strike is actually central to the novel and a key scene for the development of March as a spectator because it is not presented as an entertaining spectacle, but rather an eye-opening event that changes his perceptions about the workers. Despite her criticism, Hapke does argue that the labor texts of writers like Howells, Crane, and Riis, among others, were of a "crucial kind" in that they "reverse, question, or adapt the exceptionalist-ascension work and strike stories to tell new ones of slum immigrants [and] in so doing, they exhibit the first true interest in the artistic uses of working-class subject matter" (97). In contrast to some of Hapke's criticisms, William Alexander succinctly describes Howells' talent as his power to grasp "American reality and character and his ability to penetrate the surface of American life" (2). Additionally, Robert Hough conveys Howells' status as social commentator, arguing that the author's job, "as he [Howells] conceived it, was to reveal the defects of the old and the virtues of the new" in order to show people the benefits of innovations and set changes into motion (116).⁷

As a spectator, March challenges the notion of the detached receptor of the action. By applying his theory of realism in *Hazard*, Howells is able to use the concept of the spectator as a window into labor issues and the forces behind the strike situation. Cynthia Stretch identifies Howells' assessment of true realism as the "ability to translate objective observation into deeper truth" and describes the realist author as "uniquely positioned to see and then represent reality" (240). I argue that March as spectator functions in the same way within his narrative. He is well-positioned to see and represent reality by translating objective observations into deeper truths about society and culture.

Through March's eyes, the reader sees the action of the novel's pivotal scene unfold; the significance of the event, its causes and consequences, are conveyed to the reader through March's observations and struggles to make sense of the violence. Although March is physically unharmed, the strike scene makes a notable impact on him. As a witness of the violence, he develops from a detached and passive flâneur-type figure into a spectator whose social awareness deepens after the strike. While he had earlier considered writing city sketches of his excursions around the city, he ultimately never gets around to actually producing them, and it isn't until he experiences the strike scene that he is able to start to understand it within the larger context of the current political climate of the country.

As Mills argues, crowds were the most powerful vehicle that the workers had in the late nineteenth century to enact political and social change (79). The importance of the strike was primarily their battle to unionize without penalty, in addition to clashes over wages and work schedules. Opposition to the strikers centered on the desire to keep the workers from gaining strength by allying themselves with those who shared their economic interests. This clash over representation is at the heart of Howells' novel and reaches its height in the strike scene that March witnesses. Howells is credited as providing in *Hazard* the first comprehensive depiction in American literature of the working-class crowd that is featured as a significant element of the plot.[8]

I argue that the spectator figure provides the reader with an access point into the crowd. March takes the reader to the edge of the violence and acts as an intermediary through which we confront the discomfort and danger associated with the workers' fight for fair wages and working conditions central to the labor issue. Although *Hazard* is often considered a "stylistically imperfect novel," it was Howells' most acclaimed and in his own opinion, "the most vital" (Alexander 129). After Howells ended his work as editor of the *Atlantic Monthly* near the beginning of 1881 and was free to focus on his fiction, he soon began applying his evolving concept of realism. Both Mills and William Alexander describe a shift in the mid–1880s from more "genteel" works to writing that reflects his evolving sense of sympathy for the plight of the working poor and the influence of his readings on Christian socialism. Sender Garlin challenges the "myth of a bland Howells," and contends that "his mature awareness and literary achievement—and, above all, his criticism of society—have generally been ignored or minimized" (143). Much of the novel's importance and strength is connected to Howells' willingness to make the strike and the labor issue a key development for the plot and central to March's evolution as a spectator. Howells was among the first to address the labor movement in this way in American fiction.

Through his use of March as a spectator, Howells employs realism in order to connect with his readers and impress upon them the significance of the driving forces behind the economic situation in the country that were causing such violent eruptions. Furthermore, critical realism, as Alexander asserts, puts "the comfortable and refined in mind of the savagery and suffering all about them; and all literature, as Howells came to see it, must confront its readers with themselves and with the growing problems within our social and political systems" (5–6). This sentiment is directly present in the novel in Conrad's words to Howells about making the comfortable people understand the suffering of those less fortunate than them. After witnessing the violence himself, March is inspired to think more deeply about the situation, question the causes, and begin to imagine possible changes in the conditions, more fully embracing his role as an active spectator.

As the key spectator in the novel, March guides the reader's response, advancing the aim of realist fiction as Alexander explains it, as fiction that can and should cause the reader to contemplate and question, prompting them to work for changes to adverse conditions. In novels like *Hazard*, Howells' fiction had become "increasingly concerned with the inequities in the economic and social system and the human culpability for them" and by the late 1880s Howells was more outspoken about his view of the role of the American realist (Alexander 115). Increasingly, Howells wanted his fiction to be the kind of literature that challenged readers, particularly those who, as Alexander describes, had a "tendency to rest contented, or at least rest, in their comfortable lives and forget the problems of their society" (117). March serves as a conduit to the readers that Howells was trying to reach and by making him the spectator that witnesses the pivotal strike scene, the reader is drawn into the action too, pulling them out of their comfortable, complacent state of being and thrusting them into a space of pain, fear, and danger.

The strong connection between the novel and the actual strikes of the time period makes the significance of the fictional scene in Howells' text even stronger for his initial readers. In Paul R. Petrie's book about social consciousness, the intersection of Howells' social ethics and his aesthetic theory, as formulated in his *Editor's Study* columns, is explored. As Petrie describes, Howells' notion was that "modern literature above all else should function as a vehicle for public communication aimed at mediating the deepening alienations between classes, regions, and ethnicities" and that it should be part of a "continual, collaborative literary dialogue" to which many new American fiction writers would contribute (2, 8). This further underscores the importance of March's spectatorship and his conveying of the event's magnitude, which carries out Conrad's suggestion about making the comfortable people understand the uncomfortable people.

March's reaction to his experience as a spectator of the violence of the strike scene and his subsequent expansion of social awareness mirrors Howells' response to the Haymarket affair. Mills identifies this event as the turning point that influenced Howells' efforts to "link the world around him to the world of his fiction" (80). Sender Garlin also describes Haymarket as "like a bolt of lightning [that] was unquestionably the single searing experience that fused Howells' critique of his society and tore away the last cobwebs of illusion" (135).

Similarly, March's spectatorship of the strike scene is the point in the novel when he finds a sense of connection to the larger world around him and comes to better understand the working class. Some critics fault Howells for not using the novel to advocate a clear plan for actual social change, but that criticism fails to take into account the rich significance of the novel as a study of the "attitude and motivations that cause social evils and prevent their alleviations" (Alexander 135). Without first underscoring this level of understanding of the problem, especially during a time in history when the country's values were rapidly changing due to the new vision of the world brought on by modernity, there is no hope for eventually moving forward with any plan of action. Howells' work lays this groundwork for later acts of social change. As Alexander argues, the "representation of the facts of injustice, together with analysis of those who are accountable, *is* effective in the cause of justice ... [and] Howells' honest agony over American economic conditions" played a significant role in the late nineteenth century (121). In *Hazard*, Howells provides a mirror for Americans to see the results of their own complacency and, by doing so, creates an impetus for change.

The influence of the Haymarket event and other real-life strikes can be clearly seen in the novel's streetcar strike that culminates in a violent clash.[9] The historical context of real strikes is crucial to keep in mind when considering Howells' fictional strike, especially in relation to how labor unions were viewed. Many of the companies did not consider union representation to be valid and therefore grievances expressed on behalf of the workers by the unions were often dismissed as illegitimate. Howells does not display a bias against unions and strikers like some of his contemporary novelists, and his interest in the labor movement contributed to the production of *Hazard*.

March's relationship with Lindau highlights Howells' critical stance about America's "splendor and opulence," which owed their existence "largely to the hopeless poverty" of the working class (Howells qtd. in Alexander 128). Lindau's conversations with March echo Howells' beliefs about the inherent economic inequality in America and Howells' own complex political viewpoints. Alexander's biography of Howells portrays him as not a "tough-minded socialist, not a militant, not a Marxist by any means, not an entirely practical critic, not an organizer or fighter among the ranks," yet the realism of his works "brought into high relief a fact in American life which lays bare the fictitiousness of American equality" (Alexander 120–121). This critical perspective comes out in Lindau's questioning of how much money a man can "honestly earn without wronging or oppressing some other man" (169). Central to Lindau's argument is the assertion that "Not the most gifted man that ever lived, in the practice of any art or science and paid at the highest rate that exceptional genius could justly demand from those who have worked for their money, could ever earn a million dollars ... it is these [tyrants] that *make* the millions, but no man *earns* them" (169–170).

March laments the fact that people willing to work are not guaranteed the security of shelter, food, and rest. Scholars like Alan Trachtenberg explore the roots of these tensions between labor and capitalism. In *The Incorporation of America: Culture and Society in the Gilded Age* (1982), Trachtenberg examines the period when the rising middle-class began to view capitalism and private enterprise as more important than the value of labor, independence, and free institutions. Trachtenberg further explains this shift in thinking when he states that business used the free labor ideology to convince the middle classes that the "true America" was connected to success in competitive enterprise (87). By the late 1880s, as Trachtenberg asserts, the rise of corporations (as opposed to individual ownership or simple partnerships) had fundamentally altered the previous assumptions about the role of public service in business, placing profit-seeking above all else as the sole purpose of business (79, 83). In his essay on labor and capital, Trachtenberg traces the history of the word "strike" (with its roots in the nautical terminology for lowering or unfixing sails and putting out of use), highlighting its assertion of the power of workers over the process of production and its quality as a collective act (89). The labor movement opposed inequality (racial, sexual, and economic) and by doing so sought to uphold the "fundamental American traditions of republicanism and equality ... so far from 'foreign' as to be the most authentic voice of America itself" and strikes were "occasions of mutuality" that provided experiences of unity and equality (96–97).

The effects of the resulting class distinctions profoundly altered the cultural perceptions of American life and workers. March's opinion of the workers in Howells' novel changes when he observes them on the street as "quiet, decent-looking people" (382). The biased depiction of the strike that March has read about in the newspapers does not match what he sees, and he can't understand the violent responses of the system that subordinates the average worker.

Significantly, it is the issue of the workers' rights to organize that becomes the "point that ruptures the sense of cross-class community established through the publication of the literary magazine," forcing a breakdown of the cooperative effort between the collection of unlikely collaborators (Stretch 236). This tension erupts during the strike but as Mills asserts, Howells is careful not to use the crowd scene merely as a way to bring together loosely connected sketches of 1880s New York. Its function is much more significant than that, as March's transformation brought on by his spectatorship emphasizes the critical role of the crowd in bringing about social justice. Despite his reluctance to go near the violence, March is eventually driven to the strike by his developing social consciousness, which finally causes him to become interested in learning more about the strike.

As the prime witness to the strike, March is drawn into the action despite his wife's cautions against going near the strike site and his own ironic comment about avoiding being "the peaceful spectator who always gets shot when there is any firing on a mob" (373). Significant in this quote is the use of the term spectator and the implications of danger that proximity to the action would cause. Similar to Conrad's desire to make the wealthy class feel discomfort over the plight of the poor and working classes, Howells again underscores the need for fear, danger, and the possibility of pain in order to fully engage in the process of social awareness and change. Although he is initially hesitant to go near the violence and possibly write about the strike, once he observes the mob scene that breaks out, March finds himself siding with the workers and his perception of the police contrasts as they appear hostile.

The violent scene breaks out suddenly in a "tumult of shouting [and] cursing [as] struggling men [attack a streetcar]. The driver was lashing his horses forward, and a policeman was at their heads, with the conductor pulling them; stones, clubs, brickbats hailed upon the car, the horses, the men trying to move them" (383). The distance between the crowd and spectator melts away in this moment as March gazes at the crowd who in turn watch the people on the streetcar. I see this as a turning point that signals the shift in March from a flâneur-figure who merely watches to an active spectator who begins to understand the significance of the events he sees unfold before him. It's at this point that March's spectatorship turns the reader into an active spectator as well, forcing them to experience the violence through March's proximity to the danger. In front of March, "the mob closed upon [the streetcar] in a body, and then a patrol wagon whirled up from the other side, and a squad of policemen leaped out and began to club the rioters.... They struck them under the rims of their hats, the blows on the skulls sounded as if they had fallen on stone; the rioters ran in all directions" (383).

Howells' description falls on the side of the workers who are, as Mills asserts, "overwhelmed by the disproportionate force of the counterattack" from the police (85). Lindau arrives in the middle of the scene and is quickly struck down by an officer. As Lindau tries to shield his head, Conrad recognizes him:

> [Conrad] heard a shot in that turmoil beside the car and something seemed to strike him in the breast. He was going to say to the policeman, "Don't strike him! He's an old soldier..." but he could not speak.... The policeman stood

there; he saw his face; it was not bad, not cruel ... a mere image of irresponsible and involuntary authority. Then Conrad fell forward, pierced through the heart by that shot fired from the car [383–84].

This is another moment where the gaze between the two sides dissolves the distance between the crowd and the spectator. The narrator draws the reader in as a spectator by directing our attention to Conrad's eyes watching the officer as the fatal shot is fired, pausing to comment on how the man's face reflects the unthinking violent response to the workers' act of protest. The officer is described as not inherently malicious but rather as an instrument of the corporations used to oppose the requests of the workers with brute force instead of reason and compromise. Just like the real-life Haymarket Square riot, it is unclear who fired the shot. The police reaction to the strike is impartial until they are forced to engage in the violence that breaks out. Howells describes the officer who strikes Lindau as "not bad, not cruel." The officers seem to be fighting on the side of the corporations purely because that's what they are being commanded to do.

The portrayal of the crowd reveals that the relationship between violence and social change is not just about the violence that the mob initiates, but also the economic forces and powerful men like Jacob Dryfoos who control productivity and labor. As Mills explains, Howells' depiction of the crowd scene is markedly different than the descriptions given in real newspapers that referred to strikers as the "howling mob" and "ignorant rabble with hungry mouths" (85). Kaplan describes the strike as an undoing of "boundary lines ... between the foreground and background, between observer and spectacle, and between the home and the street. [Then] the background suddenly crashes into the foreground and kills two of its members" (77).

After witnessing the violence of the mob, March becomes more passionate about social justice and tells his wife, "What I object to is this economic chance world in which we live. It ought to be a law ... that if a man will work he shall both rest and eat.... But in our state of things no one is secure of this.... And so we go on, pushing and pulling, climbing and crawling, thrusting aside and trampling underfoot" (396). While working on *Hazard*, Howells had an experience similar to the Marches when they observed the tenements earlier in the novel, and he witnessed a poor man eating discarded food on the street. In a response comparable to March's statement above, Howells lamented the *conditions* that caused such a situation. Alexander suggests that March is not pushed as far as Howells in social outlook in the novel, but I see March's direct contact with the crowd as leading him towards an expanded sense of self-awareness and political sensitivity.

In addition, Bramen's explanation of Howells' urban aesthetic can help us to better understand March's complex role as spectator; she describes the "tension between distance and proximity, detachment and intimacy" (85) in relation to Howells' depiction of modernity and the city, but these are also the core tensions within March's position as observer and active participant for social change. March comes to understand the anguish of the poor and questions why a man like Dryfoos can accumulate more wealth in an hour on the stock market than working class people could earn in a year. He recognizes the effect that the economic conditions have on the character of individuals, saying that "conditions *make* character" and this is illustrated most clearly in the figure of Jacob Dryfoos whose greed significantly influences his character. Even Dryfoos himself finds his beliefs challenged when he reads his dead son's thoughts in his journal and finds that they were similar to Lindau's beliefs. Although he doesn't completely understand their ideas, he gains respect for Conrad, and by extension Lindau, and their viewpoints.

By the end of *Hazard*, March concludes that, although big events like violent strikes (and in Dryfoos's case, the death of his son) can deeply affect us, they alone don't have the power to *change* us; instead it is the "still, small voice that the soul heeds, not the deafening blasts of doom," and rather than change, we *develop*, because as March describes, "There's the making of several characters in each of us; we *are* each several characters" (440). For March, his spectatorship of the strike serves as a catalyst that pushes him to reassess beliefs about labor and justice, but they had been underdeveloped and dormant inside him all along.

Howells' portrayal of March seems to mirror his own struggles with the "unpleasant" side of life, but his undercutting of March and his clear flaws displays his criticism of that attitude. Within his critical depiction is the capability of his character for "self-realization and development" of his social consciousness, but, as Alexander asserts, March's development is "undramatic, and in the end, it represents no final and complete conversion [but rather the] beginning of new growth" (133). The setting of the novel contributes to March's development in that "New York forces upon March certain 'pensive questions' and a 'vague discomfort,' which bring 'nothing definite' at first but gradually deepen his insight until he recognizes his complicity in the suffering he sees" (Alexander 133). This relates back to Conrad's comment about the comfortable versus the uncomfortable people and further emphasizes Howells' attempt to use March's spectator position to rouse a sense of self-recognition and responsiveness in his readers.

Within his representation of crowds and spectatorship, Howells lays out the argument in support of the workers through Lindau's conversations with March, and the interactions between Conrad Dryfoos and Margaret Vance who clearly understand the cause of the workers; none of these characters are direct participants as strikers though, so the effect is different than that created by Theodore Dreiser who lets the strikers speak for themselves in *Sister Carrie* when they appeal to Hurstwood and the other scabs for sympathy and solidarity. In *Hazard*, we see Howells using his concept of realism to accentuate literature's connectedness to "real life," especially within social and political contexts. Trachtenberg describes Howells' conception of realism as "represent[ing] nothing less than the extension of democracy into the precincts of fiction" (184). Howells' aim was to guide his readers towards a stronger sense of brotherhood and a social purpose. Alexander offers a similar description of Howells' view of literature as "confront[ing] its readers with themselves and with the growing problems within our social and political systems" (5–6). Urban spaces allowed writers like Howells to explore sites of "constant contact and confrontation," but they also provided the opportunity to "integrate ethics and representation in order to build a modern vision of a democratic community" (Bramen 98–99). In particular, Howells and his fictional counter-part March, come to see the flaws in democracy and the inherent inequality of opportunities.

Within this context, Howells' novel can be seen not as a limited commentary, but rather as an "attack on American society [carrying] the weight of justifiable outrage and of truth" (Alexander 137). While Howells himself struggled with the effects that greed and the economic conditions during his time had on the character of his fellow Americans, he continued to see the importance of community bonds and altruism, hoping that a peaceful political movement could come out of these qualities and bring about a change in the conditions of the poor and working classes. As Alexander describes, *Hazard* "represents an effort to stimulate sensitive, responsible people to take that step toward achieving a just society" (139). The tension between unions/workers and companies in *Hazard* illustrates the struggle between the collective and the individual that Howells saw as intrinsic to American democracy.

In his fiction, Howells renders the conditions of the era which significantly contributed to the necessity of workers' strikes and in doing so, he draws his readers' attention to the plight of the working class through the spectatorship of the main character in the strike situation. March's response to the discomfort and proximity to danger that he experiences as a spectator of the crowd evolves, but ultimately his direct contact with the spectacle of the striking crowd is necessary to impart the significance of such a situation to readers. As a result of this expansion of the social consciousness, real social change can begin to occur beyond the pages of the novel. Through his use of spectatorship, Howells scrutinizes the social, economic, and political forces that lead to uprisings like strikes and riots and exposes the political responsiveness of American fiction as an important source of commentary and critique of democracy, the American city, and the role of crowds within the system of social change.

NOTES

1. Basil March and his wife were first introduced as characters in *Their Wedding Journey* (1871), and they appear in two novels post–*Hazard*, including *An Open-Eyed Conspiracy* (1897) and *Their Silver Wedding Journey* (1899).

2. Dana Brand's book on the flâneur traces the use of the figure in pre–Civil War American literature, particularly in the works of Poe, Hawthorne, and Whitman. Brand challenges notions of early nineteenth-century America as an anti-urban space disconnected from the aspects of modernity associated with metropolitan Europe. He contends that by the nineteenth century, the "consciousness of modernity" was advancing in America, and the phenomenon of the flâneur was already appearing as a type of urban spectator of modern life in the fiction of that era (13).

3. Adapted from Kennedy, Dennis. *The Spectator and the Spectacle: Audiences in Modernity and Postmodernity*. New York: Cambridge University Press, 2009.

4. For a comprehensive selection of Howells' correspondence about the Haymarket affair, see Sender Garlin's chapter on Howells in *Three American Radicals* (1991), especially pages 107–111 and 118–120. Timothy L. Parrish also provides a succinct analysis of Howells' involvement in the aftermath of Haymarket and its impact on the novel in his article "Haymarket and *Hazard*: The Lonely Politics of William Dean Howells." *Journal of American Culture* 17.4 (1994): 23–32.

5. Lamont's book *The Dignity of Working Men: Morality and the Boundaries of Race, Class, and Immigration* (2002) seeks to "amplify the muted voices of the working class" by focusing on modern American workers and the boundaries drawn between blacks, immigrants, the upper middle class, and the poor. This is a useful resource for considering how the image of the worker in the nineteenth century has influenced the conception of the modern worker.

6. Hapke asserts that anti-city biases, faceless slum dwellers, laboring masses, and emigration schemes mark the majority of fictional accounts of working people in the nineteenth century, and describes how class antagonism often surfaces in these novels. She contends that "All too often inaccurately portrayed as either falsely conscious or too fully conscious, laboring folk have been demonized, sanitized, co-opted, erased, infantilized, mythologized, depoliticized, politicized, and anesthetized. Workingmen have been called both democracy's linchpin and its enemy" (*Labor's Text* 13–14).

7. Hough's book *The Quiet Rebel* (1968) provides significant background information about Howells' involvement in reform and his concept of the novel as "an instrument of cultural advancement rather than solely as a means of entertainment ... [through which] he strove to deal with the social and economic problems of his age" (115).

8. Representations of strikes started to appear in American literature around the 1870's. Stretch explains that organized labor was usually portrayed in fiction as a "threat to national stability," and early novels involving discord between labor and capital seem to side generally with employers (235). Unlike Howells' novel, those earlier novels didn't use strikes as a climax or focal point. Fay M. Blake's *The Strike in the American Novel* (1972) contends that a look into the historical record shows us that more novelists were writing about strikes when there were actual strikes taking place, but in her opinion, most used the strike merely to draw upon sensationalism and express their (often negative) attitudes towards workers, poverty, individualism, collectivism, and minorities (2). By the turn of the century, they were being used more seriously.

9. Both Mills and Stretch also credit a streetcar strike that took place in New York soon after Howells moved there from Boston in 1889 with his wife as another source of inspiration for the strike portion of the novel. In that strike, the workers were defeated and as Stretch explains, the strike gained more attention from the press than the other strikes that year, perhaps because it affected so many commuters and marked the streetcar as a sign of modernity and urbanity (233). The major economic depressions that occurred in 1873 and 1882 had a great influence on the depiction of strikes like Howells' too. Between 1870 and 1895, there were four major strikes, including: the Railroad Strike of 1877 (the first national strike in U.S. history); the 1886 Haymarket affair in Chicago which began as a strike before a bomb was thrown (in addition to the four accused anarchists who were executed, the Knights of Labor

was also dismantled and the new American Federation of Labor later emerged); the 1892 Carnegie Steel strike (armed Pinkerton agents were used to protect strikebreakers); and the 1894 Pullman strike (the American Railway Union disintegrated and violence occurred). All of this turmoil eventually worked its way into the fiction of the time.

Works Cited

Alexander, William. *William Dean Howells, the Realist as Humanist*. New York: B. Franklin, 1981.
Blake, Fay M. *The Strike in the American Novel*. Lanham, MD: Scarecrow Press, 1972.
Bramen, Carrie Tirado. "William Dean Howells and the Failure of the Picturesque." *The New England Quarterly* 73.1 (2000): 82–99.
Brand, Dana. *The Spectator and the City in Nineteenth Century American Literature*. New York: Cambridge University Press, 1991.
Dreiser, Theodore. *Sister Carrie*. New York: Doubleday, 1900.
Garlin, Sender. *Three American Radicals*. Boulder: Westview Press, 1991.
Hapke, Laura. *Labor's Text: The Worker in American Fiction*. New Brunswick, NJ: Rutgers University Press, 2001.
Hough, Robert L. *The Quiet Rebel: William Dean Howells as Social Commentator*. Hamden, CT: Archon Books, 1968.
Howells, William Dean. *A Hazard of New Fortunes*. 1890. New York: Penguin Books, 2001.
―――. *Selected Letters*. 1882–91. Ed. Robert Leitz III. Bloomington: Indiana University Press, 1980.
Kaplan, Amy. "'The Knowledge of the Line': Realism and the City in Howells' *A Hazard of New Fortunes*." *PMLA* 101.1 (1986): 69–81.
Kennedy, Dennis. *The Spectator and the Spectacle: Audiences in Modernity and Postmodernity*. New York: Cambridge University Press, 2009.
Lamont, Michele. *The Dignity of Working Men: Morality and the Boundaries of Race, Class, and Immigration*. Cambridge, MA: Harvard University Press, 2002.
Lavelle, John F. *Blue Collar, Theoretically: A Post-Marxist Approach to Working Class Literature*. Jefferson, NC: McFarland, 2011.
Lelekis, Debbie. *American Literature, Lynching, and the Spectator in the Crowd: Spectacular Violence*. Lanham, MD: Lexington Books, 2015.
Mills, Nicolaus. *The Crowd in American Literature*. Baton Rouge: Louisiana State University Press, 1986.
Palmer, Stephanie C. "Realist Magic in the Fiction of William Dean Howells." *Nineteenth Century Literature* 57 (2002): 210–36.
Parrish, Timothy L. "Haymarket and *Hazard*: The Lonely Politics of William Dean Howells." *Journal of American Culture* 17.4 (1994): 23–32.
Petrie, Paul R. *Conscience and Purpose: Fiction and Social Consciousness in Howells, Jewett, Chesnutt, and Cather*. Tuscaloosa: University of Alabama Press, 2005.
Prettyman, Gib. "A Hazard of New Fortunes." *American History Through Literature 1870–1920*. Eds. Tom Quirk and Gary Scharnhost. Detroit: Charles Scribner's Sons, 2006. 437–443.
Scott, William. *Troublemakers: Power, Representation, and the Fiction of the Mass Worker*. New Brunswick, NJ: Rutgers University Press, 2011.
Spindler, Michael. *American Literature and Social Change*. London: Palgrave Macmillan, 1983.
Stretch, Cynthia. "Illusions of a Public, Locations of Conflict: Feeling like Populace in William Dean Howells' *A Hazard of New Fortunes*." *American Literary Realism* 35.3 (2003): 233–246.
Trachtenberg, Alan. *The Incorporation of America*. New York: Hill and Wang, 1982.

Writing the Spectacle of the Human Zoo

Literary Slumming and the Animalized Other in Maggie, A Girl of the Streets

Kailey Havelock

In the opening passage of Stephen Crane's *Maggie, A Girl of the Streets*, the narrator describes a child whose "infantile countenance was livid with fury" (3) employing the elevated poetic vocabulary of the highly-educated middle class. In a dissonant shift, the dialogue that follows is written in the localized vernacular of the impoverished tenement districts, indicated by phonetic spellings and a comparatively less complex vocabulary: a child shouts, "Run, Jimmie, Run! Dey'll get yehs!" (3). Before the reader can grasp the violent and chaotic social context indicated by this line of dialogue, the use of unconventional contractions and spellings indicates a dramatic and disconcerting shift from the register of the narration. Through this linguistic dissonance between dialogue and narration, Crane distinguishes himself from—and foregrounds his intellectual superiority to—the lower-class subjects he depicts.

By implicitly demanding a middle-class educational background for his reader to comprehend his eloquent narration, Crane invites readers to join him on the privileged side of the divide between social propriety and how the other half lives. He denies the potential for social activism in representing and advocating for the oppressed inhabitants of the tenements; instead, he uses his self-established position of intellectual superiority to exploit the impoverished Other for the entertainment of his titillated readership. In so doing, Crane takes part in the exploitative cultural fad of "slumming" and makes his implied reader complicit in this decontextualized, degrading, and dehumanizing cultural voyeurism. Through both form and content, Crane negates the humanity of his subjects and instead presents them as spectacles to entertain a middle-class audience. He uses dialect and social conduct to indicate the disruption of middle-class notions of propriety, to highlight the Otherness of his subjects. He neglects the individuating nuances of even his most central characters, instead reducing them to caricatures of poverty and animal embodiments of middle-class anxieties.

By implicating the animalization of these subjects in his presentation of them as spectacles, Crane replicates the constructed spectacle of the zoo: the inhabitants of the tenements are contained within the confines of the narrative and the tenement buildings, and their animalistic depictions emphasize a distinction from the audience, which reinforces social divisions. Drawing on historiographic scholarship on middle-class engagements with and representations of the 1890s tenement slums, I argue Crane enacts slumming through narrative by dehumanizing his subjects. I draw on a wealth of animal studies scholarship on the social, spatial, and representational power dynamics of zoos to argue that Crane's animalization of his subjects is apparent in his descriptions and inherent in his narrative structure, as a means of asserting authorial authority over his subjects.

Literary Naturalism

Crane draws on the conventions of literary naturalism, which is a late-nineteenth and early-twentieth century literary and artistic movement founded in middle-class curiosities about the Other.[1] Writers like Crane sought to create for readers a supposedly-authentic experience of an exotic, illicit, or otherwise tantalizingly-inaccessible world. All the while, readers remain at a safe distance from the perceived dangers of that reality.

Crane's work supposedly endeavors to incite readers' sympathy for his subjects, his emphasis on social difference—to the point of animalizing the inhabitants of the slums—results in a sensationalized depiction of lower-class life that ultimately prohibits empathy across classes. *Maggie* subjugates its narrative subjects through authorial process and public consumption, transforming them into objects of a middle-class gaze.

In literary criticism, there is a strong drive to distinguish between author and narrator, emphasizing a distinction between their perspectives and objectives. However, for the purposes of this essay, I refer to Crane's narrator as an extension of himself. The narrator and author provoke the same effect: the oppression of lower-class subjects. The narrative engages its audience in literary slumming, and Crane provides no ostensible intervention into the text to subvert this exploitation or offer a critical dissonance from these problematic narratorial tendencies. The narrative's effect is inextricable from Crane's implied intentions as the author—a claim supported by his documented misappropriation of lower-class experiences. As such, I will regard the narrator and author as functionally indistinguishable.

Eric Schocket defines "class-transvestite narratives" as writers' "attempts to close epistemological gaps through cross-class impersonation" (106), by adopting the caricaturized attire and physicality of lower-class persons. This practice implies the problematic assumption that subaltern perspectives can be accessed through mimicry, and yet it was praised in literary naturalism. Writers would impersonate lower-class persons to gain a superficial sense of affinity to a distinct, dramatized set of life experiences, which they then packaged in literature and sold to middle-class readers. Schocket claims these writers' "sociological authority emerges out of the ability to have an authentic experience of poverty while retaining a supposedly middle-class ability for objective assessment" (122). Their purportedly "authentic" experience of poverty is accredited by their middle-class perspectives. While Schocket makes a strenuous effort to distinguish Crane from "the distancing rhetoric of the social spectacle" (107), I argue Crane's practice of impersonation demonstrates his lack of regard for his subjects as nuanced and individuated persons whose experiences cannot be accessed through mere sartorial imitation.

Class Anxieties and Slum Characters

This historiographic background substantiates my argument for Crane's neglect of a nuanced understanding—or at least a nuanced representation—of the inhabitants of the tenement districts. Even the most central characters are reduced to caricatures that embody violations of middle-class notions of propriety. Crane describes Jimmie, the older brother of the title character, as having "studied human nature in the gutter" (14), and says, "[his] occupation for a long time was to stand on street-corners and watch the world go by, dreaming blood-red dreams at the passing of pretty women. He menaced mankind at the intersections of streets" (15). Jimmie is a manifestation of Crane's audience's perception of the inhabitants of the tenements: uneducated, unemployed, and a menace to society. Jimmie's character centers on his dissent from middle-class ideals, which Crane presents condescendingly: "Jimmie had an idea it wasn't common courtesy for a friend to come to one's home and ruin one's sister. But he was not sure how much Pete knew about the rules of politeness" (35). Crane satirizes Jimmie's distinction from propriety, through his misapplication of middle-class socialization in a lower-class setting.

Jimmie and Maggie's mother, Mary, is a caricature of the impossibility of femininity and maternity in the tenements. In the opening pages of the novella, Crane describes, "Formidable women, with uncombed hair and disordered dress" (6). He later writes, "[Mary] put her immense hands on her hips and with chieftain-like stride approached her husband" (8). The women of the tenements are made to appear grotesque, upsetting social and physical propriety. When Jimmie arrives home after a fight, Crane subverts maternal tenderness, as Mary "dragged him to an unholy sink, and, soaking a rag in water, began to scrub his lacerated face" (8). These images are a highly conscious authorial disavowal of the potential for a middle-class reader to identify with these lower-class subjects. Crane writes, "It seems that the world had treated this woman very badly, and she took a deep revenge upon such portions of it as came within her reach" (29). He transforms Mary into a caricature of the women of the slums and simultaneously contains her within the confines of the tenements, as a product of her context. Such containment has implications for Crane's audience: Mary and figures like her do not pose a threat to the middle-class, because the violations of maternity, femininity, and propriety that she represents are defined as distinctly and exclusively of the lower class.

The lack of investment in these characters as complex humans, with individuating traits beyond sensationalized markers of class, is further apparent in Crane's dismissive treatment of the deaths of his subjects and the performative manner in which he represents their grief. When Maggie's infant brother dies, Crane expresses the news in a terse, unaffected sentence: "The babe, Tommie, died" (14). This line follows Crane's extended description of Jimmie and Maggie, "crouched until the ghost-mists of dawn appeared at the window, drawing close to the panes, and looking in at the prostrate, heaving body of the mother" (14), which is poetic, imagistic, and thoroughly detailed. In contrast, Tommie "went away in a white, insignificant coffin, his small waxen hand clutching a flower that the girl, Maggie, had stolen from an Italian" (14), and remains insignificant through the novella, never again mentioned. Crane immediately refocuses his narrative attention, noting, "She and Jimmie lived" (14). Similarly, the children's father dies in a passing remark that grants no extended or affected attention to a central character of the first few chapters. Crane writes, "[Jimmie's] father died and his mother's years were divided up into periods of thirty days" (15). In this instance, the death is not significant enough to merit address in its own sentence. The narrative perspective immediately moves on to a reductive portrait of the mother, whose widowhood is defined by the financial compensation she receives each month. Both Jimmie and his mother are denied any expression of affect—grief or otherwise—in relation to this death, and once again, Crane neglects to address this character in the remaining chapters of the novella. His subjects' lives are reduced to their utility in the plot, and their deaths are brief and peripheral.

When Maggie dies at the end of the novel, Mary's grief is staged as a spectacle, rather than a humanizing, sympathetic glimpse into her maternal affections. This scene reads as a mockery of her inadequacy as a mother—and the impropriety of all mothers in the slums—rather than as a portrait of sincere grief. When Mary receives the news that Maggie is dead, she is "at a table eating like a fat monk in a picture" and "her mouth [is] filled with bread" (67). Crane juxtaposes his audience's middle-class ideals of motherhood against an increasingly grotesque caricature of the mother in the slums, who aesthetically and behaviorally defies middle-class social conduct regulations. The sobs of grieving women are described as "a high, trained voice that sounded like a dirge on some forlorn pipe" (67); the detail and obscurity of this description foregrounds his audience's detached perception of this spectacle of grief, rather than allowing the reader access to a nuanced and affected subjectivity. The reader is not invited or even enabled to empathize with these subjects. As Mary beckons her son to fetch Maggie's body, wanting to put an old pair of baby shoes on her adult feet, Crane invites his reader to be amused by the absurdity of the lower class' grief. Mary refers to Maggie's death as a "ter'ble affliction" (67), unknowingly misusing the "vocabulary [she] derived from mission churches" (67). Crane emphasizes this misunderstanding of missionary language—the middle-class moral presence in the slums—through repetition, in order to accentuate Mary's religious and maternal failures to comply with middle-class notions of propriety.

Literary Slumming

By presenting these characters as caricatures of middle-class anxieties about the tenement districts—writing to his audience rather than about the lived experiences of his subjects—Crane's text becomes a work of literary slumming. Chad Heap's book *Slumming* provides historiographic background on the practice, in the era in which Crane sets his novella: "In the mid–1880s, affluent white New Yorkers embraced a new form of urban amusement, forming 'slumming parties,' as they called them, to explore the immigrant and working-class districts of the city's Lower East Side" (17). Slumming, according to Heap, "revealed more about the women and men who participated in this activity than about the inhabitants of the urban geographies they visited" (18), and as such slummers "lacked such a nuanced understanding of the tenement districts" (23). Slumming defined the tenements as "a container for the degradation and immorality commonly associated with such racialized populations" (9)—an authorial interpellation apparent in Crane's text.

Thomas Heise argues slumming literature "[mapped] the physical, social, and moral geographies of the city for a bourgeois readership that was fascinated and repulsed by the spectacle of ethnic and class difference in the seemingly chaotic, noisome world of the slums" (33). Slumming literature not only represents the slums through a middle-class authorial perspective but furthermore enacts the social practice of slumming by presenting the slums as a fascinating and repulsive spectacle.

Crane is foremost concerned with audience entertainment and subsequently fails to attend to humanizing and individuating characteristics of his subjects. Instead, he focuses on a lack of education, unclean living conditions, and violations of middle-class notions of social propriety. This phenomenon is most prominently illustrated by the narrative's circumlocution of the title character: Maggie is scarcely present in dialogue and is often given less narrative attention than the landscapes, architecture, and peripheral characters that surround her. She is presented as the "culturally delinquent, morally destitute, and spatially marginalized underworld Other" (32) that Heise describes as a convention of slumming literature. Crane introduces and frequently refers to Maggie as "A small ragged girl" (4) in the first few chapters, and she isn't named in narration until several pages into the novella. When she is attended to in narration, it is overwhelmingly through an external perspective, rather than the free-indirect interiority granted to other characters. Crane writes:

> The girl, Maggie, blossomed in a mud puddle. She grew to be a most rare and wonderful production of a tenement district, a pretty girl. None of the dirt of Rum Alley seemed to be in her veins. [...] When a child, playing and fighting with gamins in the street, dirt disguised her. Attired in tatters and grime, she went unseen. There came a time, however, when the young men of the vicinity, said: "Dat Johnson goil is a puty good looker" [18].

Maggie is filtered through Crane's authorial bias of literary slumming—constantly projected onto the backdrop of the slum—as well as through the perceptions of other characters. Maggie lacks a nuanced and individuated subjectivity, despite being the title character. She is an object that, when gazed upon, reveals the classed lens of other characters and the classed-ness of her surroundings.

When Maggie does receive narrative focus, it is to accentuate her visual and intellectual impropriety in a middle-class setting, which further privileges Crane's middle-class narratorial perspective at the expense of his marginalized subjects. Pete is a figure of the refined lower class—familiar with some of the luxuries of the middle class due to his occupation as a bartender—and to Maggie, he represents the upwardly mobile ideal she desires. In an effort to impress him, Maggie makes a lambrequin "with infinite care" (23), attempting to emulate a fantasy of middle-class decorum. However, her decorative efforts cannot disguise her lower-class living conditions. She cannot conceal the incongruence between her concept of the middle class—wherein the adornment of a lambrequin might impress a potential suitor—and the reality of her incomprehension of that social realm: "Afterward the girl looked at it with a sense of humiliation. She was now convinced that Pete was superior to admiration for lambrequins" (23).

Maggie is frequently defined by her surroundings, most often through juxtaposition against a more vibrant middle-class backdrop or camouflage into a bleak lower-class backdrop. When Maggie is pictured at home, she is "[contemplating] the dark, dust-stained walls, and the scant and crude furniture of her home. [...] Some faint attempts she had made with blue ribbon, to freshen the appearance of a dingy curtain, she now saw to be piteous" (22). Crane draws attention to the piteousness of Maggie's attempts to emulate an ideal of middle-class propriety in her home, and in so doing, he accentuates Maggie's incompatibility with middle-class propriety herself. Her failure to recreate a middle-class aesthetic implies her failure to transcend her lower-class position. Maggie becomes the embodiment of the "dust-stained," "dingy," and "piteous" slum she inhabits. When removed from this setting, her alignment with the dreariness of the slums is made more profound by her juxtaposition against the world of the middle-class: "She saw the golden glitter of the place where Pete was to take her. An entertainment of many hues and many melodies where she was afraid she might appear small and mouse-colored" (23-24). While this passage offers a rare glimpse at Maggie's interiority, Crane's narration in no way opposes Maggie's self-effacement; rather, Maggie is transformed into an embodiment of socio-economic divisions. Not only is she made to appear inadequate in a glittering middle-class setting, but moreover she is dehumanized by the suggestion that she might appear as a mouse, which I will explore further in my section on Animalizing the Other.

In the scene of Maggie's death, Crane presents detailed descriptions of numerous men who hold negligible significance, while giving relatively little attention to Maggie herself. Maggie remains unnamed throughout the scene, only briefly gestured to as "A girl of the painted cohorts of the city" (61). In contrast, Crane offers detailed and individuated descriptions of a catalogue of passing men who are peripheral to the central narrative and moreover peripheral to Maggie's death:

> A flower dealer, his feet tapping impatiently, his nose and his wares glistening with rain drops, stood behind an array of roses and chrysanthemums [...]. A tall young man, smoking a cigarette with a sublime air, strolled near the girl. He had

on an evening dress, a moustache, a chrysanthemum, and a look of ennui [...]. A stout gentleman, with pompous and philanthropic whiskers [...]. A belated man in business clothes [...]. A young man in light overcoat and derby hat [...]. A laboring man marched along with bundles under his arms [...] a boy who was hurrying by with his hands buried in his overcoat, his blonde locks bobbing on his youthful temples, and a cheery smile of unconcern upon his lips [...]. A drunken man, reeling in her pathway [... and] a man with blotched features [60–62].

I recount these numerous descriptions with the intention of making evident Crane's extraordinary attention to detail within a relatively short scene. Maggie is scarcely present in this scene, and she is portrayed—or, more accurately, implied—only in relation to these men. Furthermore, the man who is implied to murder Maggie, or at least be the last person to see her before her potential suicide, is described in imagistic detail:

[...] a huge fat man in torn and greasy garments. His grey hair straggled down over his forehead. His small, bleared eyes, sparking from amidst great rolls of red fat, swept eagerly over the girls upturned face. He laughed, his brown, disordered teeth gleaming under a grey, grizzled moustache from which beer-drops dripped. His whole body gently quivered and shook like that of a dead jelly fish [62–63].

That this man is evidently of the lower class—indicated by his characteristically grotesque portrayal—suggests Crane's narratorial avoidance of Maggie, favoring the men that surround her, is not exclusively due to a class bias. Crane offers a profound lack of concern for Maggie as a lower-class woman and sex-worker, despite the supposed importance endowed in her character by the novella's title.

While Crane neglects Maggie's presence in this scene, he gives a great deal of focus to the architecture of the districts by the river: "The shutters of the tall buildings were closed like grim lips. The structures seemed to have eyes that looked over her, beyond her, at other things" (63). Crane personifies the surrounding buildings by describing their features as like lips and eyes, transforming the setting into an active agent in this scene. In so doing, Crane heightens the effect of Maggie's depersonalization. While Maggie only receives one line of description in this scene, Crane details the river, which "appeared a deathly black hue," and the light of a factory "that lit for a moment the waters lapping oilily against timbers" (63). Through imagistic detail, Crane paints a mimetic portrait of the setting, and infers its significance far beyond the heroine's presence by describing the water as perpetually active, "lapping" in the continuous present tense. Maggie's death is conveyed through abstract implication, as "The varied sounds of life, made joyous by distance and seeming unapproachableness, came faintly and died away to a silence" (63). Maggie's death is expressed through her surroundings; the distant and unapproachable "sounds of life" are an ostensible metaphor for Maggie herself. She "came faintly" into the world as a child of the tenements—lives that are brief and of little note to the middle class—and "died away into silence" just as unremarkably.

Exploitative Gaze

The critical discourse surrounding Jacob A. Riis's *How the Other Half Lives* illuminates equivocal narratorial tendencies in *Maggie*. Both texts present similarly reductive and degrading approaches to their subjects, through different modes of representation. Riis enacts slumming through exploitative voyeurism in his photographs of the slums and the accompanying captions. In his introduction Riis writes, "Greed and reckless selfishness wrought like results [in the tenements] as in the cities of older lands" (1), and "The story [of the slums] is dark enough, drawn from the plain public records, to send a chill to any heart" (2). He evokes sentimental language—mythical or biblical in tone and diction—to sensationalize his subject. Through this language, Riis, like Crane, distances himself from his subjects and furthermore constitutes them as *objects*. He assumes the authority to mediate their representation—through both framed shots and intrusive candids—to suit his artistic intentions. Heap describes Riis's artistic practice as "muckraking journalism" that "prompted readers to partake of a little 'armchair slumming' of their own as they followed such authors on their sensationalistic forays" (21). Likewise, Schocket argues Riis "Not only [aligned] 'neighborhoods' with corresponding 'ways,' but he depicted these ways as singularly perceptible and thus available for middle-class understanding" (119). These critics elucidate the nature of literary or artistic slumming, which reduces complex subjects into sensational and consumable aesthetic objects for a middle-class audience.

Through extended passages of detailed, sensationalistic descriptions of settings and the appearances of characters, Crane mimics Riis's photographic gaze of slumming in text. I would like to draw attention to Crane's description of the streets and corridors of the tenements (11), and the description of Pete working at the bar (58). The passage I find most striking for its sensationalistic imagism is the portrait of Maggie in her home, in the chaotic remains of her mother's rage, when Pete arrives to take her out on their first date:

> When Pete arrived, Maggie, in a worn black dress, was waiting for him in the midst of a floor strewn with wreckage. The curtain at the window had been pulled by a heavy hand and hung by one tack, dangling to and fro in the draft

through the cracks at the sash. The knots of blue ribbons appeared like violated flowers. The fire in the stove had gone out. The displaced lids and open doors showed heaps of sullen ashes. The remnants of a meal, ghastly, like dead flesh, lay in a corner. Maggie's red mother, stretched on the floor, blasphemed and gave her daughter a bad name [24].

In this passage, Maggie is again granted relatively little narrative attention; instead, Crane details and personifies her surroundings, to construct what Heise refers to as a fascinating and repulsive spectacle of the slums (33). While Maggie is static, her surroundings are active—"dangling" and "blaspheming"—which draws attention away from Maggie as a subject and towards her classed setting. Like the people in many of Riis's photographs, Maggie is seemingly at the peripheries of this portrait of slum life, as Crane's narrative lens focuses on the wreckage of the scene and its violation of propriety.

Slum Tourism Activism

Fabian Frenzel's book *Slumming It* offers a rigorous critique of contemporary practices of slum tourism. He claims, "there is arguably a difference when it comes to different practices of slumming" (164): slumming can be social activism when it "[brings] diverse resources and political capital, such as visibility, attention and financial support in campaigns for the bettering of the lives of slum residents" (162), in contrast to "the prefabricated spectacles of commercial tourist experience industries" (162). I align Crane and Riis's slumming with the latter form of slum tourism, which views slum conditions as a "spectacle" rather than as a site for action. Frenzel justifies the distinction I draw between literary slumming in *Maggie* and the potential for *productive*, non-exploitative activist representations of slums.

While "slum tourism activism [includes] critical reflection on activist practices, reverse mobilities and the struggles against gentrification" (162), Crane's text neglects this potential for activism and situates itself within the realm of commercial exploitation. Crane fixates on degrading and sensationalistic imagery, prioritizing the entertainment of his audience over the provocation of vital empathy for his subjects. Such representational inadequacies deny the possibility for a reformist activist exposure of the mistreatment of the lower-class. Instead, Crane enacts literary slumming: he exploits his subjects for sensational narrative material, without resultant benefit to the underprivileged communities of which he profits. Crane fails to represent the humanity of his subjects and, moreover, presents them as animalized figures.

Animalizing the Other

Crane frequently refers to the children of the tenements as "urchins," evoking connotations of hedgehogs and other rodents—inhabitants of the streets. These descriptions not only dehumanize the lower class through animalization, but furthermore degrade them as the lowest class of urban animals. In the initial appearance of "howling urchins [...] circling madly about the heap" (3), contextual ambiguity allows readers to surmise that "urchin" indicates an actual rodent. However, further iterations provide clarification: "The urchin raised his voice in defiance to his parent and continued his attacks" (7). Crane positions "the urchin" within this family, and with a voice capable of defying attacks within a human economy of vocalization as a means of asserting power. In so doing, he reveals the human signified by this animalizing term. This revelation has the potential to affect the sensibilities of Crane's implied middle-class audience, who discover a human subject beneath a dehumanized depiction. However, the frequent evocation of this signifier neutralizes any affective potential; repetition renders the term impotent as a source of compassionate dissonance between Crane's perspective as the author and that of a sympathetic reader.

By numbing the potential for sympathy, Crane implicates his audience in the act of literary slumming, forcing readers to be complicit in the dehumanization of his subjects. Heap states, "some affluent white pleasure seekers no doubt used the term [slumming] consciously to reinforce their sense of social and moral superiority over the residents of the districts that they visited" (11). Heap draws attention to the power language possesses in shaping perception and stratifying socio-economic classes—the same power that Crane utilizes when referring to his subjects as "urchins."

Crane further animalizes the inhabitants of the tenement districts through descriptions of their physicality. The characters are constantly described as "howling" and "roaring" (first on 3), connoting the sounds of wild animals. Crane often employs similes that liken these characters to animals: "Maggie [...] ate like a small pursued tigress" (10), and "[Jimmie] crawled [...] with the caution of an invader of a panther den" (13). When Jimmie gets into a fight, the men are "like three roosters" (41), while "The bravery of bull-dogs sat upon [their] faces" (42); and Jimmie later flees the scene "with the quickness of a cat" (42). By constantly likening them to animals, Crane portrays the lower class as an animalized Other, distinguished from the human subjectivity of his middle-class audience. Kay Anderson argues, "Animality has been a crucial reference point for constructing sociospatial difference and hierarchy in Western cultures" (4). Anderson's notion of animality extends beyond biological conceptions of the non-human animal, to encompass those groups within the human species that are socially construed as animal-like. She addresses "the discursive production of social groups identified for their base drives, proximity to 'nature,' infantility, eroticism, and absence of civilized manners" (3), applied to social groups based on race, class, gender, etc. In Crane's novella, he invokes this animalization of the social Other to present the lower-class inhabitants of the slums as non-human. He defines humanity as middle-class propriety, and the violation of those boundaries becomes an animal act.

As Anderson notes, "humanity has persistently been seen *not* as a species of animality, but rather as a condition operating on a fundamentally different (and higher) plan of existence to that of 'mere animals'" (3). The power dynamics between human and animal are at the core of the animalization of the lower class, as a means of asserting authority and distance. Schocket claims the slums "functioned crucially to define the limits of propriety by embodying the essence of impropriety" (108), articulating the distinction I draw between Crane's distinctly middle-class narrative perspective and audience, and his construction of an animalized spectacle of the slums. As I argue in the next several sections of this chapter, Crane's embrace of the sensationalizing conventions of slumming literature and his animalization of the lower class recreates the spectacle of the zoo in a human context.

Slums as Zoos

Crane presents his subjects as animalized spectacles, replicating the conditions of the Central Park Menagerie that Maggie and Pete visit together. Hoage et al. provide a history of the menagerie, tracing its social and cultural functions and development from the prehistoric period to the present day. The menagerie is any place where animals are contained and controlled for entertainment purposes, such as zoos, circuses, etc. They claim the menagerie is "primarily concerned with the symbolic role of animals" (20) who "have been singled out to be unique representatives of their species" (19). In my alignment of the middle-class consumption of the constructed zoo and the constructed slum, I observe symbolic intent in Crane's depiction of his animalized subjects: his subjects are manifestations of violations of middle-class notions of propriety—with propriety signifying the boundaries of humanity.

At the menagerie in Crane's novella, "Pete occupied himself in returning stony stare for stony stare" (30), effectively mimicking the physicality of the animals. Similarly, Pete "went into a trance of admiration before the spectacle of a very small monkey threatening to thrash a cageful because one of them had pulled his tail and he had not wheeled about quickly enough to discover who did it" (30). The literal animal—the monkey—is explicitly addressed as a "spectacle" for entertainment of the human observers outside its cage. Pete's "admiration" for the monkey relates him to the figure of the animal; this scene mirrors the aforementioned scene in which a young Pete and Jimmie fight in the streets of the slums, described as "urchins." By constructing a parallel between Pete and the monkey, Crane implicitly animalizes Pete and relates the spectacular violence in the slums to that in the zoo.

Hoage et al. state "menageries have remained an urban phenomenon. [...] Perhaps the rise of cities created a nostalgia for the wild environment, and in response the menagerie evolved as the 'art form' of encountering the wild" (20). The slum districts are likewise a uniquely urban phenomenon. While the advent of the menagerie exploited the new exoticism of animals in an increasingly urban society, the practice of slumming emerged as a parallel form of entertainment out of the unintended propagation of impoverished immigrant populations in the city. Furthermore, Hoage et al. state, "The issue of context [in the presentation of menagerie subjects] may no longer be valid in a culture that believes the entire planet can be enjoyed from the comfort of one's easy chair" (28). This quotation echoes criticism of Riis's—and, by extension, Crane's—degrading and sensationalistic representations of his subjects, which "prompted readers to partake of a little 'armchair slumming' of their own" (Heap 21). In both the menagerie and the slum, the object of entertainment is decontextualized for the privileged audience and transformed into a spectacle of Otherness.

The inhabitants of the tenements are contained within the confines of the narrative and the tenement buildings, just as the animals in the menagerie are contained within their cages and pseudo-habitats. Their animalized depictions emphasize a distinction from the audience, which reinforces social and spatial divisions. Heap claims, "slumming made manifest the profound physical and demographic transformations that reshaped U.S. cities [...] the practice reinforced the public perception of the American city as a segregated place" (18). Both the slum and the menagerie signify a profound change in the social and spatial landscape of the city and are exploited as a source of entertainment through their transformations into sites of spectacle. Both the literal animals and the lower-class persons portrayed as animals are removed from their contexts and displayed as embodiments of the boundaries of middle-class notions of humanity.

Slumming at the Zoo

The final sections of this essay will consider a selection of animal studies theories on the conditions, functions, and power dynamics of the menagerie—specifically the zoo—and apply these theories to Crane's representation of the slum, to make an argument for a parallel between the middle-class relationship with the zoo and with the slum. In *Animals on Display*, Dodd et al. offer a thorough study of the implications of how cultures have displayed animals throughout history. They claim, "scientific and cultural practices collaborate to transform animals from complex, multiple creatures into standardized, singular idealizations" (8). The same "standardized, singular idealizations" are clearly observable in Crane's representation of his human subjects, which furthers his problematic animalization of the inhabitants of the tenement slums. The gaze of the zoo-visitor and the gaze of the slummer share an obscuring lens of distance and superiority that degrades their subjects.

Ralph Acampora presents a critical animal studies reading of the relationship between subject and observer in zoos. He writes, "People come to zoos with an expectation of entertainment, not education" (503), and consequently, "zoos teach poorly or, worse, leave their visitors to formulate distorted and even quite detrimental impressions of animals and their relationships to human beings" (502–503). I observe the same investment in entertainment at the expense of education—or entertainment paired with miseducation—in both the practice of slumming and its manifestation in Crane's narrative. Beyond the fundamental problem of viewing either subject—the caged animals or the impoverished inhabitants of the tenements—as spectacles for entertainment is the lens through which they are viewed. Both practices are grounded in the middle-class assumption that these subjects "exist, at least in their placement in the zoo [or slum], specifically to entertain us humans" (503), which implicitly denies the subjectivity of these subjects, transforming them into objects of entertainment. As Acampora argues in relation to the zoo, both forms of middle-class entertainment depend upon "an overexposure that degrades [the] real nature" of these subjects (502), resulting in a "paradoxical form of pornography defined as visive violence" (502). The voyeuristic gaze of the slummer commodifies and perpetuates the dehumanizing exploitation of these subjects.

Within the exploitative relationship between zoo-visitor and animal—or slummer and slum-inhabitant—the subjugated subjects are constructed into "fetishes of the exotic, underlying fear of nature, fantasies of illicit or impossible encounter" and are depended upon "a powerful presumption of mastery and control" (503). Both relationships—in the slum and in the zoo—are premised on a sense of control that mediates the middle-class audience's engagement with the illicit. In the zoo, this control takes the form of cages or glass walls that maintain the boundary between the human space and the animal space, enabling nearness to a dangerous wildness without the threat of harm. For the slummer, these conditions are recreated by the association of the lower class with the tenement districts, removed from the space of the middle class, and through the voluntary nature of these recreational excursions—often with a police escort (Heap 17)—that maintains the slummer's control. In slumming literature, this sense of control is made more profound by the containment of these subjects within the bindings of a book, while allowing for a more intimate view into the slums as they supposedly exist in the absence of spectators. The likeness between descriptions of both cultural phenomena emphasizes the parallel between the middle-class gaze in zoos, slums, and slumming literature.

Spectacle of the Slum-Zoo

Warwick Frost and Jennifer Laing theorize the cultural function of zoos within an experience economy. They state, "The experience economy is a seductive idea, promising an appealing combination of higher revenue and satisfied visitors. For [the proprietors of] zoos, it is easy to be attracted by this and overlook the negative implications of the concept" (141). Zoos operate to receive economic capital—from an almost exclusively middle-class audience—in exchange for cultural capital as experience. The experience is culturally received as education but, due to the financial dependence of the zoo on its visitors, predominantly functions as entertainment with trivial attention given to the consequences of commodified representations of animals. I align this distinction between educational function and financially-motivated entertainment with Frenzel's aforementioned distinction between slum tourism as activism and "the prefabricated spectacles of commercial tourist experience industries" (162). In both dichotomies, the middle-class exploits constructed, commodified subjects and neglects a productive, educational, and socially active engagement.

Frenzel also considers the socio-economic structures that both enable and necessitate the practice of slum tourism, which "directly points to inequality and the injustice of the distribution of wealth in this world" (18). The practice is constructed through an economic disparity, wherein one group has sufficient disposable income to engage in recreational tourism while another must depend upon the marketability of their suffering. This statement holds different—but arguably related—implications in the contexts of zoos and slums: the zoo inhabitant is forcibly contained within the cage and has negligible agency in the efficacy of their function as entertainment; the slum inhabitant is more acutely aware of the potential for direct profit resulting from an appeal to slummers. Slumming literature robs lower-class persons of representational agency and allows the middle class to maintain inviolable control over the slum. Authorial mediation enables the seamless exploitation of the lower class as fetishized objects—particularly, I argue, as animalized figures that serve to define the boundaries of human propriety.

Through ideological and linguistic dissonance between the narratorial perspective and the lower-class subjects, Crane transforms the slums into a spectacle for voyeuristic consumption by a sensationalized middle-class readership. Crane's denial of nuanced subject-hood and frequent alignment of his subjects with animals dehumanizes the lower class. In his presentation of his narrative subjects as animalized spectacles, Crane replicates the fraught power dynamic of the zoo in his portrayal of the slums, wherein animals are decontextualized and presented as distinctly Other, for the profitable entertainment of a middle-class audience. In so doing, Crane deprives his subjects of empowering self-representational agency and endows himself with inviolable authorial authority in the decontextualization, degradation, and dehumanization of an already subjugated social group. Literary slumming enables authorial profit off the voyeuristic exploitation of the inhabitants of the slums, without perceived risk on the part of the reader or perceived social and factual accountability on the part of the author. Crane's text demonstrates the necessity of a self-aware engagement with privileged representations of subjugated subjects, to avoid becoming complicit in highly problematic social and literary practices.

Note

1. I use the proper noun Other as both a gesture to the Other indicated in the title of Jacob Riis's *How the Other Half Lives*, a contemporary to Crane, as well as the conceptual post-colonial Other defined in Edward Saïd's *Orientalism*.

Works Cited

Acampora, Ralph. "Zoos and Eyes: Contesting Captivity and Seeking Successor Practices." *The Animal Ethics Reader*, 2nd ed. Eds. Susan J. Armstrong and Richard G. Botzler. New York: Routledge, 2010. 501–506.

Adams, Carol J. "The Rape of Animals, the Butchering of Women." *The Sexual Politics of Meat*. New York: Continuum Publishing, 2002. 50–73.

Anderson, Kay. "'The Beast Within': Race, Humanity, and Animality." *Environment and Planning D: Society and Space*, vol. 18, 2000. 301–320.

Crane, Stephen. "Maggie, A Girl of the Streets." *Maggie, A Girl of the Streets and Other New York Writings*. New York: Modern Library, 2001. 3–69.

Dodd, Adam, Karen A. Rader, and Liv Emma Thorsen. "Introduction: Making Animals Visible." *Animals on Display: The Creaturely in Museums, Zoos, and Natural History*. Ed. Adam Dodd, Karen A. Rader, and Liv Emma Thorsen. University Park: Pennsylvania State University Press, 2013. 1–11.

Frenzel, Fabian. *Slumming It*. Chicago: Zed Books, 2016.

Frost, Warwick, and Jennifer Laing. "Up Close and Personal: Rethinking Zoos and the Experience Economy." *Zoos and Tourism: Conservation, Education, Entertainment?* Ed. Warwick Frost. Bristol, UK: Channel View Publications, 2011. 133–142.

Gandal, Keith. *The Virtues of the Vicios: Jacob Riis, Stephen Crane, and the Spectacle of the Slum*. New York: Oxford University Press, 1997.

Gullason, Thomas A., ed. Maggie, A Girl of the Streets: *An Authoritative Text, Backgrounds and Sources, the Author and the Novel, Reviews and Criticism*. New York: W.W. Norton, 1979.

Hayes, Kevin J., ed. Maggie, A Girl of the Streets: A Story of New York. London: Bedford Cultural Editions, 1999.
Heap, Chad. "Into the Slums: The Spatial Organization, Cultural Geography, and Regulation of a New Urban Pastime." *Slumming: Sexual and Racial Encounters in American Night Life 1855-1940*. Chicago: University of Chicago Press, 2009.
Heise, Thomas. "Going Down: Narratives of Slumming in the Ethnic Underworlds of Lower New York, 1890s-1910s." *Urban Underworlds: A Geography of Twentieth-Century American Literature and Culture*. New Brunswick, NJ: Rutgers University Press, 2011. 30-76.
Herring, Scott. "Introduction: Queer Slumming." *Queering the Underworld: Slumming, Literature, and the Undoing of Lesbian and Gay History*. Chicago: University of Chicago Press, 2007. 1-24.
Hoage, R.J., Jane Mansour, and Anne Roskell. "Menageries, Metaphors, and Meanings." *New Worlds, New Animals: From Menagerie to Zoological Park in the Nineteenth Century*. Ed. R.J. Hoage and Willian A. Deiss. Baltimore: Johns Hopkins University Press, 1996. 19-29.
Jones, Gavin. "'What Deh Hell?': Stephen Crane's Bad Language." *Strange Talk: The Politics of Dialect Literature in Gilded Age America*. Berkeley: University of California Press, 1999. 141-150.
Link, Eric. *The Vast and Terrible Drama: American Literary Naturalism in the Late Nineteenth Century*. Tuscaloosa: University of Alabama Press, 2004.
Linke, Sharon, and Caroline Winter. "Conservation, Education or Entertainment: What Really Matters to Zoo Visitors?" *Zoos and Tourism: Conservation, Education, Entertainment?* Ed. Warwick Frost. London: Channel View Publications, 2011. 69-81.
Riis, Jacob A. "Introduction." *How the Other Half Lives*. Mineola, NY: Dover Publications, 1971, pp. 1-4.
Schocket, Eric. *Vanishing Moments: Class and American Literature*. Ann Arbor: University of Michigan Press, 2009.
Westgate, J. Chris. "The Courage to See the Sights of the Tenement." *Staging the Slums, Slumming the Stage: Class, Poverty, Ethnicity, and Sexuality in American Theatre: 1890-1916*. London: Palgrave MacMillan, 2014.

Social Radicalism in Sherwood Anderson's *Winesburg, Ohio*

Deborah Giggle

In his *Memoirs*, Sherwood Anderson states that his best known work, *Winesburg, Ohio* (1919), was "universally condemned" at the time of its publication:

> What names I was called. They spat upon me, shouted at me, used the most filthy of words and I remember one letter, in particular, from the wife of a man who had been my friend. She said she had once been seated beside me at a dinner table. "I do not believe that, having been that close to you, I shall ever again feel clean," she wrote [154].

These reactions, in combination with a flood of letters of complaint (and the burning of his book in a public square of a New England town) led Anderson to claim that *Winesburg, Ohio* was "generally recognized as in some way a powerful book" (154).

For today's student of literature it is difficult to understand why this book provoked such extreme responses from the early twentieth-century establishment and reading public. While Anderson's experimentation with modernist techniques and candid treatment of the sexual lives of his characters might explain these early negative reactions to his work, there remains compelling evidence for a third point of contention. The language employed in these contemporary criticisms draws upon discourses of hygiene and disease associated closely with social class in literature of the late nineteenth and early twentieth centuries. Both *Winesburg, Ohio* and its author are condemned using terminology of dirt and contagion drawn upon in discourses of working-class living conditions and moral attitudes during this period.[1] This essay will therefore argue that the "powerful" controversy at the heart of this work must be considered in terms of Anderson's treatment of social class, in particular his experimental approach to representation of "ordinary people." By depicting characters from *all* social backgrounds as individuals with rich and complex inner lives, Anderson forced privileged early twentieth-century readers to confront their own class bias. Expressing the complex humanity and sensitivity of characters from across the social hierarchy, Anderson challenged discourses of class permeating literature of the preceding period, which aimed to condone economic inequality based on assumptions of psychological and intellectual inferiority of the working classes. Kevin Swafford's study of British texts from the late Victorian period, for example, notes how working-class characters are "flattened" providing "general representations" which depict them as "mere types" such as "potentially dangerous ignoramuses or essentially good-hearted simpletons in need of charity and guidance" (29). The denial of a distinct working-class culture, and the reductive treatment of these characters (often attributing comic or eccentric traits) enabled novelists of the period to reinforce hegemonic ideologies of class.

Anderson's stories, by contrast, harness emerging modernist techniques to depict the complex interiority of "ordinary people." In a letter to George Freitag, Anderson states: "Love, moments of tenderness and despair, came to the poor and the miserable as to the rich and successful" (404). By refusing to "flatten" his characterizations of the inhabitants of Winesburg, he challenges the discourses of class in small town America which provided justification for economic inequality in this period. It will be argued that the extreme reactions described by Anderson can be attributed to the way in which the book forced privileged readers to confront uncomfortable truths of social complacency. In this essay, conventional depictions of working-class characters in this period will be analyzed (via a close reading of the short story "Between Rounds" by O. Henry), to demonstrate why and how Anderson's approach challenged early twentieth-century social attitudes in such a radical manner. This essay will also propose that the default theoretical frameworks employed for literary critical analysis of class have, in recent decades, served to conceal the true social radicalism of Anderson's work.

The Nineteenth Century Legacy of Working-Class Representation

While *Winesburg, Ohio* was published just after the end of World War I, Clarence Lindsay argues that Anderson looks back to the late nineteenth century "when America was emerging from its pre-industrial, pastoral and agrarian, and significantly puritanical past, into the modern age" (92). One of the many dichotomies of *Winesburg, Ohio* is that an emerging modernist aesthetic is employed to recreate an historical, cultural, and social context which had, to a large extent, already passed. Stuart Downs argues, similarly, that Anderson spans the "fault line of America's transformation from an agrarian to an industrial society" (25). Furthermore, he argues that *Winesburg, Ohio*, marks the transition in American writing "from external literary structures to internal psychological concerns" and notes that Anderson was "embroiled in the two faces of the American dream, industrialism and socialism" (25). To these interpretations of Anderson (as an author who explores the marginal and the transitional), I would add my own observation that *Winesburg, Ohio* marks an evolution in working-class representation. Anderson's work moves away from a reductive nineteenth-century approach to working-class representation (characterized by the need to create "legibility" of the "lower classes," and to redefine class difference) towards twentieth-century forms of representation which challenged earlier discourses around assumptions of the aesthetic and intellectual inferiority of "ordinary" people.

In order to provide explanations for the extreme reactions to Anderson's work, it is necessary to place *Winesburg, Ohio* within the wider context of working-class representation in literature, and the attitudes expressed towards this stratum of society during earlier decades. The leading British art critic of the Victorian period, John Ruskin, exemplifies the problematic attitudes towards the working class during this period in his essay "Of Vulgarity" (published posthumously in 1906).

> The old English rough proverb is irrevocably true,—you can make no silk purse of a sow's ear. And this great truth also holds—though it is a disagreeable one to look full in the face—that, named or nameless, no man can make himself a gentleman who was not born one. If he lives a right life, cultivates all the powers, and yet more all the sensibilities, he is born with, and chooses his wife well, his own son will be more of a gentleman than he is, and he may see yet better blood than his son's in his grandchild's cheeks, but he must be content to remain a clown himself—if he was born a clown [202].

Ruskin draws on a long-standing discourse of class in which the qualities associated with superior social standing (those of a "gentleman") are seen to be inherited (passed down through subsequent generations). In doing so, Ruskin rejects the notion that individuals can attain a higher social status through their own efforts (the concept of the self-made man which underpins notions of the American Dream). In addition, his use of the term "clown" suggests that the man of lower standing does not excite dignity or respect. He lacks credibility, and his contribution to society is described in terms of light relief or entertainment. Most importantly, the criteria Ruskin applies, to segregate society along class lines, have at their heart an assumption of the intellectual and aesthetic inferiority of the working classes:

> [T]hough rightness of moral conduct is ultimately the great purifier of race, the sign of nobleness is not in this rightness of moral conduct, but in sensitiveness.

When the make of the creature is fine, its temptations are strong, as well as its perceptions; it is liable to all kinds of impressions from without in their most violent form; liable therefore to be abused and hurt by all kinds of rough things which would do a coarser creature little harm [45].

While Ruskin acknowledges the necessity for all individuals to live respectable lives, he argues that superior class status is associated with a degree of sensitivity and emotion unavailable to those at the bottom of the social hierarchy. He asserts that the "coarser creature" does not have the capacity to feel as deeply as individuals placed higher in the social scale.

Kevin Swafford argues that these attitudes towards the working classes are exemplified in canonical English literary texts of the late Victorian period. Swafford argues, for example, that Anthony Trollope was "personally invested in a concept of innate distinctions" between the classes as it provided a means by which to "order and generate his narrative practice within the contentious social realities of the nineteenth century" (14). In order to position his work within the inequities of his own historical and social context, the author needed to draw upon those dominant ideologies of class which provided a moral justification for economic inequality. P.J. Keating also argues that, where working-class characters feature in Victorian novels, class-related implications of texts are often nullified through a "process of avoidance," characterized by a "refusal or inability to break away from the literary and social conventions governing the role that a working man could be allowed to play in a novel" (46). Keating argues that this resulted in the presentation of working-class characters as stock types: the respectable, skilled artisan; the working-class intellectual (such as George Eliot's creations Felix Holt and Alton Locke); the object of pity; the debased (often defined by alcohol addiction or violent behavior); the eccentric (characterized by idiosyncrasies such as unusual occupation or dialogue); and the criminal (often portrayed as a corrupter of children) (26–28).

Jonathan Wild argues that Victorian critics often *expected* authors to reduce working-class characters to stock types in this way. He quotes a late nineteenth century review of George Gissing's *Eve's Ransom* (1895) in the *Manchester Guardian* which queried: "Is it really true, that the average clerk leads the consciously repressed life of Maurice Hilliard before his emancipation? In other words, is the case selected by Mr. Gissing for presentation typical?" (34–35) A sense of realism in the novel is equated with the provision of a generic portrayal of a stock type which calls upon the lowest common denominators of the "average" clerk. A more rounded, individualized depiction of the character (this review suggests) was neither desirable nor encouraged. Wild's study notes that clerks of the period protested against reductive literary representations of members of their profession, making a "reasonable plea ... for variety in representation" (51).

Late nineteenth century authors such as Henry James, of course, struggled to overcome the problems associated with working-class representation at this time, with the aim of achieving greater complexity and depth. Keating notes the Preface to *The Princess Casamassima*, in which James comments:

> [T]he agents in any drama, are interesting only in proportion as they feel their respective situations; since the consciousness, on their part, of the complication exhibited, forms for us their link of connexion with it. But there are degrees of feeling—the muffled, the faint, the just sufficient, the barely intelligent, as we may say; and the acute, the intense, the complete, in a word—the power to be finely aware and richly responsible [47].

James implies that, if working-class characters are not generally acknowledged as fully cognizant of the nuances of emotion associated with the dramas in which the narratives place them, the author is at risk of over-attribution or exaggeration. The resulting portrayals therefore risk appearing untruthful, as they assume a degree of sensitivity available to the working-class characters that might be considered, by the reader, to be unrealistic. James also had concerns that placing a working-class protagonist in the foreground of the narrative could risk alienating readers. He wrote: "[O]ur curiosity and our sympathy care comparatively little for what happens to the stupid, the coarse, and the blind" (47). In common with other authors of his period, James was concerned that the primarily middle-class readership of the late nineteenth century would not be sufficiently interested in the outcomes of narratives featuring working-class characters, and that readers would find it difficult to empathize and associate with characters of a lower social standing.

Working-Class Representation and the Early Twentieth-Century American Short Story

While the literary critical analyses informing this argument, by Swafford, Keating, Wild and others, refers to English literature of the pre-World War I period, it is clear that similar discourses of class, and reductive approaches to working-class representation, were also shaping popular American short stories in the period in which Sherwood Anderson was writing *Winesburg, Ohio*. In his *Memoirs* Anderson discusses his determination to reject these approaches, writing that *Winesburg, Ohio* "broke the O. Henry grip, de Maupassant grip. It brought the short story in America into a new relation with life" (155). In his letter to Freitag, Anderson objects to the short stories of O. Henry (William Sydney Porter) on the grounds that they are "nice little packages, wrapped and labelled" adding that his own stories, by contrast, "were obviously written by one who did not know the answers" (149). Anderson appears to reject the degree of authorial control exerted by O. Henry over the reader's attitudes towards his working-class characters, and challenges the way in which the narratives convey value judgments, with the aim of restricting the reader's interpretation to that of the author himself.

O. Henry's short story "Between Rounds" exemplifies this perceived manipulation of reader responses. It chronicles events in a boarding house on a May evening. The narrative focuses on Mrs. Murphy (the owner of the boarding-house), her tenants Mr. and Mrs. McCaskey, and Policeman Cleary, who is passing by. The short story adopts a humorous, sardonic tone throughout, with comedy generated through O. Henry's witty description of the nightly fights between Mr. and Mrs. McCaskey, involving the hurling of kitchenware and food:

> "Pig's face, is it?" said Mrs. McCaskey, and hurled a stewpan full of bacon and turnips at her lord.
> Mr. McCaskey was no novice at repartee. He knew what should follow the entrée. On the table was a roast sirloin of pork, garnished with shamrocks. He retorted with this, and drew the appropriate return of a bread pudding in an earthen dish. A hunk of Swiss cheese accurately thrown by her husband struck her below one eye. When she replied with a well-aimed coffee-pot full of a hot, black, semi-fragrant liquid the battle, according to course, should have ended.
> But Mr. McCaskey [...] sent the granite-ware wash basin at the head of his matrimonial adversary. Mrs. McCaskey dodged in time. She reached for a flat-iron, with which, as a sort of cordial, she hoped to bring the gastronomical duel to a close [29].

This scene is a slap-stick comedy in which the McCaskeys are reminiscent of two-dimensional cartoon characters. The reader is encouraged to enter into a shared joke with the author to laugh at their antics, understanding that no actual harm will come to either party. The author provides no context by which their violent interactions, and their underlying grievances, might be explained. The art of hurling objects is described as "repartee," and the acts of throwing are described in terms of speech/rhetoric. Mr. McCaskey "retorts" by throwing a roasted joint of meat, and Mrs. McCaskey's "appropriate return" of the bread pudding takes the place of a verbal rebuttal. Mrs. McCaskey is then said to have "replied" with "a well-aimed coffee-pot." These acts of throwing take the place of dialogue in the scene. This has the dual effect of representing the characters as inarticulate, at the same time as removing the opportunity for the characters to communicate their emotions and attitudes. As a result, the reader is unable to access the stated viewpoints or interiority of either character. The author's interpretation of the scene is therefore imposed on the reader, due to the lack of evidence by which to arrive at an alternative perspective. The extended metaphor of the fight, as a meal made up of a series of courses, is too self-conscious to suggest objective observation, and the scene is reported in a distinct narrative voice.

Later in the story it emerges that Mrs. Murphy's son has gone missing:

> Mrs. Murphy shrieked to the moon: "Oh, ar-r-Mike, f'r Gawd's sake, where is me little bit av a boy?"
> "When'd ye see him last?" asked old man Denny, with one eye on the report of the Building Trades League.
> "Oh," wailed Mrs. Murphy, "twas yesterday, or maybe four hours ago! I dunno, But it's lost he is, me little boy Mike. He was playin' on the sidewalk only this mornin'—or was it Wednesday? I'm that busy with work, 'tis hard to keep up with the dates" [30–31].

In this excerpt also, the reader is encouraged to collude with the author to laugh at the working-class characters. The mother's dialogue infers, in subtext, that she has paid insufficient attention to the boy's welfare until his disappearance. While she is portrayed as hard-working, the unsympathetic tone of the passage renders the scene condemnatory.[2] This siding of the reader against Mrs. Murphy transforms her distress into a source for comedy. Old man Denny, similarly, is portrayed as having only a limited interest in the boy's welfare. He does not give the boy's disappearance his full attention, continuing to read the sports pages.

The conventions of working-class representation in late nineteenth century English literature, described earlier, are clearly evident in this early twentieth-century short story by O. Henry. These conventions include, most notably, the deployment of the characters for comic purposes, and the "flatness" of the characterization (due to authorial distance and the absence of access to interiority of characters). In addition, the short story might be said to resonate with earlier Victorian discourses of class, such as those of Ruskin, in which it is assumed that the lower classes have a greater capacity for coarseness and inarticulacy, and a limited ability to feel depths of emotion or pain. The McCaskeys fight regularly (seemingly as a substitute for communication) and appear unharmed, while Mrs. Murphy's distress is conveyed in comic, rather than tragic, terms.

Sherwood Anderson's Innovation in Working-Class Representation

Anderson made clear his determination to reject the conventions of short story writing exemplified by writers such as O. Henry. Anderson's vision was more ambitious, intending to convey objective truthfulness (without the imposition of value judgments or inferred interpretations), and desiring to explore and communicate the complex interiority of people from all social backgrounds. In a letter to Waldo Frank, Anderson described *Winesburg, Ohio* as "a series of intensive studies of people of my home town, Clyde, Ohio" (4) aimed at suggesting "the real environment out of which present-day American youth is coming" (5).[3] His aim for greater truthfulness is combined with an essentially democratic vision in which characters from all strata of society are approached with similar depth and narrative investment. In his letter to Freitag, Anderson relates an encounter, from his early life, with "a violent, dangerous man, said to be a killer." Anderson writes, "One night he walked and talked with me, and became suddenly tender. I was forced to realise that all sorts of emotion went on in all sorts of people" (149). While critics have noted Anderson's tendency to "embroider" his reminiscences, it is undeniable that his representation of working-class characters reflects his intention to communicate on behalf of those individuals often silenced in literature. Kim Townsend argues: "His subject was the common people of America, his task to give them their voice" (207). This aspect of Anderson's work has continued to attract critical attention since the publication of *Winesburg, Ohio*. As long ago as 1936, for example, Robert Morss Lovett stated: "Humble and sordid realities, the trivia of observed phenomena, bring to him an emotion which is the essence of poetry" (100). Anderson was recognized for finding beauty and lyricism in the mundane. In addition, recent criticism has expanded considerably upon our understanding of Anderson's creative process. Lindsay, for example, describes *Winesburg, Ohio* as, "a great, swirling democracy of absolutely equal oddities" (xxi). Noting the authorial egalitarianism of Anderson's work, Lindsay argues: "The related-tale format itself is a formal expression of the digressive impulse expressing a democratic multiplicity of claims on the narrator's attention" (14). Lindsay's interesting argument sees Anderson's rejection of a central, foregrounded, protagonist (in favor of an "inexhaustible carnival of narrative possibility") as a deliberate strategy by which Anderson removes a sense of hierarchy from this text through the adoption of the short story cycle form, and the meandering narrative course achieved. He explains: "The democracy of the narrator's fascination subverts the traditional novel's insistence on the centered individual" (15). The notion of an exceptional central character (Lindsay likens this to the heroic individual of Romanticism) is purposely problematized by Anderson's choice of form, and the reader is presented with a series of intensely-felt moments (described by Martin Bidney as "impressively complex psychological portraits"), in the lives of an entire community of characters (234). In comparison to nineteenth century novels with exceptional working-class "heroes" (for example Pip in Dickens's *Great Expectations*), the implication is that each "ordinary person" in *Winesburg, Ohio*, while unheroic in the Romantic sense, is nonetheless important and interesting, regardless of his or her social class.

Biographer David D. Anderson has argued that Sherwood Anderson's own working-class background contributed to this egalitarian approach towards characterization. He writes, "Unconsciously, through the stories of his father, the talk at the local race track, and his everyday contacts and activities, Sherwood absorbed the sense of closeness to others. [...] Above all, he became aware of people and the bitter-sweetness of their lives" (6). It must be acknowledged that interpreting the creative outputs of authors in terms of influences in their own lives is problematic. Sherwood Anderson's letters and memoirs, however, appear to support the argument that his work was shaped fundamentally by his direct experiences of economic inequality and social marginalization during his childhood and early adulthood. Responding to criticism from the Rev. Arthur H. Smith, of an actual town called Winesburg in Ohio, Anderson argued that "real" citizens of the "real" Winesburg had no justification in feeling "arrogant" towards his imaginary citizens. He added that his fictional characters did not "become bankers, or stockbrokers, establish any of our great modern industries or rise to the management of great businesses" (143). He asserts, however, that they were "simple, good people" who were "at bottom as decent" with "as much inner worth" as the inhabitants of the real Winesburg. He reacts angrily to Smith's accusation that his characters are a "burlesque," emphasizing that his book was an "effort to treat the lives of simple ordinary people with sympathy and understanding."

Anderson describes himself as both intrinsically linked and psychologically detached from the citizens whose narratives he creates. He empathizes with them from a position of peer, rather than superior. Marcia Jacobson notes Anderson's reaction to Burton Rascoe's review of the book, in which Anderson comments, "Whatever is wrong with the people in the book is wrong with me" (10–11). In another excerpt from his *Memoirs* he describes a sense of detachment:

> Sometimes it had seemed to me when, as a young man, I sat at the window of that room, that each person who passed along the street below, under the light, shouted his secret up to me. [...] What dreams. What egotism. I had thought then, on such evenings, that I could tell all of the stories of all the people of America [157].

He imagines himself channeling the narratives intuitively, rather than arriving at them via a conscious creative process and, perhaps disingenuously, wonders at his own audacity in speaking on their behalf.

Fictional Exploration in "The Book of the Grotesques"

The challenges inherent in telling "all of the stories of all the people of America" involved Anderson in a lifelong exploration of form, stylistic experimentation, and intensive observation of the class divisions of his day, as well as the wider experience of humanity. His creative journey towards more nuanced and egalitarian representation of "ordinary lives" is, in itself, the inspiration behind a number of the stories in *Winesburg, Ohio*.

The opening story, entitled "The Book of the Grotesque," employs the imagery of a procession or cavalcade once again, to describe the writer's creative process. The writer—"an old man with a white mustache"—has a dream in which a "long procession of figures" is driven "before his eyes" (6). The passage continues:

> They were all grotesques. All of the men and women the writer had ever known had become grotesques.
> The grotesques were not all horrible. Some were amusing, some almost beautiful, and one, a woman all drawn out of shape, hurt the old man by her grotesqueness. When she passed he made a noise like a small dog whimpering [6].

This description of the characters in *Winesburg, Ohio* as "grotesques" has attracted much literary critical debate. The concept of the grotesque was clearly of importance. Anderson originally intended to use the title *The Book of the Grotesque*, before being persuaded by his publisher to adopt the title *Winesburg, Ohio*.[4] The opening story of *Winesburg, Ohio* establishes that the work, stylistically, breaks away from the conventions of social realism. The allegorical tone suggests that the use of the term "grotesque" should be interpreted metaphorically rather than literally. While David Stouck notes that Anderson makes a number of his characters "memorable by means of a bizarre physical trait or a stylized gesture that isolates the individual from society" there is, nonetheless, broad agreement that Anderson refers to a form of spiritual rather than physical distortion (41). Martha Mulroy Curry, for example, argues: "The short story by Sherwood Anderson is usually an idea about the hidden beauty and sweetness twisted into a form called 'grotesque' by the indifferent and unsympathetic" (94). Similarly, Kim Townsend places Anderson in the Emerson and Whitman tradition and notes the influence of Edgar Lee Masters's *Spoon River Anthology* on Anderson's work. Townsend argues that Anderson infers that the inhabitants of Ohio "become grotesque when they or others take attraction to be the truth about them" (203–204). David D. Anderson proposes that, in describing his characters as "grotesques," Sherwood Anderson's intended interpretation is that people are transformed into "spiritual grotesques" by the "indignities" inflicted upon them. He argues that individuals experience "spiritual distortion" due to the "narrowness of human vision," and that Anderson "employs empathy, compassion and intuition rather than analysis or fierce desire to cure" (40). Some early literary critical interpretations saw this imposition of grotesqueness in terms of the book's historical and social context. Lionel Trilling, for example, argued that "the loneliness and solitude of the grotesque were by-products of the materialism and industrialism of the end of [the nineteenth] century and the early decades of the twentieth" (27). Benjamin T. Spencer, drawing on Anderson's *Memoirs*, also argued that "blind faith in machines had not brought beauty but had left a residue of fragmented grotesques" through the "disintegration of the agrarian community" (8).

The text itself provides an (albeit enigmatic) explanation of how the people were rendered grotesque:

> [I]n the beginning when the world was young there were a great many thoughts but no such thing as a truth. Man made the truths himself and each truth was a composite of a great many vague thoughts.... It was the truths that made the people grotesques ... the moment one of the people took one of the truths to himself, called it his truth, and tried to live his life by it, he became a grotesque and the truth he embraced became a falsehood.

Anderson makes a distinction between the instinctive response to the human condition (thoughts), and a taught/learned response, arrived at through the opinions, and indeed prejudices, of society as a whole (truths). Anderson warns that internalizing the opinions acquired from others damages and distorts us and that only individual beliefs gained through personal experience are of value. This might be seen in terms of discourse, as described by Michel Foucault, in which "truths" can be associated with societal control.[5] *Winesburg, Ohio*, of course, predated the publication of Foucault's theories and, as such, these concepts were not available to Anderson at the time of writing. I would argue, instead, that Anderson interprets "truths" in terms of prejudices (in particular class-related bias), which act as distorting forces. Seen in this context, the Edenic metaphor, identified by Clarence Lindsay in this extract, has a clear relevance. Lindsay sees the rendering of the people as "grotesques" in terms of an aesthetic fall from grace (xiv–xv). I would argue that this passage can also be interpreted in terms of a political loss of innocence. Class bias, which provides the distorting force in this context, can be seen as the outcome of the materialistic imperatives of a capitalist culture. The "truths" underpinning class division, including justifications for economic inequality predicated on assumptions of aesthetic and intellectual inferiority of the socially-marginalized, can be seen to render grotesque, both those who accept them and those oppressed by them. I would argue, therefore, that Anderson expresses, in this extract, the ugliness of the capitalist system and its adverse impacts on humanity. Some individuals almost escape the misshaping effects: "The grotesques were not all horrible. Some were amusing, some almost beautiful." Some, however, are entirely disfigured: "[O]ne, a woman all drawn out of shape, hurt the old man by her grotesqueness. When she passed he made a noise like a small dog whimpering." Those most afflicted by class bias provoke in the old man an indescribable sense of helplessness and fear, rather than a more predictable sense of anger and resentment. Anderson's choice of metaphor is interesting. While the writer could have been represented as a champion of the oppressed, Anderson describes the writer as a "small dog whimpering." The writer is insignificant and powerless rather than authoritative and powerful. He expresses his pain, from his position as an equal of the old woman, rather than as a philanthropic superior. The writer, like Anderson himself, was "one who did not know the answers."

It can therefore be argued that Anderson's overarching intention, in this opening story, is to guide the reader towards a deeper understanding and sense of connection with others. Readers are to develop their own impressions of this procession of characters, shedding the preconceptions of current discourses of class, unhampered by their own prejudices. Anderson is all too aware, however, that this is difficult for the reader to achieve. What's more, it demands an entirely new approach from the author, if the preconceptions underpinning class bias are to be circumvented. I would argue that, in the story "Loneliness," Anderson describes the challenges inherent in this process for the writer.

The Dark Spot by the Road: The Challenges Facing the Artist in "Loneliness"

In his story "Loneliness," Anderson explores the difficulties of communicating without imposing meaning. The story relates the reminiscences of Enoch Robinson, a failed artist, who confides in the aspiring journalist George Willard. As a young man, Enoch became part of a circle of friends, described as "artists of the kind that talk." While these friends "talked and talked with their heads rocking from side to side" about Enoch's paintings, Enoch was "too excited to speak coherently":

> "You don't get the point," he wanted to explain.... The dark spot by the road that you might not notice at all is, you see, the beginning of everything ... in among the elders there is something hidden. It is a woman.... She has been thrown from a horse and the horse has run away out of sight.... She is hurt and suffering but she makes no sound.... I didn't try to paint the woman of course. She is too beautiful to be painted [93].

Enoch deliberately omits a key element of his painting. This "dark spot by the road" is the key to the painting's meaning and beauty. Enoch's reason for not painting the woman is that "She is too beautiful to be painted." There is a sense that depicting the painting's essence cannot do justice to its complexity. If the artist renders this part of the canvas in paint, he will, in the very act of reproducing it, reduce its meaning to a two-dimensional, physical interpretation. This destroys the opportunity that viewers of the painting might otherwise have, to experience their subconscious reactions more fully. The viewer's reaction to the artist's creative process becomes a cerebral one (understanding the meaning dictated by the artist, which carries with it a degree of ideological freight) rather than a visceral one (by which the individual searches for meaning within his/her subconscious). Enoch recognizes that, in withholding interpretation, his work becomes the conduit for a more open and nuanced connection. He is unable to vocalize this, however. The artist aches to be understood, while simultaneously needing to withhold meaning.

This dichotomy is mirrored in Enoch's personal life. Surrounded by the imaginary characters of his inner world, Enoch is able to reconcile these oppositions. When his marriage fails, Enoch withdraws from human company in his New York room. He finds a degree of security with "two dozen" imagined characters, he refers to as "shadow people," whose identities had been "invented by the child-mind of Enoch Robinson, who lived in the room with him" (95). Enoch imagines living alongside an unsullied, innocent part of his own persona. While he is able to isolate himself from the world beyond his room (and its prejudices), he is able to imagine these "shadow people" into being. When the prejudices of the outside world encroach upon him, however, his creative process is destroyed. A new relationship with a woman who "was too big for the room" disrupts Enoch's fragile balance (97). Enoch breaks his own rule and, apparently with a degree of violence, forces the woman to listen to his inner thoughts: "I wanted her to understand but, don't you see, I couldn't let her understand. I felt that then she would know everything, that I would be submerged, drowned out, you see" (97–98). Enoch confronts the dichotomy of being understood and the effect is devastating: "Out she went through the door and all the life there had been in the room followed her out. She took all of my people away" (98). It can be argued that Anderson sees the dichotomy of being understood as irreconcilable for the artist. If you dictate the meaning of your work, its beauty and imagination is destroyed, along with your peace of mind. Yet withholding its meaning risks criticism based on misinterpretation. There is also the sense that it was Enoch's innocent, child-like self which had brought the "shadow people" into being. In telling the woman who was "so grown up" about his people, he unleashes violent emotions and conveys them angrily and too vehemently (97). Anderson expresses all that can be lost if the artist/author coarsely imposes his interpretations on the viewer/reader. The "grown up" opinions formed by the prejudices, or "truths," of society have the ability to destroy the output of the artist and, at the same time, are able to nullify the fragile, vulnerable sense of openness to stimuli which makes the creative process possible.

Sherwood Anderson's Social Radicalism

Within the context of Anderson's wider humanitarian message, this dichotomy of aching to be understood, but needing to withhold meaning, can be seen in terms of the author's conflicting attitudes towards polemic. *Winesburg, Ohio* is, arguably, a socially-radical book, challenging readers to tackle their own class bias and to relinquish the reassuring discourses of class which salved the consciences of privileged Americans. As Enoch's story seems to suggest, however, Anderson was aware that stating his position directly would drive away his audience and, simultaneously, abstract from him the creative impetus necessary to convey his ideas in the future. In preference, Anderson adopts a subtle and ambiguous approach to social critique which, like the "dark spot by the road," has remained largely hidden. *Winesburg, Ohio* is, clearly, a text with a deep social conscience, but the extent of its social radicalism has, until recently, been underestimated within its literary critical legacy. The reasons for this appear to be four-fold: Anderson's rejection of polemic as a conduit for social change; his stylistic choices; his political allegiances; and the traditional theoretical approaches employed for the analysis of texts by "working-class writers."

Absence of polemic: Firstly, as the story "Loneliness" appears to articulate, Anderson's ambitious artistic journey necessitated narratorial ambiguity, with the associated risk of misinterpretation. Anderson was clearly aware of the class bias of his historical, social, and cultural moment. In "The Modern Writer" (1925), Anderson wrote: "There is always that huge, comfortable, self-satisfied American audience made up of all kinds of people with little prejudices, hates and fears that must not be offended" (89). David D. Anderson argues that Sherwood Anderson's response was more confrontational prior to writing *Winesburg, Ohio* (169). He asserts that the polemical "protest and rejection" of materialism in Anderson's two earlier works, *Windy McPherson's Son* (1916) and *Marching Men* (1917), gave way to experimentation with modernist ideas in *Winesburg, Ohio*. As a result, social critique is encoded within Anderson's privileging of the complex emotional lives of the "ordinary" inhabitants of Winesburg. As Lindsay explains:

> Class divisions, awareness of class, social status, and social aspirations appear with some significance in nearly every tale in this work, although it is a theme that is craftily hidden deep, hidden by the absence of a class rhetoric [35].

Issues of economic inequality are neither dealt with directly, at a thematic level, nor expressed through an authorial or narrative voice. I would argue that, as a result, the book has not traditionally been categorized as a vehicle for driving social change, despite its intensive engagement with issues of class.

Stylistic choices: Secondly, I would argue that Anderson's aesthetic approaches in *Winesburg, Ohio*, have tended to mask the text's engagement with matters of economic inequality. Anderson rejects the use of a realist style in favor of experimentation with modernist techniques. In 1924 Anderson wrote, "[T]he story or novel will not be a picture of life. I will never have had any intention of making it that" (93). He admits that it is "Easy enough to get a thrill out of people with reality" but argues that no-one mistakes sensational events (such as a "child falling out at the window of a city office building") as art. "Art is art. It is not life," he emphasizes (90). In rejecting realist form in favor of a modernist aesthetic, Anderson was able to defamiliarize the familiar, forcing readers to look at small town America in new ways. Lindsay articulates this characteristic perfectly, arguing, "Anderson's art doesn't quite let the reader get the emotional or moral purchase that he expects" (12). Modernist techniques enabled Anderson to remove the authorial clues that might otherwise manipulate a reader's response to the narrative, or present the reader with pre-determined attitudes towards the contents of the text. The reader must rely on his or her own reactions to the text to find meaning.

The modernist aesthetic in which Anderson chose to work is not widely seen as a conduit for social critique in this period, however. Prior to this point, texts engaging with issues of economic inequality had favored a realist aesthetic. By contrast, as critics such as John Carey have discussed, modernist texts of this period and their authors have been associated with thematic disconnection from social comment, and individual writers have been considered, by some, to be elitist. Carey notes, for example, that Ezra Pound wrote in 1914: "The artist has no longer any belief or suspicion that the mass, the half-educated simpering general [...] can in any way share his delights" (72). In terms reminiscent of Ruskin's, Pound perpetuates notions of intellectual and aesthetic inferiority of the socially-marginalized, which are entirely at odds with Anderson's world view. Downs notes:

> No sooner than [Anderson] was hailed, the modernist movement closed ranks under the dominance of Eliot and Pound. Both writers privileged reason and intellect over the emotional and native intelligence favored by Anderson. Critics followed suit, and Anderson's ensuing work was often maligned for sentimentalism and lack of form [26].

Winesburg, Ohio, therefore, harnesses modernist techniques to achieve egalitarian ends that are not characteristic of other texts within this stylistic category. This factor can be seen to have contributed to the underestimation of the text as a vehicle for social comment.

Anderson's political allegiances: Thirdly, while authors of socially radical works are often associated with clear political standpoints and allegiances, Anderson's own views in this regard have proved difficult to categorize. Welford Dunaway Taylor describes Anderson's political views as "chameleon-like" (68). David D. Anderson also comments that Anderson was never "seriously interested in practical politics" (105). He notes that, when editing a newspaper in the 1920s, Anderson "farmed out the political editorials to local politicians," rather than taking the opportunity to promote his own views. Anderson was clearly opposed to aspects of capitalism. John W. Crowley argues that Anderson spent his "creative life" disavowing the materialist values that had "pursued him to the edge of his sanity" in his earlier life as a businessman (5). Equally, however, Anderson professed little allegiance to left-wing political ideologies. While earlier critics, such as John Ditsky have discerned in Anderson's work "the inexorable clicking-into-place of a process of dialectic," more recent interpretations have stressed Anderson's ideological distancing from Marxist ideologies (114). Later in life, Anderson wrote, "It is the one thing I would go to any lengths for, to defeat dictatorship, either Communist or Fascist" (150). David D. Anderson argues that, in Anderson's view, Communism was too simplistic an answer to the problems of society. The solution was not to be found in alternative political ideologies, but in the essential humanity of the individual. Jon S. Lawry commented: "[H]is concern is only for the individual man, and, moreover, for that man as an imaginative rather than as an historical realization; the expression of sympathy was to result in artistic rather than political or social expression" (309). Anderson's standpoint, I would argue, is socially radical in that it rejects *all* existing political systems of his historical moment on the basis of their potential to subjugate the individual. The form of revolution that Anderson imagines has to take place within the psyche of every individual. Social reform cannot be brought about by political process, as the ability to change society is only possible through new levels of consciousness at the level of the individual in which citizens are able to see one another anew, and without bias relating to class, race or gender. His vision was an optimistic one. In one of his last letters, Anderson wrote to Mrs. William Brown Meloney: "I have lived long enough, travelled wide enough, and have known the so-called common people enough in the United States to believe that there is, at bottom, a great store of common sense and of belief in democracy in our American people" (466). In many ways, Anderson's approach is counter-cultural, existing outside mainstream political positions, pre-empting ideas that were to emerge in America in the hippie movement of the 1960s. I would argue, therefore, that Anderson's work responds to a secular, counter-cultural vision of the potential for social reform. This form of resistance to hegemonic ideologies of class presents particular challenges for literary critical analysis.

Theoretical Approaches for Analysis of Working-Class Writing

As John F. Lavelle describes, in *Blue Collar, Theoretically: A Post-Marxist Approach to Working Class Literature*, the theoretical frameworks employed traditionally to analyze issues of class in literary texts can prove particularly problematic when critiquing the texts of socially-marginalized authors. Asserting that "Marxism is hegemonic within working-class literature studies" (42), Lavelle argues that, when analyzing texts which fall outside the "golden period of proletarian writing," critics are forced to "try to shoehorn texts not really fitting within their [Marxist] tenets into the parameters, often making assertions with little or no textual evidence" (77). Theoretical positions predicated upon collectivist notions of social reform become increasingly untenable when critiquing texts by authors who rejected such metanarratives. Lavelle explains: "Although workable at a macro level, [Marxist tenets] fall apart at the micro level," and as literature is (overwhelmingly) the creative output of an individual, "written at the micro level of the population," there is a disconnection between theory and text which can result in misinterpretation, or analyses based on insufficient textual support (85–92).

Aspects of Lavelle's argument are demonstrated in Thomas Yingling's Marxist interpretation of *Winesburg, Ohio*, published in 1990. Yingling discerns "nostalgic moments of cultural non-differentiation" in the text, which he sees as the only remaining traces of a "vanished harmony and collectivity" (103). I agree that Anderson appears to hanker after America's agrarian past. Yingling adds however:

> [T]his loss of collective identity places a terrible burden on interiority, on how an individual may fashion the meaning of his or her life [...]. It is this theory of twisted characters as originating in an inaccessible but determining interiority that accounts for the utter desolation of so many lives in Winesburg [103].

I would argue that this Marxist perspective of the text overlooks significant evidence to the contrary in Anderson's correspondence and the comprehensive body of literary critical opinion, which provides the opposite view. Anderson (in my view) articulates, values and celebrates the interiority of Winesburg's inhabitants, seeing problems of communication as aspects of the human condition, not as the undesirability of individual agency. In instances such as this, traditional approaches to literary critical analysis of class risk arriving at interpretations which, while interesting, fail to take into consideration important textual evidence. Marxist-derived theoretical approaches, therefore, do not provide a comprehensive framework within which to analyze Anderson's highly individual forms of resistance to dominant ideologies of class. This is part of a larger discussion regarding textual analysis of work by socially-marginalized authors. New literary critical methods are needed, capable of unpacking complex social critiques in literary texts which have, to date, been overlooked due to the difficulties of analyzing the textual evidence with the available literary critical tools.

To conclude, Sherwood Anderson's *Winesburg, Ohio*, has an extraordinarily ambitious social objective. Anderson rejects reductive representations of working-class characters by other writers of short stories, which were predicated upon assumptions of aesthetic and intellectual inferiority of ordinary people. He refuses to structure his work in a manner that would establish a sense of hierarchy in his narrative. He replaces the traditional "heroic" protagonist at the center of his text with a procession of equally compelling psychological portraits of "all the people of America." Each is defined by nuanced emotion and sophisticated self-awareness of the epiphanic moments of his or her life, irrespective of their social status. In breaking these conventions of working-class representation, Anderson identifies a way forward for writers of a later generation, such as William Faulkner and Ernest Hemingway.[6] By understanding the problems inherent in realist styles and forms, and experimenting with emerging modernist techniques, he was able to take small town life in the early twentieth century and "make it new" (as Ezra Pound insisted was necessary). At the heart of his text, however, Anderson placed a dichotomy. His white-haired writer, and the misunderstood artist Enoch Robinson, do not have the answers, but they feel the need for change acutely. They urge the individual reader to start the revolution, beginning with his or her own impact on the world, rather than relying on the potential of political ideologies (of any flavor) to bring about change. His rallying call is extraordinarily relevant, I would argue, to our own historical moment.

NOTES

1. Lara Baker Whelan's chapter entitled "Dying of One's Neighbours: Victorian Suburban Literature and its Deconstruction of the Suburban Ideal" in *Class, Culture and Suburban Anxieties in the Victorian Era* places these discourses of class in context. In addition, Victoria Kelley's article "'The Virtues of a Drop of Cleansing Water': Domestic Work and Cleanliness in the British Working Classes, 1880–1914" is a useful source for understanding the link between hygiene and moral attitudes in this period.

2. As the character's name and dialogue clearly delineate Mrs. Murphy as being from an Irish background, there are important issues relating to representation of race in this short story that also deserve further literary critical analysis.

3. In his *Memoirs*, however, Anderson claims that the inspiration for the *Winesburg* stories came from the "unsuccessful Little Children of the Arts" with whom he shared a Chicago rooming house (155).
4. Publisher B.W. Huebsch's recommendation to change the book's title is discussed by John Updike in his 1984 article for *Harper's Magazine*.
5. For more information, refer to Michel Foucault, *The Archaeology of Knowledge* (1969).
6. Refer, for example, to Martin Bidney's 1993 article "'Windy McPherson's Son' and Silent McEachern's Son: Sherwood Anderson and 'Light in August'" for more information on Anderson's influence on William Faulkner.

Works Cited

Anderson, David D. *Sherwood Anderson: An Introduction and Interpretation*. New York: Holt, Rinehart and Winston, 1967.
Anderson, Sherwood. "Letter to George Freitag, August 27th, 1938." *Letters of Sherwood Anderson*. Eds. Howard Mumford Jones and Walter Rideout. Boston: Little, Brown and Co., 1953. 403–407.
_____. "Letter to Mrs. William Brown Meloney, December 27th, 1940." *Letters of Sherwood Anderson*. Eds. Howard Mumford Jones and Walter Rideout. Boston: Little, Brown and Co., 1953. 466–467.
_____. "Letter to Reverend Arthur H. Smith." Reprinted in *Winesburg, Ohio*. New York: W.W. Norton, 1996. 142–144.
_____. "The Modern Writer." Reprinted in *Sherwood Anderson: A Study of the Short Fiction*. Ed. Robert Allen Papinchak. Woodbridge, CT: Twayne, 1992. 89.
_____. "A Note on Realism." Reprinted in *Sherwood Anderson: A Study of the Short Fiction*. Ed. Robert Allen Papinchak. Woodbridge, CT: Twayne, 1992. 90–93.
_____. *Sherwood Anderson: Selected Letters*. Ed. Charles E. Modlin. Knoxville: University of Tennessee Press, 1984.
_____. *Sherwood Anderson's Memoirs*. Rpt. *Winesburg, Ohio*. New York: W.W. Norton, 1996.
_____. *Winesburg, Ohio*. New York: W.W. Norton, 1996.
Baker Whelan, Lara. *Class, Culture and Suburban Anxieties in the Victorian Era*. New York: Routledge, 2010.
Bidney, Martin. "Refashioning Coleridge's Supernatural Trilogy: Sherwood Anderson's *A Man of Ideas* and *Respectability*." *Studies in Short Fiction*, 27, 2, Spring 1990. 221–235.
_____. "*Windy McPherson's Son* and Silent McEachern's son: Sherwood Anderson and *Light in August*." *The Mississippi Quarterly*, vol. 46, no. 3, Summer 1993. 395.
Carey, John. *The Intellectuals and the Masses: Pride and Prejudice among the Literary Intelligentsia, 1880–1939*. London: Faber, 1992.
Crowley, John W. "Introduction." *New Essays on* Winesburg, Ohio. Ed. John W. Crowley. New York: Cambridge University Press, 1990.
Ditsky, John. "Sherwood Anderson's *Marching Men*: Unnatural Disorder and the Art of Force." *Twentieth Century Literature*, vol. 23, no. 1, 1977. 102–114.
Downs, Stuart. "Thirteen Poems: Sherwood Anderson." *The American Poetry Review*, May-June 2007, pp. 25–30.
Dunaway Taylor, Welford, "Anderson and the Problem of Belonging." *Sherwood Anderson: Dimensions of His Literary Art*. Ed. David D. Anderson. East Lansing: Michigan State University Press, 1976. 61–74.
Henry, O. "Between Rounds." *The Four Million*. New York: Doubleday Page, 1906.
Jacobson, Marcia. "*Winesburg, Ohio* and the Autobiographical Moment." *New Essays on* Winesburg, Ohio. Ed. John W. Crowley. New York: Cambridge University Press, 1990. 53–72.
James, Henry. "Preface to The Princess Casamassima," Reprinted in P.J. Keating, *The Working Classes in Victorian Fiction*. New York: Routledge and Kegan Paul, 1971.
Keating, P.J. *The Working Classes in Victorian Fiction*. New York: Routledge and Kegan Paul, 1971.

Kelley, Victoria. "'The Virtues of a Drop of Cleansing Water': Domestic Work and Cleanliness in the British Working Classes, 1880–1914," *Women's History Review*, 18:5, 2009, pp. 719–735.

Lavelle, John F. *Blue Collar, Theoretically: A Post-Marxist Approach to Working Class Literature*. Jefferson, NC: McFarland, 2012.

Lawry, Jon S. "*Death in the Woods* and the Artist's Self in Sherwood Anderson," *PMLA*, vol. 74, no. 3, 1959. 306–311.

Lindsay, Clarence. *Such a Rare Thing: The Art of Sherwood Anderson's* Winesburg, Ohio. Kent, OH: Kent State University Press, 2009.

Morss Lovett, Robert. "Sherwood Anderson (1936)." Reprinted in *Sherwood Anderson: A Study of the Short Fiction*. Ed. Robert Allen Papinchak. Woodbridge, CT: Twayne, 1992. 98–104.

Mulroy Curry, Martha. "Anderson's Theories on Writing Fiction." *Sherwood Anderson: Dimensions of His Literary Art*. Ed. David D. Anderson. East Lansing: Michigan State University Press, 1976. 90–109.

Mumford Jones, Howard, and Walter Rideout, eds. *Letters of Sherwood Anderson*. Boston: Little, Brown and Company, 1953.

Ruskin, John. "Of Vulgarity." 1906. Public domain ebook.

Spencer, Benjamin T. "Sherwood Anderson: American Mythopoeist," *American Literature*, vol. 41, no. 1, March 1969, pp. 1–18.

Stouck, David. "Anderson's Expressionist Art." *New Essays on* Winesburg, Ohio. Ed. John W. Crowley. New York: Cambridge University Press, 1990. 27–51.

Swafford, Kevin. *Class in Late-Victorian Britain: The Narrative Concern with Social Hierarchy and its Representation*. Amherst, NY: Cambria Press, 2007.

Townsend, Kim. "The Achievement of *Winesburg*." *Winesburg, Ohio*. New York: W.W. Norton, 1996. 203–210.

Trilling, Lionel. *The Liberal Imagination*. New York: Viking Press, 1950.

Updike, John. "Twisted Apples," *Harper's Magazine* 268, March 1984.

Wild, Jonathan. *The Rise of the Office Clerk in Literary Culture, 1880–1939*. London: Palgrave Macmillan, 2006.

Yingling, Thomas. "*Winesburg, Ohio* and the End of Collective Experience." *New Essays on* Winesburg, Ohio. Ed. John W. Crowley. New York: Cambridge University Press, 1990. 99–128.

Losing Control
Contrasting Identity Constructs in Jean Toomer's Cane

CHARLENE TAYLOR EVANS

> I am of no particular race. I am of the human race, a
> man at large in this human world, ...
> I am of no specific regions. I am of earth.
> —Jean Toomer

In his autobiographical essay "On Being American," Jean Toomer asserts his position on being born "mixed race" and the difficulties associated with living within the rigid racial categorizations of late nineteenth and twentieth century America. Additionally, in a 1923 missive to his publisher Horace Liveright, Toomer was adamant that his racial composition and position in the world were realities that he alone could determine and that he did not expect to be told what he should consider himself to be. Jean Toomer's strong feelings about the right of self-definition contextualize his view of the fact of race as the major determinant of a person's identity in America having a negative effect on the class identity of "racial" and "racially ambiguous" minorities. Accordingly, Cane (1923), Toomer's semi-autobiographical modernist text, is comprised of poignant sketches or vignettes of characters who struggle against the debilitating effects of their social environments in a fashion that demonstrates Toomer's philosophy of social formation and critiques racial caste and classification.

In Cane, Toomer portrays the impact of race and miscegenation on the lives of his characters, both black and white, living in the North and South. Toomer's characters are faced with societal pressures that are physically, spiritually, and psychologically destructive. Some of them attempt to increase their cultural, economic, and political power while others acquiesce to the seemingly insurmountable forces against them. Characters grapple with issues of gender and class, and many are labeled as social outcasts and are isolated and alienated within the larger communities. For example, female characters rendered helpless by their gender appear particularly damaged and vacuous in Toomer's sketches. Although there is an implication that one can find escape through creative works as an artist, in general, there is little resolution for the problems faced by these characters. Toomer's dysfunctional protagonists are embroiled in cycles of confusion and chaos. Many of the characters in *Cane* appear weak, vulnerable, and oftentimes dysfunctional, for race and gender dictate social class which is, in turn, a contributing factor to their victimization.

In short, the narration of identity through class ideologies and the separation of social classes are evidenced in *Cane*. Although the novel does not conform to traditional narrative models and is experimental in form and content, the unifying aspects are spiritual; they communicate the "controlling" values and beliefs of the status quo. The elemental thematic concerns of the search for self-realization; the relationships between individuals, families and community; issues of race, gender and socio-economic class; and pressures to conform in a dominant society are all operatives in this work. The theme of the intuitive-self juxtaposed to the conflicting internalized mores of society, the developing consciousness of representative characters linked to societal entrapments, the use of language as a method of entrapment and escape (creating a dialectic and using language against itself) and the rejection or acceptance of values and norms associated with hegemony will all be explored in the novel as appropriate.

In the late 1960s, there was a renewed interest in Toomer, and the sheer volumes of scholarship concentrating on his life and oeuvre are noteworthy considering the general consensus that *Cane* is his only work of any real merit. One might surmise that Waldo Frank's introduction to the first edition of the book identifying Toomer as a "Negro," Liveright's request to highlight Toomer's "Negro" ethnicity for marketing purposes, and Toomer's objection and resistance to being classified racially as a "Negro" or to have his work included in Alain Locke's *The New Negro: An Interpretation* (1925) and other black anthologies were all hindrances to his initial reception and publication efforts. Although the Harlem Renaissance provided publishing opportunities for black writers, Toomer held that his identification as a part of a group would have been reductive, and if he were considered "Negro," he would be relegated to an inferior social status or caste. In *Jean Toomer and Nella Larsen: The Invisible Darkness*, Charles Larson affirms Toomer's reluctance to being promoted as a black writer:

> In *Cane*, Toomer had reached out and attempted to embrace his darkness but ... if he continued to identify himself as a black man his life would always bear the stigma of restriction. Instead of expanding his perspective, blackness, he feared,

would limit it.... What he wanted was something larger, bigger, wider: completeness [38].

Seeking knowledge of his paternal heritage, Toomer was awakened to his black roots in the South; however, he did not want to deny the other parts of his ontology.

In addition, Toomer's association and psychological alignment with the spiritual teachings of Georges Ivanovitch Gurdjieff, the influential, yet controversial Eastern mystic, as well as his immersion into Quakerism, did little to benefit him with his mainstream publication efforts. Toomer's failure to publish any other works of major significance was not for a lack of effort on his part, however, because he labored assiduously for most of his life in an attempt to sustain his literary voice and support himself with his writings. His blatant rejection of racial categorizations and his rather dogged search for "harmony and wholeness" placed him outside of the norm and restricted him to a life of isolation in his later years. Though Toomer grew up living in black and white communities, he was generally considered a member of the Washington Negro "elite" and was aware of the challenges associated with being black in America; this led him to refuse to accept the binary racial structure thrust upon him by the status quo.

In "The Negro Artist and the Racial Mountain," Langston Hughes examines Toomer's literary success in *Cane* as well as issues associated with the black/white dichotomy and contrastive reactions to the book's publication:

> The Negro artist works against an undertow of sharp criticism and misunderstanding from his own group and unintentional bribes from the whites.... Both would have told Jean Toomer not to write *Cane*. The colored people did not praise it. The white people did not buy it. The colored people who did read *Cane* hate it. Although critics gave it good reviews, the public remained indifferent. Yet (excepting the work of W.E.B. Du Bois) *Cane* contains the finest prose written by a Negro in America [1313].

Hughes's assessment and his interesting comparison of Toomer to Dubois is high praise, and an indication of Hughes's belief in the social significance of Toomer's work.

Du Bois published a book review of *Cane* in *The Crisis* magazine, applauding Toomer's impressionistic style and provocative presentation of the sexual conventionality of his female characters; however, overall, Du Bois found the work to be somewhat dense and almost impenetrable:

> The artist, of course, has a right deliberately to make his art a puzzle to the interpreter (the whole world is a puzzle) but on the other hand, I am myself unduly irritated by this sort of thing.... All of these essays and stories ... have their flashes of power, their numerous messages, and numberless reasons for being [171].

Unlike Du Bois, Toomer utilizes a modernist canvas in *Cane*, providing an innovative portrayal of the issues of social stratification and racial inequality that both see facing blacks in twentieth century America. Connecting with his audience on numerous levels, Toomer elicits a more visceral, multi-faceted response to his work, leaving the "puzzle" for the "interpreter" to solve. A metaphor of black life, the literary form of *Cane* defies categorization as it crosses genres of fiction, drama, and poetry, with its tripartite structure and settings forming a circular pattern: with action beginning in the South, followed by movement paralleling the Great Migration with action taking place in the Washington D.C. and Chicago areas, and finally returning to the South in rural Georgia.

Initially, the ebbs and flows of critical interest in *Cane*, by both black and white critics, focused on Toomer's avant-garde literary style and thematic concerns relative to black life in urban and rural environments; however, Toomer's own racial exoticism as well as his, unabashedly, unconventional lifestyle seemed to overshadow his literary talents, and though these factors were deterrents to his financial success as a writer, they became points of interest for subsequent generations of Toomer scholars. After all, Toomer had refused to conform to societal dictates, exposed racial issues that had been camouflaged and ignored, and had asserted his own forms of control and authority on his personal life, as reflected in his revelatory depictions of race relations in *Cane* as well as his flamboyant relationships and violations of legal norms with his marriages to white women. On the whole, his partners, seemingly, had few, if any, problems with his being labeled "Negro" or with providing him financial support. Some believe that Toomer's decision to marry outside of his designated racial caste was indicative of his choice to become a part of the white race, but another likelihood is that this was an act of rebellion against the status quo and an assertion of the "power" and control he maintained over his life. Indeed, Toomer's protean racial identity, coupled with his desire to repurpose the racial narrative in *Cane*, has generated myriad theoretical analyses and has had a dramatic effect on American racial discourse.

The unique issues and restrictions associated with race and racial fluidity, particularly as it relates to blacks, gave rise to destructive psychological and spiritual problems for Americans with long term implications for race relations. This topic forms the crux of Toomer's work. The idea of an individual's losing control, or never having control, of his own person, his body, or physical space is reflected in the lives of the male and female characters in *Cane*. The characters' lack of control or "position" in life is relegated by race and, subsequently, confines them into a social class or caste. In "Jean Toomer's Washington and the Politics of Class," Barbara Foley contends that in many readings of *Cane*, race has been decoupled from class and that Toomer's articulation of racial identification is construed largely in isolation from considerations of economic power and social stratification (315). Foley suggests that

> Toomer's formative experiences among the capital's "blue-veined" aristocracy of color, as well as his engagement with socialist politics, had a profound impact upon the categories through which he perceived and articulated racial issues in his writings of the early 1920s—especially the Washington, D.C., portion of *Cane* [315].

While one of the most striking aspects of Toomer's *Cane* is its lyrical style, inherent in its lyricism is his depiction of race, and the concomitant issues of racial inequality and class are major thematic concerns; thus an examination of many of the subtexts in the novel juxtaposed to Toomer's historical awareness and sensitivities regarding these issues confirms an important, and discernible, understanding of his desire to escape the race/class dichotomy in America. Ostensibly Toomer's consciousness was informed by his racial heritage and ambivalence, his familiarity with life behind and beyond "the veil," a deep and abiding understanding of his social environments, as well as his knowledge of legalistic issues related to social class and caste.

After the Emancipation Proclamation in 1863, which granted freedom to the slaves in Confederate states, and the 13th Amendment in 1865, which abolished slavery in the United States, freedom for blacks was illusory. "That problem of the past," according to Du Bois, "so far as the black American was concerned, began with caste—a definite place preordained in custom, law and religion where all men of black blood must be thrust" ("Evolution of the Race Problem"1). America's racial caste system undergirds and binds the narratives, poetry, and drama in *Cane* thematically. Based on inequality and comprised of a group of people locked into an inferior position, no dynamic change or recourse can occur within a racial caste. Blacks of any racial composition, as graphically portrayed in Toomer's characterizations in *Cane,* are immobilized and in anguish because they do not have the power of self-determination. A common option of social mobility for blacks of mixed racial heritage was to "pass for white," and to separate themselves from the social paralysis and stigma of being relegated to a racial caste. An individual generally has to relocate and live a life of secrecy, abandoning black familial ties and basically reinventing him or herself. One of the key aspects of "passing" is concealment, and an individual must possess the mental fortitude to repel the demeaning fictions assigned to the black race as well as accept and assume the identity of the oppressors. The consequences of passing were psychologically overwhelming, as illustrated in "Bona and Paul."

In "Bona and Paul," a sketch in the second section of *Cane,* which takes place in the North, there is a "likeness of Toomer in the character of Paul who prefigures Toomer's personal dilemma with racial matter" (Larson 32). Paul is racially self-conscious because he is attempting to "pass" for white. Although Bona is white, she is drawn to Paul's swarthy complexion and his "difference"; she knows that he is black because the whole dormitory had whispered that he was "nigger," and even then she finds him attractive.

> "She [Bona] explains to herself by a piece of information which a friend of hers had given her: men like him can fascinate. One is not responsible for fascination. Not one girl had really loved Paul: he fascinated them" [*Cane* 78].

Paul does not believe that Bona truly cares for him; he feels awkward and is uncomfortable with Bona and his group of white friends as he enters a segregated nightclub at Crimson Gardens in Chicago. Paul feels that someone will see his blackness:

> People.... University of Chicago students, members of the stock exchange, a large Negro in crimson uniform who guards the door ... had watched them enter. Had leaned towards each other ... and whispered. What is he, a Spaniard, an Indian, an Italian, a Mexican, or a Japanese? [*Cane* 76].

The fear of recognition is a major challenge for Paul, and he is tormented by the contradictory narratives which define his identity in binary terms. According to societal standards, Paul is supposed to be repulsive, yet Bona is drawn to him; his internal conflict with America's social taboos prevents him from reciprocating her feelings. Paul's identity is unreconciled in cultural discourse, and he is indecisive and struggles within the boundaries of the black/white dichotomy. In a letter to Georgia O'Keeffe, Toomer's friend and confidant, he asks if she has read "Bona and Paul," and he shares with her his belief that the reader will not understand the narrative because of restrictive racial categorizations:

> Most people cannot see this story because of the inhibitory baggage they bring with them. When I say "white," they see a certain white man, when I say "black," they see a certain Negro [Rusch 280].

The racial complexities related to Paul's neurotic behavior represent the impact of societal norms on individuals and community. Both language and social stratification cause Paul's anxiety and paranoia, leaving him unable to function within the cultural framework of his white friends or the black doorman. Paul believes that the doorman can *see* his blackness, and he feels compelled to inform him that he is wrong about his race or the likelihood of his having a successful relationship with Bona. Paul addresses him as "Brother," and tells him of his error, and the doorman answers "Yassur," in the servile tone of one who is still enslaved and accepting of his caste. The doorman's eyes show that he sees Paul and his black mixed-race reality. Paul says, "I came back to tell you, to shake your hand, and tell you that you are wrong" (80). Since Paul is "passing," he can live outside of the restrictions of the racial caste only on a physical level; however, both he and the doorman are victimized and imprisoned psychologically.

As inheritors of America's dehumanizing system of chattel slavery, Blacks have remained bound by the harsh strictures of a society that enslaved them and after emancipation unleashed Jim Crow and other insidious and systemic restrictions on their lives. Blacks were released from the subjugation they suffered on the plantations to another form of enslavement—a racial caste. Even racially indeterminate individuals who successfully "passed" and were assimilated into white communities were haunted by guilt and fears of discovery, and they were tormented by social fictions of inferiority assigned to the black race.

With that in mind, German sociologist Max Weber's views on social stratification and class as well as his focus on individuals and "life chances" provides an additional lens for textual analysis of *Cane*. Moreover, a Weberian perspective of "class," in conjunction with several ideological views and theories developed by Du Bois offers even more insight into the challenges of blacks and the persistence of racial conflict in modern and postmodern America. In 1904, while visiting the Universal Exposition in St. Louis, Missouri, Weber met with DuBois and asked for a German translation of *Souls of Black Folk* (1903), Du Bois's seminal work, and it is from this work that Du Bois makes the powerful, visionary statement that "the problem of the twentieth century is the problem of the color-line" (692); also, Weber collaborated with Du Bois on *Die Negerfrage in den Vereinigten Staaten: The Negro Question in the United States (1906)*; and, finally, in a meeting of the German sociological society in Frankfurt, Germany, in 1910, Weber issued a resounding endorsement of Du Bois, claiming that "the most important sociological scholar anywhere in the Southern States of America, with whom no white scholar can compare, is a Negro—Burckhardt Du Bois" (Weber, 1910/1973, 312; 1910/1971). Albeit Weber qualifies Du Bois as "Negro," his comparison of Du Bois to white scholars is significant and a denunciation of racial fictions that challenge the intellectual abilities of blacks. Though some of Du Bois's views were considered paradoxical, his pre-eminence, both nationally and internationally, especially as it relates to race, class, and social stratification, remains foundationally unchallenged.

Like Weber, Du Bois understood fully that any theories which do not examine the social relations between exploiters and those who are exploited, or that disregard this relationship altogether, are unable to explain the reality of the human condition fully and, therefore, are likely to provide an empty or bankrupt perspective ("Du Bois and Rushton Coulborn" *The Journal of Modern History*, 14 [December 1942]: 500–21).

When asked about how the class struggle was applied to blacks in America, Du Bois responded in an essay in *The Crisis* magazine:

> Theoretically we (blacks) are part of the world proletariat in the sense that we are mainly an exploited class of cheap laborers; but practically we are not a part of the white proletariat to any great extent. We are the victims of their physical oppression, social ostracism, economic exclusion and personal hatred ["The Class Struggle" 141].

As Toomer consistently demonstrated in *Cane*, racism prevented blacks from achieving "wholeness" as individuals within the context of standards set by the white power structure. Consequently, and in response, blacks began to create their own racial hierarchies, elitist divisions/groups within their communities. The "feigned" upward social mobility of blacks during the post Reconstruction era was pitiable, as white racist groups, indiscriminately, regardless of skin color or socio-economic level, shattered their attempts of property ownership and self-sufficiency by inflicting numerous obstructions and horrific acts of violence on them. Moreover, because of the heterogeneity within black communities, it was difficult to build solidarity among black groups; fear and distrust were rampant, and this did not create a climate for unity or cohesion. Although survival was a common interest for all, most blacks bore irreversible emotional scars that served as tools of separation and confusion. Even though Toomer was aware of the racial challenges blacks faced in Washington, D.C., and Louisiana, his "watershed" moment was crystallized after his trip to Sparta, Georgia, and its surroundings with Waldo Frank. Earth or Georgia red clay was an epistemology for Toomer as he saw his kinship to the natural surroundings and the folk culture. He witnessed the tragedy of the South found in the ravaged land and in the faces of the people he encountered. Miscegenation had been rampant in the South during slavery; black mothers had been victims of sexual exploitation by their white slave owners, and the remnants of these numerous violations were in the mixed-race progeny, who in time populated America's caste system and became the embodiment of the black race in America. In "Race Problems and Modern Society," Toomer illustrates the prevalence of race mixing:

> This mingling of bloods has been recognized and formulated as a maxim of anthropology. Even so, because of the American social system that keeps racial, national and cultural groups "divided and repellent," the consciousness of most so-called Americans lags far behind the organic process [168].

In "Race, Ethnicity, and the Weberian Legacy," John Stone addresses the general belief about the enmity that southern whites harbor against blacks, and he debunks the belief that whites have a natural repulsion towards blacks because of the occurrence of "the large number of mixed-race offspring from interracial unions and sexual relationships" (2). Also he notes

America's inconsistency that any visible trace of black blood in an offspring of this kind relegated an individual to a subordinate social status "whereas significant amounts of 'Indian blood' did not" (Stone 2). According to Stone, "Weber's explanation for this strange differential rests with the institution of slavery, which was unique to the black experience in America" (Stone 2). The rule of hypodescent or "one drop" of black blood served as an authorized social code followed in the United States during and after Reconstruction. The problem, of course, is that the "one drop" rule, or the composition of a person's blood, could not be determined scientifically. Moreover, one's race is not corporeal and cannot be determined by blood or physical appearance, specifically, hair texture, physical traits, and, most importantly, the color of a person's skin. The overriding fear of racial amalgamation was the impetus for the development of this code, and the cause of the high incidence of mixed-race births rests squarely on the hands of the people in control, southern whites and the plantation system. Rebecca Nisetich suggests that the legal discourse on racial identity was codified by the 1896 Plessy v Ferguson decision that ignored, concealed, and simplified the gaps in knowledge inherent in a structure that defined identity by "drops of blood." From a racial standpoint, one's identity is nebulous at best, and race is a social construct with no intrinsic connection to human variations. These ambiguities paved a small avenue for self-determination, and blacks persisted and continued the struggle for equality within America's socio-economic systems.

In his unpublished essay "The Negro Emergent," Toomer addresses the issue of social divisions/elitist groups within black communities and the seemingly disproportionate opportunities afforded blacks of a lighter complexion. He states that "the split within the Negro group is due to differences in skin color and economic preferences, which is often stimulated by the white group, and that this creates disdain and contempt on the part of those of lighter color and better position" (87). Imbedded in miscegenation, the idea of light-skinned privilege or "colorism" has persisted into the twenty-first century and continues to create schisms within black communities. Toomer's perceptions of colorism and his own racial indeterminacy afforded him the opportunity to live in the world of "socially elite" blacks and whites, particularly his early life with Pinckney Benton Stewart Pinchback, his maternal grandfather, who himself vacillated between races. In an excerpt from Toomer's "Outline of an Autobiography," he speaks of the innocence of light skinned blacks and their commonalities with whites:

> My new friends were ... no different from the boys and girls ... in white groups. They behaved as American youths of that age and class behave ... new friends of mine were not conscious of being either colored or white. They had no active prejudices against black people or white people.... Segregation if known to them meant nothing. They had never run up against the color line [Turner 85].

Outside of the confines of the black bourgeoisie community, things were different, and as Toomer matured, he sought an even higher level of freedom, perhaps realizing that this lifestyle was transitory. Taking control of his life, Toomer assumed black and white identities periodically as it suited his personal needs, forgetting that once he was racially identified as black, he could no longer live comfortably in certain regions of the United States.

In his autobiography, *The Big Sea*, Langston Hughes reveals a negative side of the upper class society and culture created by blacks living in Washington, D.C., and other affluent areas during the Harlem Renaissance:

> The "better class" Washington colored people ... drew rigid class and color lines within the race against Negroes who worked with their hands, or who were dark in complexion and had no degrees from colleges.... They were ... unbearable and snobbish.... They lived in comfortable homes, had fine cars, played bridge, drank Scotch, gave exclusive "formal" parties, and dressed well, but seemed to me altogether lacking in real culture, kindness, or good common sense [206–07].

Mirroring the behavior of upper class whites, the so-called black elite were condescending and contemptuous of the less fortunate of their race. They sincerely believed that they had escaped the caste system and were superior to the majority of struggling blacks. Furthermore, Hughes notes that some members of the black bourgeoisie boasted of being directly descended from the leading Southern white families, "on the colored side"—which meant the "illegitimate side" (*The Big Sea* 208). The notion of blacks taking pride in being related to members of a so-called genteel southern aristocracy is ironic, and members of the black elite were delusional to think that they would receive any real honor from their white heritage. Generally speaking, blacks of any racial composition were relegated to the caste system and unable to enjoy the equal status of their white counterparts on any level.

In their comprehensive biography *The Lives of Jean Toomer: A Hunger for Wholeness*, Kerman and Eldridge cite the constant struggle that Toomer and his grandfather had engaged in as it relates to power, status, and control:

> Class and status, wealth, loyalty, fine appearance, and power were held up against sensitivity, fantasy, intricate blood-confused human relationships, pain, beauty, and truth. Yet even rejecting his grandfather and stubbornly choosing his own way to fame, Jean was reflecting his grandfather's independence and grasp of power [74].

Admittedly, Toomer acknowledged his grandfather's influence on his life, but his desire for control was self-motivated. His functioning as part of the black elite obviously left him unfulfilled, and his numerous unsuccessful stints in college demonstrate his future patterns of nonconformity and independent spirit. Perhaps his physical appearance would have allowed him to live as a white man, but once he was published as a black writer, the option was no longer available to him.

Toomer's rendering of negotiations of identity through class ideologies and the separation of social classes is evidenced in "Kabnis," the final section of *Cane*. Ralph Kabnis, Toomer's alter ego, struggles with the subtexts of elitism, fear, and paranoia in this drama. Kabnis is an educated Northerner of mixed ancestry who accepts a post at a black agricultural and mechanical school in a small town in Georgia. He has been recruited by Hanby, a caricature of a member of the southern black upper class and president of the colored school. Hanby's responsibilities include raising operational funds, hiring teachers, and interacting with the school's white benefactors. He is inebriated by his "authority" and "position" and is out of touch with the dangerous realities of the South. Kabnis, Professor Layman, and Fred Halsey, a middle-class black shop owner, are sharing a bottle of whiskey and discussing the random and widespread violence and victimization of blacks of any complexion or occupation, including "preachers and school teachers an everybody" when Hanby comes to visit. Heedless of their conversation, Hanby enters Kabnis's room with an obliviousness to his own relative unimportance and actual position in the larger society:

> He [Hanby] is a well-dressed, smooth, rich, black-skinned Negro who thinks that no one is quite as polished as himself. To members of his own race, he affects the manners of a wealthy white planter.... To white men he bows, without ever completely humbling himself. Tradesmen in the town tolerate him because he spends his money with them. He delivers his words with a full consciousness of his moral superiority [95].

Hanby is annoyed by Kabnis's lack of decorum and inappropriate lifestyle of drinking and smoking, and he has planned to relieve Kabnis of his duties. Hanby is unaware that Kabnis's behavior is a coping mechanism to counteract his fear of the rampant southern violence toward blacks as well as his problem with his deplorable physical space. Kabnis is haunted by the "ghosts" of Blacks who suffered the atrocities of slavery, and, in a Faulknerian sense, he believes that the past is never dead and is ever-present. Kabnis is unable to find solace in his status as a mixed race, educated Northerner, and Hanby views his behavior as weak and cowardly. Kabnis's behavior is contrary to Hanby's psychological position and his misguided ideas about what his education has done for him. Hanby's hope for "coloreds" and allegiance to his goal of setting a good example is captured in this declaration of his own self-importance:

> Hum. Erer, Professor Kabnis, to come straight to the point: the progress of the Negro race is jeopardized whenever the personal habits and examples set by its

guides and mentors fall below the acknowledged and hard won standard of its average member. This institution ... has been maintained at a cost of great labor and untold sacrifice. Its purpose is to teach our youth to live better, cleaner, more noble lives, to prove to the world that the Negro race can be just like any other race [95].

Though Hanby is dark skinned, he feels that he is in a privileged class. Although well-intentioned, he erroneously believes that his position and educational accomplishments have somehow made him superior to other blacks and immune to the dangers of the Jim Crow South.

Marcus Garvey, Pan-Africanist and civil rights activist, referred to the groups of people like Hanby as belonging to "bastard aristocracies" who were trying to maintain themselves at the expense of the masses:

> The Negro has had enough of ... race superiority as inflicted upon him by others; therefore, he is not prepared to tolerate a similar assumption on the part of his own people. In America ... we have Negroes who believe themselves so much above their fellows as to cause them to think that any readjustment in the affairs of the race should be placed in their hands for them to exercise ... control as others have done to us for centuries [Garvey 999].

Based in Harlem, New York, the Universal Negro Improvement Association (UNIA) and its weekly publication, were efforts to establish racial unity and pride among blacks. Although Garvey's success was short-lived, his attempts to create jobs and provide blacks an opportunity to re-connect with their African heritage were important steps toward the development of a more unified presence. With no desire for assimilation or participating in America's racial hierarchy, Garvey initiated a "Back to Africa" movement with a platform that was an attractive option to many. On the other hand, and perhaps unwittingly, some blacks had surrendered their identities and lost themselves in the throes of a false hope to advance in the chaotic American experiment that would not embrace them and, conceivably, never accept them as equals.

The self-importance of the "black bourgeoisie" and the professional and financial accomplishments they had attained were soon to be undone after sweeping violence in a number of American cities erupted during what is referred to as the Red Summer in 1919; the riots broke out a year after the end of World War I. Although blacks willingly volunteered for the military, they were assigned to menial positions and were not treated as men for their service. Suffering from feelings of guilt and a paranoia which stemmed from the brutal treatment they had inflicted upon blacks during slavery, many whites assumed that blacks would seek revenge, so they were reluctant to put guns in the hands of former slaves and allow them to join in the war. The jaws of the rigid caste system had not been loosened, and blacks suffered unrelenting discrimination even while trying to protect "their" country.

When blacks returned to their homes after the war, they observed that white oppression was alive and well and little had changed. Moreover, when lower class white veterans returned, they were displeased and envious of the economic progress that had been made by the black elite, so they fabricated reasons to justify violence against them. The Red Summer was a catalyzing event for black World War I veterans, family men, and entrepreneurs who refused to be slaughtered and have their homes and businesses destroyed by their white countrymen; the black community took up arms to defend themselves. The rise and dominance of the Ku Klux Klan terrorized blacks through numerous acts of brutality, and Blacks met violence with violence.

Whites were not accustomed to the openly combative, widespread responses by Blacks to their onslaught of brutal attacks. While the number of white supremacist organizations and hate mongers increased, the former enslaved Blacks were emboldened to defend themselves and their families, and the black women could not have been happier. In an unsigned letter published in *The Crisis* magazine, Paula Giddings cites a black woman's response to the bravery of the black men who fought back during the riots:

> The Washington riot gave me the thrill that comes once in a lifetime.... At last our men had stood like men, struck back, were no longer dumb driven cattle.... Oh I thank God ... a woman loves a strong man, she delights to feel that her man can protect her, fight for her if necessary, save her... [184].

In "Reflections on the Race Riots" (1919), Toomer presents a contrary position on what he refers to as the true nature of the "fighting psychology" of Blacks:

> The central fact emerging from the recent series of race riots is not so much that the Negro has developed an essentially new psychology.... The Negro has always been conspicuous for his aggressiveness.... What is significant is that the Negro, for the first time in American history, has directed his "fight" against the iniquities of the white man in the United States. It is, of course, obvious that this fighting spirit received a decided stimulus in the form of the world war [qtd. In Scruggs and VanDemarr 226].

In Toomer's essay, he boldly lists current and historical indignities hurled against Blacks, and as citizens, he maintained that they had a responsibility to launch a full-fledged defense. Critics who have classified Toomer's retreat from black communities as cowardly should remember that he never really chose to be white; his objective was always to transcend racial delineations. Even though black men had formally re-established the manhood that had been taken away from them during slavery, and they had exhibited great courage in defending their families, after the Red Summer all knew that the idea of a black aristocracy was an oxymoron in the larger society. Blacks of any racial composition remained in the caste system, and there was little real progress being made toward racial equality in the United States.

Conceivably, we might also use Weber's concept of "life chances," (*Lebenschancen*), as an operative term for sociological analysis of Toomer's characters in Cane because if an individual is born poor and/or black, his/her life chances are low. Post-slavery, blacks had few possibilities of obtaining a quality education, fair employment, housing, food, and other necessities; hence, opportunities for advancement were little to none, and women were even less fortunate. In poignant examinations of the absence of life chances in the South, Toomer's perceptions of the intersectionality of race, class, and gender are shown in his several scenarios of women in *Cane*.

In the first section of the text, comprised of six vignettes of women living in the South with prose poems interspersed among their impressionistic portraits, Weber's concept of life chances provides additional insight into their situations. Karintha, Becky, Carma, Fern, Esther, and Louisa are tragic representations of women who are victims of a misogynistic society wherein women have been abused and defiled by men; they are victims of oppressive traditions and customs. Their life chances are worse than those of black men, and they have been misused and are powerless with no options or control of their lives. Although many of the women are shown as sensuous and irresistible, they have been objectified, and, as such, they appear soulless with no interior lives. While most are strangely beautiful and desirable, they are remote and unapproachable; both black and white men find communication with these women impossible, and search as they may, they cannot make meaningful connections with them. According to Paula Giddings, Toomer's *Cane* likens feminine beauty to the ultimate pleasures of the senses; complexions are compared to ginger, honey, cinnamon, dusky sunsets, and the like (185) Toomer's tantalizing images of these black women are analogous to images of nature and its natural beauty that have been ravaged by man and machine.

In *Jean Toomer, Artist: A Study of His Literary Life and Work, 1894–1936*, Nellie Y. McKay focuses on the tension between the powerless and the powerful in the beautiful portrait of Karintha whose skin is the color of "dusk on the eastern horizon ... when the sun goes down":

> Although internal sexual oppression is the most obvious factor in the abuse of Karintha, race, class, and economics are the factors that perpetuate the cycle of poverty in which she—and those who follow her—live. In a world in which men manipulate the souls of women, Karintha is a paradigm for the black community's powerlessness over the control of its own class and economic status in a white, capitalistic society [McKay 95].

Compared to a child of the earth, a natural beauty, defiled by men of all ages who used their power over an innocent because of their own greed and lasciviousness, Karintha is irreparably damaged and has no life chances. Her disadvantage parallels the black community's lack of control against the white hegemonic class. She and the other members of her racial caste have no opportunities for social mobility. Thus the men choose to create and exert their power over the beautiful woman/child who is subsequently transformed into a cold, barren, hollow figure. "The interest of the male, who wishes to ripen a growing thing too soon, could mean no good to her" (*Cane* 3). Karintha has been objectified and is mute, she is, according to McKay, "…a reflection of the moral and psychological deprivation that the community generates against itself" (94).

The story of Louisa's ultimate destruction is examined in "Blood Burning Moon." Like Karintha, she is voiceless and totally diminished throughout the narrative; however, she joins the community of women who sing an ominous song to counteract their sense of forthcoming violence and their utter helplessness. "The women sang lustily. Their songs were cotton-wads to stop their ears. Louisa came down into factory town and sank wearily upon the step before her home" (31). Toomer's use of metaphors paints a naturalistic image of Louisa, comparing her to things in nature: "Her skin was the color of oak leaves on young trees in fall. Her breasts, firm and up-pointed like ripe acorns. And her singing had the low murmur of winds in fig trees" (*Cane* 30). Louisa is of the earth, and Bob Stone and Tom Burwell are drawn to her.

Utilizing the stream-of-consciousness technique, Toomer presents a psychological snapshot of the fragmented and confused thoughts of Bob Stone, the younger son of Louisa's employer and her white lover. Stone is involved in a love triangle with Louisa and Tom Burwell, her black lover. Bob Stone exerts his white privilege and feels empowered to have Louisa; he showers her with gifts and meets her in the cane brake for his sexual rewards. Although she had a "warm glow" when she thought of him, the reader is not privy to her inner thoughts. When she considers both of them, the narrator tells us that Tom's "black balanced, and pulled against the white of Stone, when she thought of them" (30). Bob Stone struggles to understand his fascination with Louisa and on his way to meet her, he invokes a semblance of confidence from his privileged status as a white man as he reminisces about the antebellum South and questions his feelings for her:

> His mind became consciously a white man's.… He went in as a master should and took her. Direct, honest, bold. None of this sneaking. The contrast was repulsive to him. His family had lost ground. Hell no, his family still owned the niggers, practically. Damned if they did, or he wouldn't have to duck around so.… He was going to see Louisa to-night, and love her. She was lovely—in her way. Nigger way. What way was that? Damned if he knew. Was there something about niggers that you couldn't know? Nigger was something more [*Cane* 32].

The interconnected constructs of identity, gender, family, and class are intertwined in Bob Stone's reveries as he struggles with his position in the

Jim Crow South and the enigma associated with his lusting/loving Louisa. Their sexual rendezvous are in secret because he does not want public scrutiny; interactions with a woman from a racial caste was a taboo and no longer a birthright for young Stone. Communication was impossible between any of the characters because of the racial barriers/class differences of separation. In addition, Tom Burwell, Big Boy, has been incarcerated three times, is uneducated and so mesmerized by Louisa that he is totally inarticulate when he is around her and historically resorts to brutal violence as a defense. Both men sacrifice their lives for a woman that neither can possess. They suffer graphically depicted, horrific physical deaths, and Louisa is left on the verge of insanity. Knowing his own death was imminent, Tom hesitated before killing Bob Stone. Toomer's depiction of mob rule and Tom's cruel death was reminiscent of Twain's chapter on the cowardice and insanity of mob violence in *Adventures of Huckleberry Finn*. The race/class divisions created barriers that spawned unspeakable crimes in the South that followed blacks and persisted after the Great Migration.

Toomer's portrait of "Esther" is a disturbing examination of the alienation and dysfunctionality that stems from being part of the mixed-race black elite class in the rural South. Esther is not connected to the other desirable women of this section of *Cane*, and neither black nor white men hold any interest in her; she, too, is victimized and powerless as she experiences estrangement from community. Esther is white in physical appearance:

> Esther's hair falls in soft curls about her high-cheek-boned chalk-white face. Esther's hair would be beautiful if there were more gloss to it. And if her face were not prematurely serious, one would call it pretty. Her cheeks are too flat and dead for a girl of nine. Esther looks like a little white child, starched, frilled as she walks slowly... [22].

Esther is Jim Crane's daughter, and he is the richest colored man in the town.

The black community labels Esther and her father as "dictie," and although they have a place in the business community, they are outcasts socially. One would assume that their mixed race heritage would have placed them in better social standing, but Esther has experienced no value in having money or being near white. She has no maternal presence in her life and little interaction with her father. A nameless, omniscient narrator provides a panoramic view of her at nine, sixteen, twenty-two, and twenty-seven years old. At nine, she is enthralled by witnessing the spectacle of a powerful, spiritual Africa epitomized by the "clean muscled, magnificent, black-skinned Negro, King Barlo." His prodigious figure has a spiritual effect on Esther as she witnesses King Barlo's powerful transcendence from society and his inspired message of God's wrath and the Middle Passage; shortly thereafter, he departs. "King Barlo became the starting point of the only living patterns that her mind was to know" (*Cane* 23).

Although Esther's father has taught her the rules of economics and the importance of money as social uplift, she is listless and in a dream-like state. At twenty-two, Esther has completed her education and lives an unfulfilling life working in her father's grocery store. She is scorned by the young men in the town and fantasizes about Africa and having a child with King Barlo. At twenty-seven, Esther is downtrodden, and has aged considerably. Her hair has thinned and her face is compared to "the color of gray dust that dances with dead cotton leaves" (25). Finally, King Barlo returns and Esther decides to pursue her dreams of a relationship with him, only to be shamefully rejected. Amongst jeers of ridicule, she leaves the tavern where she had confronted him demanding him to leave with her. "A coarse woman's voice remarks, 'So thats how th dictie niggers does it…. Mus give em credit fo their gall" (27) Toomer's use of the vernacular shows the gulf between the two groups and the disdain that they had for each other. Although Esther's family has money and status, she is still classified as a "nigger." She has an existential crisis, and leaves the tavern in a fragmented state: "She steps out. There is no air, no street, and the town has completely disappeared" (27).

The most optimistic view of blacks' resistance to the racial caste system is depicted in Toomer's prose poem entitled "Seventh Street." He presents a Whitmanesque view of Blacks in Washington, D.C., people who are striving for and achieving a freedom that they had been denied in the South. There is a vibrancy, and one can feel their urge toward procreation. After the Great Migration and post–World War I, the political and socio-economic challenges in America forced blacks to adjust to the city:

> Money burns the pocket, pocket hurts,
> Bootleggers in silken shirts,
> Ballooned, zooming Cadillacs
> Whizzing, whizzing down the street-car tracks. (41)

Toomer calls Seventh Street "a bastard of Prohibition and the War" (41). Robust and full of life, the language of the poem contains a series of interrogatives answered by the "whizzing" and movement of the streetcars. Blacks improvised a new level of existence for themselves; although through illegal means, they were finally creators and controlled their own lives, albeit temporarily. Blacks of various hues formed a rainbow of colors and discarded their old selves which were relegated by class divisions; they were transformed and created a new culture. Escaping the pretentiousness of the black bourgeoisie, Langston Hughes joins Toomer in his perception of Seventh Street:

> Seventh Street is the long, old, dirty street, where the ordinary Negroes hang out, folks with practically no family tree at all, folks who draw no color line between mulattoes and deep dark-browns, folks who work hard for a living with their hands.... Their songs ... had the pulse beat of the people who keep going [*The Big Sea* 208–09].

The portraits of individuals and black life in *Cane* are fragmented, diverse and kaleidoscopic. In "The Negro Emergent," Toomer details sociological and psychological factors relative to black emancipation and America's history of slavery:

> It (the Civil War) freed the Negro nominally; it increased the Negro's bondage to white resentment and white fear, (and, in a large measure added political exploitation to the already existent forms, while doing little more than modify these forms) ... and, ever since emancipation, well intentioned white men aided by Negroes, have been trying to plaster a white image on a black reality [Rusch 88].

Du Bois's idea of double-consciousness is analogous to Toomer's reference to a "white image on a black reality." The concept of assimilation or losing oneself into a dominant culture creates a type of racial schizophrenia and gives rise to a fractured being, a dysfunctional mime, not having a sense of self. Although issues of race/racial identity, and more importantly colorism, have prevailed as topics in modern and post-modern America, the issues of the powerless versus the powerful persist.

A major challenge Toomer encountered while writing *Cane* is the racism that is inherent in language itself. The inadequacies of language as a tool of expression presented far too many barriers that even Toomer's experimentation in technique and form could not adequately address. His characters' concepts of themselves are largely controlled by the language of the larger society in which they live. In Book X of his autobiography, Toomer challenges conventional and "distorting" terms for communicating his racial message and laments the reductive aspect of orality and literacy. Toomer's desire to know and to express his own reality was impossible through conventional avenues: "It seems axiomatic to us that the social milieu helps one to define his self-concept, and the self-concept that evolves affects the manner in which one person communicates with another" (Hall and Freedle 129). Language is one of the vehicles of the expression of one's identity, and Toomer believed that the problems with language were so severe that he stopped writing for a time because he felt that what he was producing reinforced the emasculating ideology and racial caste he was trying to escape.

> The dilemma of the writer happens to strike me with peculiar force. It impresses and sometimes depresses me and makes me beat my brains almost to the point that I voluntarily seal my lips and stop writing. Indeed in the past there was a time when I did become mute, owing to a realization of this very matter which, as I saw then as I see now, involved the entire use of words with reference to any and all aspects of life [Toomer, Preface 12].

Repudiating the constructs of racism inherent in language, Toomer sought other mediums of expression, such as music, meditation, and physical exercise. In the "Kabnis" section of *Cane,* Toomer uses his alter ego to raise the issue of the limitations and philosophy of words. Kabnis tells Halsey that he is an orator and begins a discussion of the symbolic representation of words as tools of language:

> "I've been shapin words after a design that branded here."
> "Know whats here?" M soul… "Been shaping words to fit m soul."
> "An it lives on words. Not beautiful words. White folks feed it cause their looks are words. Niggers, black niggers feed it cause they're evil an their looks are words. Yallar niggers feed it. This whole damn bloated purple country feeds it cause its goin down t hell in a holy avalanche of words" [*Cane* 111].

Eventually, Toomer sought anonymity and began to withdraw from society. His life had become an improvised series of adaptations, as he continually resisted categorization, discarding the racial binary and selecting American.

> I wrote a poem called "The First American," the idea of which was that here in America we are in the process of forming a new race, that I was one of the first conscious members of this race. I had seen the divisions, the separatisms, and antagonisms…. And in this America I saw the divisions mended, the differences reconciled—saw that (1) we would in truth be a united people existing in the United States, saw that (2) we would in truth be once again members of a united human race [qtd. in Turner, *The Wayward and the Seeking* 121].

Cane anticipated much of the interracial debate that emerged decades after its publication and explored the notion of American hybridity long before it came into vogue. A view of his text as a metaphor of race captures Toomer's own battles with racial diversity, racial categorizations, white prejudice, and black resistance. Toomer's multi-genre approach captures the essence of man's racial strivings.

Works Cited

Alexander, Michelle. *The New Jim Crow: Mass Incarceration in the Age of Color-Blindness.* New York: The New Press, 2010.

Byrd, Rudolph P., and Henry L. Gates, Jr., Eds. "Song of the Son: The Emergence and Passing of Jean Toomer," in *Cane.* New York: W.W. Norton, 2011.

"The Class Struggle," *The Crisis*, vol. 22 no 4 (August 1921): 151. *The Philadelphia Negro*. Philadelphia: University of Pennsylvania Press, 2017.
Coser, Lewis A. *Masters of Sociological Thought. Ideas in Historical and Social Context*. New York: Harcourt Brace Jovanovich, Inc, 1971.
Cox, Oliver Cromwell. *Caste, Class & Race: A Study in Social Dynamics*. New York: Monthly Review Press, 1948.
Du Bois, W.E.B. Review of *Cane* in Darwin Turner's edition of *Cane*. New York: Liveright. 1975. *The Crisis* 27 (February 1924), 161–162.
_____. "Souls of Black Folk." *The Norton Anthology of African American Literature*, vol. 1. Eds. Henry L. Gates and Nellie McKay. New York: W.W. Norton, 2004. 692–777.
Early, Gerald. Ed. *Lure and Loathing: Essays on Race, Identity, and the Ambivalence of Assimilation*. New York: Penguin, 1993.
Ellison, Ralph. "What America Would Be Like Without Blacks" *The Collected Essays of Ralph Ellison*, Ed. John Callahan. New York: Modern Library, 1995. 582–583.
Farebrother, Rachel. "'Adventuring Through the Pieces of a Still Unorganized Mosaic': Reading Jean Toomer's Collage Aesthetic in *Cane*." In *Journal of American Studies*, 40 (2006), 3, 503–521.
Foley, Barbara. "'In the Land of Cotton': Economics and Violence in Jean Toomer's *Cane*." *African American Review* 32.2 (Summer 1998): 181–98.
_____. *Jean Toomer: Race, Repression and Revolution*. Champaign: University of Illinois Press, 2014.
_____. "Jean Toomer's Washington and the Politics of Class: From 'Blue Veins' to Seventh-street Rebels." Reprinted in the 2nd Edition of *Cane*. Eds. Byrd, Rudolph P. and Henry L. Gates. New York: W.W. Norton, 2011. *Modern Fiction Studies* 42.2 (1996): 289–321.
_____. "Roads Taken and Not Taken: Post-Marxism, Antiracism, and Anti-Communism." *Cultural Logic: An Electronic Journal of Marxist Theory and Practice* 1.2 (Spring 1998): 11 paragraphs.
_____. *Spectres of 1919: Class & Nation in the Making of the New Negro*. Champaign: University of Illinois Press, 2008.
Garvey, Marcus. "Africa for Africans." *The Norton Anthology of African American Literature*. Eds. Gates, Henry Louis and Nellie McKay. New York: W.W. Norton, 2004.
Gerth, H., and C.W. Mills, Eds. *From Max Weber*. London: Routledge, 1948.
Giddings, Paula. *When and Where I Enter: The Impact of Black Women on Race and Sex in America*. New York: Bantam Books, 1988.
Green, Dan S., and Earl Smith. "W.E.B. DuBois and the Concepts of Race and Class." *Phylon*. (1960) Vol. 44, No. 4 262–272.
Guterl, Matthew Pratt. *The Color of Race in America, 1900–1940*. Cambridge, MA: Harvard University Press, 2001.
Hall, William S., and Roy O. Freedle. *Culture and Language: The Black American Experience*. Washington D.C.: Hemisphere Publishing Corporation, 1975.
Hughes, Langston. *The Big Sea: An Autobiography*. New York: Knopf, 1940.
Hutchinson, George. "Jean Toomer and American Racial Discourse." *Texas Studies in Literature and Language*. 35.2 (Summer 1993): 226–250.
Johnson, E. Patrick. *Appropriating Blackness: Performance in the Politics of Authenticity*. Durham, NC: Duke University Press, 2005.
Jones, Robert B. *Jean Toomer and the Prison-House of Thought: A Phenomenology of the Spirit*. Amherst: University of Massachusetts, 1993.
Kerman, Cynthia Earl, and Richard Eldridge, Eds. *The Lives of Jean Toomer: A Hunger for Wholeness*. Baton Rouge: Louisiana State University Press, 1987.
LaMothe, Daphne Mary. "*Cane*: Jean Toomer's Gothic Black Modernism." *The Gothic Other: Racial and Social Constructions in the Literary Imagination*. Ed. Ruth Bienstock Anolik and Douglas L. Howard. Jefferson, NC: McFarland, 2004. 54–71.
Larson, Charles R. *Invisible Darkness: Jean Toomer and Nella Larsen*. Iowa City: University of Iowa Press, 1993.
Manasse, E. "Max Weber on Race." *Social Research*. 14, 191–221.

Marvin, Tom. "Jean Toomer's 'Kabnis.'" *Explicator* 67.1 (Fall 2008): 43–45.
McKay, Nellie Y. *Jean Toomer, Artist: A Study of His Literary Life and Work, 1894- 1936*. Chapel Hill: University of North Carolina Press, 1987.
Myrdal, Gunnar. *American Dilemma: The Negro Problem and Modern Democracy*. New York: Harper & Brothers, 1944.
Nicholls, David. "Jean Toomer's *Cane*, Modernization and the Spectral Folk." *Modernism, Inc.: Body, Memory, Capital*. Ed. Jani Scandura and Michael Thurston. New York: New York University Press, 2001. 151–70.
Nisetich, Rebecca. *Contested Identities: Racial Ambiguity, Indeterminacy and Law in the American Novel, 1900-1942*. 2014. University of Connecticut, PhD dissertation.
Peckham, Joel Bishop, Jr. "Jean Toomer's *Cane*: Self as Montage and the Drive Toward Integration." *American Literature* 72.2 (June 2000): 275–90.
Rex, J. "The Theory of Race Relations: A Weberian Approach." *Sociological Theories: Race & Colonialism*. Paris: UNESCO, 1980. 117–142.
Rusch, Frederik L. *A Jean Toomer Reader: Selected Unpublished Writings*. New York: Oxford University Press, 1993.
Scaff, Lawrence A. *Max Weber in America*. Princeton, NJ: Princeton University Press, 2011.
Scruggs, Charles, and Lee VanDemarr. *Jean Toomer and the Terrors of American History*. Philadelphia: University of Pennsylvania Press, 1998.
Sollors, Werner, ed. *Theories of Ethnicity: A Classical Reader*. New York: New York University Press, 1996.
Taylor, Kirstine. "Untimely Subjects: White Trash and the Making of Racial Innocence In the Postwar South." *American Quarterly* 67 (March 2015) 55–79.
Toomer, Jean. *Cane*. New York: W.W. Norton, 1988.
_____. *The Collected Poems of Jean Toomer*. Eds. Robert B. Jones and Margot Toomer Latimer. Chapel Hill: University of North Carolina Press, 1988.
_____. "Jean Toomer: Exile." In *In a Minor Chord: Three Afro-American Writers and Their Search for Identity*, pp. 1–59. Carbondale: Southern University of Illinois Press, 1971.
_____. *Essentials: Definitions and Aphorisms*. Chicago: Lakeside Press, 1931.
_____. "Letter to Georgia O'Keefe, Sunday, January 15, 1924," in *A Jean Toomer Reader*, Ed. Frederik L. Rusch. New York: Oxford University Press, 1993. 280.
_____. "The Negro Emergent," *A Jean Toomer Reader: Selected Unpublished Writing*. Ed. Frederik L. Rusch. New York: Oxford University Press, 1993. 86–93.
_____. "Race Problems and Modern Society," *Theories of Ethnicity: A Classical Reader*. Ed. Werner Sollors. New York: New York University Press, 1996. 168–190.
Turner, Darwin T. "Introduction." *Cane*. By Jean Toomer. New York: Liveright, 1975.
_____. *The Wayward and the Seeking: A Collection of Writings by Jean Toomer*. Washington, D.C.: Howard University Press, 1980.
Whalan, Mark, Ed. *The Letters of Jean Toomer, 1919-1924*. Knoxville: University of Tennessee Press, 2005.

"One had to have castes"
Class, Culture and Ideology in American Tragedy

Adam Nemmers

The second act of Theodore Dreiser's *An American Tragedy* (1925) introduces the fairy godfather figure of Samuel Griffiths, a wealthy manufacturer traveling on business to Chicago. In an incredible bout of serendipity, the mail is delivered by his long-lost nephew Clyde, a hotel bellboy who occupies such a lowly position because of his itinerant missionary upbringing. Face-to-face for the first time, Samuel is impressed by the youth's industry and appearance; Clyde flatters his uncle's achievements; both are pleased to find a contrast to their mutual connection, the "short, fat and poorly knit mentally as well as physically" Asa Griffiths (192). In short order, the relatives come to an arrangement: Clyde will move east and take up a position in the Griffiths Collar Company of Lycurgus, New York. All that remains is for Samuel—"a kind of Croesus, living in ease and luxury" (26)—to decide what role Clyde should play (whether family or stranger, equal or subordinate) in the drama that proceeds. Returning home, Samuel confers with his son Gilbert. As the didactic Dreiser relates, "Neither could tolerate the socialistic theory relative to capitalistic exploitation. As both saw it, there had to be higher and higher social orders to which the lower social classes could aspire. One had to have castes" (196). According to this rationale, the Lycurgus Griffithses offer Clyde "the munificent sum of fifteen dollars" a week and place him at "the very bottom of the business," reasoning that if he is worthy of the Griffiths name, he will work his way up (195). Although sensitive to the reputation of their surname, they resolve that their relative must receive no preferential treatment. Clyde, like others of the lower class, must "become inured to a narrow and abstemious life" so as to arrive at "a clear realization of how difficult it was to come by money" (196). As both father and son believed, such treatment "was good for their characters. It informed and strengthened the minds and spirits of those who were destined to rise. And those who were not should be kept right where they were" (196). The posited binary outcome—whether Clyde is "destined to rise" or "should be kept right where [he is]"—becomes the central tension in the action that follows. For though Clyde does aspire to "higher and higher social orders," he finds the longstanding American ideology of class mobility incompatible with his lived reality.

The Griffithses' pronouncement, though merely an aside in the text, was well in line with popular American ideology during the long nineteenth century, which promoted the "bootstraps" mentality and notion of the self-made man, and held that competition determined a natural (and therefore just) social hierarchy based on genetics. Indeed, as Louis Zanine argues, "*An American Tragedy* can be read as the tragedy of the 'unfit' individual [in this case, Clyde Griffiths], who [is] driven by internalized social values to achieve, but who was destined by innate biological inabilities to fail in the competition for power, prestige, and pleasure" (107). In their subscription to Social Darwinism and the social caste system, the Griffiths eschew the compelling and competing Marxist ideology of the same period, which stipulated an economic explanation for the development of classes and culminated with the Russian Revolution of 1917. While others in the United States saw trust busting, violent strikes, and the rise of Socialism throughout the early twentieth century, Dreiser's characters are insulated from and uninterested in "the socialistic theory relative to capitalistic exploitation." Indeed, for a novel sorely concerned with class and situated in a factory environment, *An American Tragedy* does not lend itself well to traditional three-class Marxist analysis. To begin, the family of oppressed proletariat to whom Clyde belongs (the Griffiths of Kansas City) is in fact impoverished by choice, owing to their missionary work and faith in God's providence. The rest of the novel's "working class" are not wretched victims, but contented and prosperous, from the hedonist hotel bell-boys to the industrious farm girls employed at the Lycurgus shirt-collar factory. At the top of the supposed Marxist structure, the capitalist Samuel Griffiths is neither rapacious nor exploitative, but wise and judicious, and seems more concerned with achieving social distinction than turning a profit. Finally, protagonist Clyde Griffiths provides a connective thread between these groups, moving with determined agency across status boundaries and demonstrating that personal and ideological factors may supersede one's position in the economy. It turns out that "the socialistic theory relative to capitalistic exploitation" does little to explain the attitudes of the novel's characters, much less their behavior. Rather than sorting themselves among the landlords, bourgeoisie, or proletariat, they exhibit class consciousness only regarding social matters: whom one is related to; what status one has in local society; and especially what one owns, wears, and looks like.

In *American Tragedy*, class identity is based not upon one's relationship to the means of production, but instead markers of cultural capital and difference. The ideology to which the novel's characters subscribe (including in-group/out-group interpellation and inclusion/exclusion dynamics) positions them on a fluid class gradient, forcing them to acquire fetishized commodities, display luxury consumption, and adopt higher-class speech and actions in order to increase their status, all the while remaining vigilant against any act or association that might lower their standing. As Dreiser demonstrates, it is these factors, not Marxist economics, which configure each character's self-identified position on the socioeconomic spectrum. Though placed at the bottom of the industrial ladder, Clyde Griffiths' discontent is not due to exploitative capitalism, but rather his subscription to popular American ideology, which offers the pervasive illusion that moving up in the world ("rising from the ranks") is as simple a matter as proving one's mettle.[1] Paternalism aside, Samuel and Gilbert Griffiths arrive at the right idea: because American class-ways apparently depart from the rigid caste systems of England or India, those from the lower classes can be deceived and harmed by the American Dream, broadly defined. The novel's primary tragedy, then, is not inherent to the capitalist system, but rather due to the characters' failure to comprehend and navigate the invisible ideological dynamics operating upon them. That such a misconception still recurs in the United States underscores the power and clarity of Dreiser's vision, published across nine hundred pages nearly a century ago.

"Plainly there was something wrong somewhere": Clyde in Kansas City

In a sense, Clyde Griffiths' fate was determined at birth. Instead of belonging to the prosperous Griffiths family of Lycurgus, Clyde is born to Samuel's brother Asa, who, as an urban missionary, leads his family through the greater Midwest—Grand Rapids, Detroit, Milwaukee, Chicago, Kansas City—in pursuit of souls to save. Beyond his deficiencies in vigor and intelligence, Asa has also drawn the short straw of the family inheritance. While Samuel and his brother Allen were bequeathed the bulk of their father's property (along with thirty thousand dollars), Asa received only "a petty thousand" (193) and was turned out at a young age, highlighting the keen deficiency that Clyde later feels with regard to his cousin Gilbert. Rather than growing up as scion to a rich and respected factory owner, Clyde is impoverished and itinerant with little cultural capital. Dreiser reports that "there were times when, the work proving highly unprofitable and Asa being unable to make much money ... they were quite without sufficient food or decent clothes, and the children could not go to school" (23). The pitiful account that opens the novel illuminates the Griffithses as a member of the urban poor. Yet they cannot be counted among the proletariat or working class, as they eschew employment in favor of religious providence and an alternative ideology. Indeed the Kansas City Griffithses are unembarrassed by their penury, counting it as parcel of their faith and calling. In light of continued financial difficulties, Mrs. Griffiths repeats such blandishments as "God will provide" and "God will show the way" (18). Asa, while allowing that "the pleasures and cares of the world hold a very great many," believes that "the love of Christ must eventually prevail" (21). Despite frequent downturns, they "remained as optimistic as ever" and "had unwavering faith in the Lord and His intention to provide" (23). Plainly the Griffiths are content with their material state and, "determined upon spiritualizing the world as much as possible" (19), would reject an increase in wealth or change in class were it available to them.

As John Lavelle argues in *Blue Collar, Theoretically*, all ideology "exists within a feedback loop" and is "passed down through families, and modified by state ideological apparatus and various organizations, such as religious groups" (153). Yet Clyde, while born into the Kansas City Griffithses, does not share their spiritual attitude. By nature he is "as vain and proud as he was poor," looking upon himself as "a thing apart—never quite wholly and indissolubly merged with the family of which he was a member, and never with any profound obligations to those who had been responsible for his coming into the world" (27). Clyde's self-conception as "a thing apart" endures throughout the novel (whether as a neophyte among the Green-Davidson's bellhops or on-the-outside-looking-in among Lycurgus's smart set), but originates with the missionary work of his family, where Clyde emerges as a malcontent in contrast to the cheerful singing of his brothers and sisters. Paul Orlov characterizes Clyde as "a socially dislocated being" who simultaneously "feels trapped outside the mainstream of American life, superior to his parents, and committed to (worldly) values antithetical to those his family supports as well as embodies" (104). As a passer-by observes the Griffiths troop, he remarks that Clyde apparently "don't wanta be here. He feels outa place.... He can't understand all this stuff, anyhow" (19). "A thing apart," "out of place"—what Clyde does understand is the yawning gap between him and others, and how the cheerful spirituality of his family prevents him from realizing his materialist dreams. As Dreiser reports, matter of fact: "plainly there was something wrong somewhere" (18).

From an early age Clyde exhibits the tragic flaw of discontent, a characteristic incubated by American culture and encouraged by the cornucopia he finds around him. Unlike his parents, who rely upon God to provide for their needs, Clyde sees only what they (and he) lack. According to his perspective, his family is "always 'hard up,' never very well clothed, and deprived of many comforts and pleasures which seemed common enough to others" (18). More specifically, he feels that "he and his parents looked foolish and less than normal—'cheap' was the word he would have used if he could have brought himself to express his full measure of resentment" (20). As a teenager Clyde compares himself to the general community, finding himself "less than normal," and lacking that "which seemed common enough to others." As he grows, however, he finds that the mean is not enough, and begins to compare himself to the best and richest of Kansas City. Thus Clyde becomes consumed by invidious comparison (or distinction), a concept introduced by Thorstein Veblen in *The Theory of the Leisure Class* (1899). According to Veblen, invidious comparison began among nomadic tribes, when hunter-gatherers began to make comparisons between the wealth of relative tribes, and also between individuals within a tribe—particularly hunters who returned with wild game as a kind of trophy. With the shift of society to a capitalist system, Veblen theorized, invidious comparison became "primarily a comparison of the owner with the other members of the group. Property is still of the nature of trophy, but, with the cultural advance, it becomes more and more a trophy of successes scored in the game of ownership carried on between the members of the group" (18). The "game of ownership" to which Veblen refers grew rapidly when imbricated with late capitalist culture, where the accumulation of goods became the chief marker of status among owners in a given society—in this case, the "commercial heart of an American city" (15). Under siege by forces beyond his comprehension, young Clyde becomes obsessed with worldly matters in inverse proportion to the spirituality of his parents. His materialist desires are summarized in an early passage:

> He had always told himself that if only he had a better collar, a nicer shirt, finer shoes, a good suit, a swell overcoat like some boys had! Oh, the fine clothes, the handsome homes, the watches, rings, pins that some boys sported; the dandies many youths of his years already were! Some parents of boys of his years actually gave them cars of their own to ride in. They were to be seen upon the principal streets of Kansas City flitting to and fro like flies. And pretty girls with them. And he had nothing. And he never had had [28].

For Clyde, the vision of "nice clothes and handsome homes" has "all the luster and wonder of a spiritual transfiguration" (38). Dreiser goes on to label it "the true mirage of the lost and thirsting and seeking victim of the desert" (38), combining the power of "spiritual transformation" with the pejorative of a "mirage"—something that seems tangible but is actually ephemeral. Clyde, then, emerges as a "lost," "thirsting," and "seeking" victim who may never find what he desires. As Veblen explains, "since the struggle is substantially a race for reputability ... no approach to a definitive attainment is possible" (21). This is the "mirage" to which Dreiser refers, the same aspirational illusion represented by a host of American expressions: "the rat-race," "keeping up with the Joneses," and perhaps even "the American Dream," the last of which receives extended treatment in the novel. In his perpetual desire for "more," Clyde similarly fulfills the pronouncement of Max Weber, who theorized that under late capitalism people become "dominated by the making of money, by acquisition as the ultimate purpose of his life" and that "economic acquisition is no longer subordinated to man as the means for the satisfaction of his material needs" (78).

Clyde needs money to satisfy his material "needs," yet the job he secures, as a bellhop at the "lavish" Green-Davidson hotel, only serves as a self-fulfilling prophecy that exacerbates his fantasy. Working in "an essential hotel in a great and successful American commercial city" Clyde is immersed in an environment "almost too luxurious" and "too richly furnished, without the saving grace of either simplicity or necessity" (42). The hotel's "gauche luxury of appointment ... as some one sarcastically remarked, was intended to supply 'exclusiveness to the masses'" (42). Such a trenchant comment is well over Clyde's head; to him the hotel is not gauche but fantastic, "for his ideas of luxury were in the main so extreme and mistaken and gauche—mere wanderings of a repressed and unsatisfied fancy, which as yet had had nothing but imaginings to feed it" (45). It is at the Green-Davidson, and especially among fellow bellhops, that Clyde has his first real experience with hedonism and wealth. There he observes the "pleasures and privileges of the wealthy, the 'correct' fashions and manners, and, most crucially, the socio economic significance of identities" and becomes "fully initiated into the religion of worldly values and ways of seeing" (Orlov 78). Witness to the grandeur and wealth of guests in the Green-Davidson lobby, Clyde dreams of making enough money to become a "person of consequence in the world" (58) and unwittingly becomes a "modern, urban Tantalus, a dupe of the 'American Dream's' popular myths about the quick climb to fortune possible for individuals like himself" (Orlov 113). Like other analogues between books I and II, the Kansas City Clyde is an inchoate version of the social striver made manifest in the Lycurgus portion of the novel.

Clyde is not the only character "duped" by the American Dream, for the rest of the Green-Davidson's bellhops are similarly taken with their good wages and the freedom money allows. Though part of the working-class and purportedly exploited for their labor, the bellboys do not consider themselves part of the proletariat, but are instead happy to take advantage of the capitalist system to fulfill their own desires: namely, alcohol, prostitutes, and "a good time." Again we see the disconnect between

Marxist and post-Marxist explanations for systems of economics, especially when complicated by the American ideology of wealth, ascendency, and consumption. Situated in a lavish milieu, working at the pleasure of the wealthy, the bellhops have every reason to engender resentment and class consciousness; to unionize and demand better working conditions, or to commit crimes to get rich quick. Yet, as Phillip Neel points out, "what holds the characters back from a full militancy is simply their own inability to politicize their situation—to actively and consciously take sides in the class struggle ... they imagine themselves as seamlessly interwoven into the social narrative, engaged in an ascent toward higher social strata and material satisfaction" (172). Opting for materialism over militancy, Dreiser's working-class characters consistently exhibit satisfaction and subjective well-being despite their lowly economic positions.

Clyde's abiding material desire is on full display during his involvement with a particular item of attraction, the crude shop girl Hortense Briggs, whom he meets on a double date. Though "not a little coarse and vulgar," and a "very long way removed from the type of girl he had been imagining in his dreams" (84), Hortense captures Clyde's heart, then skillfully manipulates him into doing her bidding. The prolonged episode illustrates the power of another of Veblen's terms: "conspicuous consumption," or the purchase of goods or services for the specific purpose of displaying one's wealth. In this case, Hortense is captivated by a fur coat she desires from the shop of Mr. Isadore Rubenstein, a local Jewish merchant, by which she hopes she might become "the smartest-dressed girl in Kansas City" (120). Conspicuous consumption, from Veblen's perspective, is intended to show off one's status, especially when the items exhibited appear surplus to the means of a person's peers. The coat on display in the window of Rubenstein's shop is clearly too expensive for Hortense to purchase, unless she can find a suitor like Clyde to buy it for her on installment. Reasoning that he "seemed to have real money" (120), Hortense inveigles him with her feminine wiles, and though the besotted Clyde complies, the irony is that he intends for the well-dressed Hortense to become his own object of conspicuous consumption, which he intends to put on display in order to distinguish himself from the fellow workers in his class.

Such superficiality—though common in Kansas City society—is a strong determinant of Clyde's behavior, catalyzing his trajectory in the very American drama that proceeds in the second act. Though pivotal toward establishing Clyde's character, the Kansas City section is mere prelude to the novel's main action, which replicates the first volume's trajectory through the fictional technique of doubling. In a harbinger of the tragedy to come, under an assumed name, Clyde flees a fatal accident, takes a series of odd jobs across the Midwest (St. Louis, Peoria, Milwaukee), and lives undercover until the fateful encounter with his uncle in Chicago. Poised to migrate east and begin a new life, Clyde takes up his pursuit of the Dream anew, imagining himself "in an ascent toward higher social strata and material satisfaction" (Neel 172).

"Cut by a knife or divided by a high wall": Class Dynamics in Lycurgus

With his role in the Griffiths Collar Company decided, Clyde begins work in the factory's "enormous basement," where his task is to shrink collars among a dozen men wearing "armless undershirts" and "a pair of old trousers belted in at the waist" (206). The men, Clyde decides at first glance, are "rather below the type of individuals he hoped to find [t]here" (207)—beneath, he feels, even the bellhops of the Union League and Green-Davidson whom he had once been glad to join. By design, this is the "lowest of all the positions the factory had to offer" (232). Nevertheless, Clyde accepts his lot, believing he is destined to rise in the company. Samuel Griffiths eventually provides wish fulfillment. While inspecting the factory, he observes Clyde sweating and working along with the common men of the shrinking department. "Jealous of the ... name" and "general social appearance of the Griffiths," he decides that his nephew "ought not to be compelled to continue at this very menial form of labor any longer" and promotes him to a foreman on a higher floor of the factory, where he might wear a suit and sit above common workers (248). In a few years Clyde has made a rapid climb in the world: from missionary to bellhop to factory manager—where might the next act take him? To this end, Shawn St. John observes that "Clyde simply cannot help mindlessly pursuing the American Dream as he conceives it: better jobs bring more money and possessions, hence higher social status" (68). While better jobs are attainable, "higher social status" proves elusive, as Clyde makes little headway on the Lycurgus scene despite his good looks and even better surname. His prospects are buoyed by an initial invitation to the Griffithses' Sunday dinner but stymied thereafter, as the family leaves for the summer and worries itself with other social concerns. "Herein," Clare Virginia Eby claims, "lies the seed of the tragedy: the Griffithses cannot behave consistently toward Clyde, much less become the new family he desires" (138). Deterred but not defeated, Clyde focuses on his work at the factory, where he discovers a mutual attraction with one of his employees.

From a Marxist perspective, the sprawling factory of the Griffiths Collar Company might resemble an exploitative sweatshop (like those immortalized in the 1911 Triangle Shirtwaist Factory fire or the 1912 Lawrence

Textile Mills strikes): that is, a site of potential conflict between capital and labor, as was common in the United States during the early twentieth century. The factory itself is literally formed in a typical Marxist pyramid, with the proletariat (factory girls and working men) at the bottom, the bourgeoisie (such as clerks and managers) in the middle, and the capitalist (the Griffiths family) at the top. Certainly, the Griffiths Shirt Collar Factory is practicing capitalism on a mass, industrial scale. When Clyde first arrives he finds a red brick building six stories high and almost a thousand feet long; we are told that in his department "there were so very, very many women—hundreds of them—stretching far and away between white walls and white columns to the eastern end of the building" (256). Yet when we become acquainted with one of those women, Roberta Alden, she is not a pitiful, exploited worker, but rather (like the bell boys of the Green-Davidson) contented with her position. For Roberta, who grew up on a poor farm upstate, the position is an opportunity to transcend her mean and parochial upbringing ("where she felt that she could no longer endure") and act for herself. Agency in this case means gaining employment outside the home, a product of cultural factors that provides her freedom, a decent wage, and the opportunity to meet a husband. Her decision to leave the farm for a factory job echoes Lavelle's claim that "once happiness (subjective well-being) is added to economics and working conditions, the idea of exploitation becomes complex and must be studied at an individual level—whether a person's overall circumstances allow for a feeling of fulfillment" (140). At the Griffiths Collar Company, Roberta learns, "Girls ... were always started at nine or ten dollars, quickly taught some of the various phases of piece work and then, once they were proficient, were frequently able to earn as much as fourteen to sixteen dollars, according to their skill" (271). For Roberta as for Clyde, a position at the factory is a springboard—means for upward mobility, to achieve her "dream" of learning bookkeeping or stenography (270) or marrying someone of a higher class. On the former count, she makes steady progress; on the latter count, she, like Clyde, is stymied, finding that the social mores of the company (and Lycurgus at large) prevent her from a legitimate relationship with anyone above her station. Such artificial barriers belie the mirage of class mobility inculcated in young Americans, for, as the lovers discover, "the line of demarcation and stratification between the rich and poor in Lycurgus was as sharp as though cut by a knife or divided by a high wall" (274–5). The meeting of Roberta and Clyde, then, is a star-crossed intersection of two young Americans consumed by dreams (one might say illusions, or mirages) of the better life that surely awaits them. The problem is not economic progress—for each is making plenty of money, and has come a long way from humble beginnings—but rather social ascendancy, which is governed not by economics, as Marxism would maintain, but instead by culture and ideology. The same social caste system that the Griffithses consider "good for the characters" of the working class prevents those workers from achieving the status they believe they deserve, for "all the social norms [in Lycurgus] are drawn along strict class lines" (Spindler 72).

The entrenched social dichotomy is highlighted when Clyde is juxtaposed with his cousin Gilbert, who serves as his double and doppelganger. Of similar age, intelligence, and appearance, their likeness is not only a key plot mechanism, but also underscores the fundamental inequality of American society: one is high-caste and the other low solely due to the happenstance of birth. Throughout the novel Gilbert presses this inherited advantage in order to keep his cousin in his place, partially out of spite and partially to preserve his family's distinction among the upper-class of Lycurgus. As Pierre Bourdieu discussed in his *Distinctions*, the Lycurgus Griffithses are a compelling case study regarding his theory of the stasis and reproduction of cultural and social formations, especially within class divisions. As Bourdieu postulated, society is broken down not just by social classes but by class fractions therein. In the upper class for example, there exists strong tensions between old money and the nouveau riche, who marshal newly created wealth in an attempt to rise in status. As a family belonging fully to neither set, the Griffiths are forced to thread the needle between two Lycurgus sets: the "old-fashioned," well-established, and conservative families such as the Anthonys, Nicholsons, and Taylors; and the "too showy and too aggressive," though "solid enough financial element" such as the Cranstons and Finchleys (167–69). While Clyde is overawed by all the residents of Wykeagy Avenue, there does exist a subtle difference, and "that the social distinction between Finchleys and Griffithses is so fine as to prove invisible" Eby asserts, "only confirms its value: the truly elite ... discover subtle ways to display their wealth to distinguish themselves from more conspicuous arrivistes" (138). Doing so, as Bourdieu outlines, requires frequent subtle expressions of class and taste, from the type of boat one owns (thirty-foot electric launch is the new standard) to how one speaks (slang such as "swell" and "huh" is considered low-class) to where and how long one summers (Twelfth Lake is currently preferable to Greenwood Lake). The fiercest struggle for distinction is often within the dominant class, between those who have status but may lack economic capital and those wealthy bourgeois who are rich but may lack culture. Such is life among the upper-caste of Lycurgus, a "very limited world, where quite everyone who was anything at all knew every one else, [and] the state of one's purse was as much, and in some instances even more, considered than one's social connections" (394).

Beyond the obvious arena of material wealth, one of the chief avenues by which the elite achieve distinction is through social proxy—whom they and children socialize with, and particularly whom they marry. As Dreiser explains:

> for these local families of distinction were convinced that not only one's family but one's wealth was the be-all and end-all of every happy union meant to include social security. And in consequence, while considering Clyde as one who was unquestionably eligible socially, still, because it had been whispered about that his means were very slender, they were not inclined to look upon him as one who might aspire to marriage with any of their daughters [394].

Eby views such ceremonial distances as an "inevitable consequence of invidious comparison" (138); the sanction cuts both ways, however, extending to the debutante Sondra Finchley, who as the daughter of nouveau riche is "similarly the victim of a class definition, for she is allowed to court only young men of wealth" (Spindler 73). Though much of their courtship is for show Sondra does seem to genuinely care for Clyde, especially when compared with the odious Gilbert Griffiths. Straitjacketed by social pronouncement, Sondra cannot publicly date Clyde, offering yet another example of the primacy of status and reinforcing Lavelle's claim that ideology "limits or gives access to codes for entry into power structures within fields" (157).

Thus the American mythos of social mobility (in either direction) proves increasingly untenable in the twentieth century, when class identity is rooted in history and cemented by social more.[2] A pair of brief passages illustrate Clyde's dispirit regarding the immutability of social identity. Of himself, Clyde asks, "Who was he anyway? And what did he really amount to? What could he hope for from such a great world as this really ... all at once he felt himself very much of a nobody" (210). Of Roberta, Clyde likewise, asks "for after all, who was she? A factory girl! The daughter of parents who lived and worked on a farm and one who was compelled to work for her own living" (330). Clyde's personal interrogation—"who was he?" "who was she"—speaks to a working-class crisis of identity that blossoms into full-blown transformation. While Roberta, even through marriage, will always remain a farm-to-factory girl, Clyde attempts to refashion his public identity (a la James Gatz) into an upper-class gentleman, first by obscuring his humble beginnings, then by disassociating himself from Roberta and cleaving to Sondra. In this way, the latter functions as "the ultimate trophy, arousing in him not sexual passion but the pangs of emulation: 'a curiously stinging sense of what it was to want and not to have'" (Eby 144). When Roberta probes his interest in Sondra, Clyde confesses, "I like her some, sure. She's very pretty, and a dandy dancer. And she has lots of money and dresses well," though "outside of that Sondra appealed to him in no other way" (391). By his own admission, he is attracted not to Sondra's personality or sexuality, but her dressing, dancing, appearance, and particularly her purse, all of which are status markers Clyde wishes to attain through a liaison. Donald Pizer agrees, noting that Sondra "is a princess in her realm, and Clyde, desiring above all to enter this realm, wants her not for sex—the principal force in his desire for Hortense—but rather to share in her wealth and status" (Pizer 128). In his fantasy of becoming a Lycurgus socialite, Clyde plays upon a rags-to-riches archetype of yore: the chivalrous knight who is made royalty through marriage to the princess.

Roberta's retort cuts to the quick: "Yes, and who wouldn't, with all the money she has? If I had as much money as that, I could too" (391). Later on the same count, she speculates that "If I'd ever had a chance like some girls—if I'd ever been anywhere or seen anything! But just to be brought up in the country and without any money or clothes or anything—and nobody to show you" (393). Like Clyde, Roberta is hamstrung by her humble beginnings and concomitant lack of social and cultural capital, only she has not even the benefit of relation to the upper class to provide a foot in the door. Yet in mixing with his betters, Clyde is saddled with an additional insecurity, a class anxiety diametrically opposed to "the very definite sense of social security and ease that seemed to reside in everybody" else (347). Often these displays of capital are purposeful, as when Sondra, "realizing ... he had not been accustomed to equipment of this order before coming to Lycurgus," sweetly asks Clyde, "aren't all kitchens as big as this?" (396). Other instances are off-hand and random, as when Freddie Sells, a Now and Then Club party-goer, leverages his educational capital to wonder "just what, outside of money, there is to the collar business. Gil and I used to argue about that when we were down at college. He used to try and tell me that there was some social importance to making and distributing collars, giving polish and manner to people who wouldn't otherwise have them, if it weren't for cheap collars" (352). His pontification not only discloses that he (and Gilbert) are college-educated, but also calls out Clyde, the very sort of person who believes he can dress his way to social success. For Clyde, who received intermittent schooling and never so much as conceived of college, the banal statement carries an air of mysticism and erudition, exposing the gap between him and them. He is overawed by the phrase "social importance," and wonders, "just what did [Mr. Sells] mean by that—some deep, scientific information that he had acquired at college" (352). As Lavelle contends, "A person takes up a position within a social field depending on how much and what type of economic, cultural, social, or symbolic capital the person has accumulated. This position is in relation to a system or network of power within the field" (158). As much as he tries to blend in with the upper-class society, Clyde cannot help his ignorance and naiveté. He simply has not acquired the capital (educational and otherwise) to belong in such a group.

Both episodes exemplify Bourdieu's notion of habitus—the "internalised form of the class condition and of the conditionings" (101) by which "a member of a certain class internalizes how one should react to different cultural stimuli, what he or she finds 'pretentious' or 'vulgar' or 'gaudy' rather than 'attractive' or 'dignified' or 'beautiful'" (Blundren).[3] Habitus, as Andy Blunden explains, "is not a direct reflection of the conditions of existence of a class, but a sensibility acquired through a life-time and an upbringing in those conditions and the possibilities they include or exclude." That both Clyde and Roberta have descended from weak fathers highlights the hereditary relationship among wealth, class, and taste, and underscores how difficult it is to escape the inertia of a low-class background. As a member of the Kansas City Griffiths, Clyde is too impoverished to gain legitimacy in social circles, yet considers himself "really too good for the commonplace [factory] world by which he was now environed" (343). On the other hand, as a member of the Lycurgus Griffiths, Clyde faces resentment from the working people of the company, who reason that "he was not one of them" and, because he was "in touch with those who were above them.... He was, as they saw it, part of the rich and superior class" (215). Their subsequent judgment—that "the poor must stand together everywhere"—is the nearest the novel comes to Marxist sentiment, but is quickly abandoned in favor of a detailed exploration of the post–Marxist considerations heretofore.

By dint of his ambition and pretension, Clyde is doubly bound; he can neither assume a stable class identity nor consort with women socially lower (Roberta) or higher (Sondra) than himself. Trapped in a clandestine and illegitimate relationship, with an impending child threatening to reveal his double life, Clyde must gain release of low-class ballast in order to continue his rise. The long-budding tragedy flowers one afternoon on Big Bittern Lake, a direct consequence of Clyde's social encumbrance as a man who subscribes to American ideology yet lacks a stable social identity.

"Left to starve between social strata": Clyde Griffiths on Trial

The final book of *An American Tragedy* offers a fitting terminus to the narrative arc of Clyde Griffiths, whose ambitious ascendency into the upper levels of Lycurgus society is accompanied by an Icarus-like punishment and fall. Whatever the exact nature of his fatal act on Big Bittern Lake (murder? accident? unconscious wish-fulfillment?), his plot to kill Roberta can be symbolically read as ridding himself of his low-class portion and past, especially as he returns to the company of Sondra and the rest of the social elite at the Casino thereafter. With Roberta sunk to the bottom of the lake, he is free to rise, to dream of permanent entry into the upper caste. When his crime is discovered, however, the inelastic societal forces he has stretched bring him crashing down to earth, and eventually remove him from society and then his walking life. Though American ideology is the root cause of his tragedy, Clyde is ultimately the agent of his own destruction, for, as Yoshinobu Hakutani reminds us, he "is not merely ... a victim of society but more importantly ... a victim of his own illusions about life" (270).

The Clyde of the final act is no longer a good-looking social striver, but rather a cornered criminal whose artifice has been exposed. Eby rightly claims, "it is difficult to imagine a character more self-alienated than Clyde becomes" (141); it is this pronounced self-alienation (or abnegation?) which allows for his subsequent re-creation, both by himself and others. Clyde's fluid identity is contested at the trial, where his defense team settles on the construction of Clyde as an innocent, confused boy—a "mental and moral coward"—while the prosecution (and the press) portray him as a cold-blooded climber who killed to rid himself of an inconvenience. Thus the third act "emphasizes in brutal detail the extent to which Clyde's self is constructed in the eyes of his beholders" and "Clyde becomes, to all intents and purposes, an image of himself drawn from how others view him" (Eby 143). The chief agent of influence is Orville Mason, the District Attorney of Cataraqui County, who creates a public spectacle in order to further his own political prospects. The mountain of evidence left by Clyde makes for an open-and-shut case which could be tried entirely on its factual merits, yet Mason skillfully utilizes class resentment to set the twelve common men of the jury (farmers, clerks, and storekeepers) against Clyde. His primary rhetorical technique is juxtaposition, whereby he introduces a series of comparisons that prey upon working-class resentment for the wealthy. The first contrast is between the poor farm-girl Roberta, who "went to the city of Lycurgas in order that by working with her own hands she might help her family" (691), with "the rich and beautiful" socialite Sondra, whose servants attend to her daily needs (691). He proceeds to contrast Clyde with Roberta, informing the jury that Clyde's salary was "such that he could afford to keep a room in one of the better residences of the city, while the girl he had slain lived in a mean room in a back street" (692). Finally, Mason cunningly offers a reminder that Clyde "has had more social and educational advantages than any one of you in the jury box," and had become "part of as smart a society and summer resort group as this region boasts" (692). The series of comparisons whips up the jury's anger against Clyde, portraying him as a class traitor who has slain one of their own, a "poor little murdered country girl" (797). Thus beyond their basic mandate to fairly execute the law, the jury is tasked with enforcing the working-class conviction that "the poor must stand together everywhere" (215). During the trial Mason assumes the mantle of "the true hero—the nemesis of Clyde—the avenger of Roberta" (796), asking the assembled country folk to police and punish one of their own.[4] As Gregory Phipps writes, "Clyde's fate exemplifies the way the social collective both encourages and condemns the superficial and illusory display of wealth. After all, if Clyde were an affluent person with solid connections to the Lycurgus crowd, he might be able to escape punishment.[5] But then, if this were the case, he would not be following the American Dream" (229). And, as Zanine submits, Clyde is foremost guilty of rising in class, "the kind of thing which Americans should and would have said was the wise and moral thing for him to do had he not committed a murder" (103). So it is that Clyde faces the sanction of the working class for having successfully risen from their ranks. Just as George Wilson does Tom Buchanan's dirty work in murdering Jay Gatsby, it is left to Clyde's erstwhile peers to carry out his execution.

In addition to the scorn he receives from the working-class, Clyde is ostracized by the rich, who close ranks in order to deny and diminish his importance within their world. The Finchleys and Cranstons immediately flee to remote summer resorts under assumed names, while the Griffithses eventually decamp to south Boston. Though his uncle does hold off judgment and supply funds for lawyers, his primary concern is not to prove Clyde's innocence, but rather to "see that all blatant and unjustified reference to the family on the part of the newspapers was minimized" (636). While Roberta's pitiful missives are aired for maximum exploitation, Sondra is anonymized as "Miss X" and her letters withdrawn from the record. The absence of his family and friends at the trial is just as well, for as Samuel Griffiths realizes, "the public was so prejudiced against wealth in such cases" (635). Even after Clyde is convicted, Griffiths does not recoil at the nature of Clyde's crime, but instead quails at the "awful public picture" the proceedings entailed (801). The best Sondra can do is send an anonymous letter months after Clyde's conviction in order to wish him "freedom and happiness" and disclose that "she has suffered much, too" (847). The Lycurgus elite, cautious of Clyde's bona fides to begin with, quickly disavow him when he proves of a baser pedigree during the trial.

So it is that the social climber is again doubly bound by the American class system, with Clyde, as Phillip Neel puts it, "left to starve between social strata" (172). In the same way that social stricture prevented him from a legitimate liaison with Roberta or Sondra, Clyde can neither draw support from the upper-class or lower, for each consider him an abject member of the other. Orlov explains "although he has no money, he is hated by the backwoods folk and their legal spokesman for being related to those who do; his own poverty prevents him from circumventing the law, and his uncle's wealth keeps him from pleading temporary insanity, the means of defense which his lawyers see as his only hope" (87). Clyde is neither rich nor insane but has merely the misfortune of being caught in the no-man's-land between classes; squarely in the public eye, he faces crossfire from each.

The trial concluded, his legal remedies exhausted, Clyde has only the last resort of his family and their cold comfort of religion. In a way, this completes the narrative circle and serves as his final atonement, for his family's was the lowest position he'd known, and theirs was the first ideology he abandoned "to try and ascend the social ladder, an ascent governed by secular values" (Cassuto 122). Nearly a decade after departing, Clyde is a complete stranger to his parents. The ascetic Asa, with no knowledge of his son's "motivating forces of passion," tells reporters "he has never understood Clyde or his lacks or his feverish imaginings. ... And preferred not to discuss him" (800). His mother similarly states that "she would never understand his craving for ease and luxury, for beauty, for love—his particular kind of love with went with show, pleasure, wealth, position, his eager and immutable aspirations and desires" (866). As ever, the yawning disconnect between his family's Spartan spirituality and Clyde's materialist hedonism is a cultural divide exacerbated by American ideology. Nevertheless, his mother resolves to save his soul, if she cannot his life, and enlists the Rev. Duncan McMillian to counsel Clyde in prison. For the last time, Clyde plays chameleon and undergoes a long, halting transformation from hardened criminal to repentant sinner. Though professedly heartfelt, Clyde's conversion is as suspect as his letters to Roberta; his confession is composed "at the request of the Reverend McMillian, and his mother," and edited thereafter so as to better appeal to "young men of his own years" (867). Even then, the short note speaks of "the joy and pleasure of a Christian life," a spiritual hankering for the same quantities that Clyde sought in the secular realm. To the end, Clyde is a man apart, his identity insecure. His final words sound like they "emanated from another being walking alongside of him, and not from himself" (870).

After Clyde's death, Dreiser appends a brief "Souvenir" featuring three generations of Kansas City Griffithses, now plying their spiritual trade in San Francisco. In addition to Asa, his wife, and their daughters, there appears "a boy of not more than seven or eight": Russell, the bastard son of Elsa, an analogue for young Clyde, and a stand-in for Roberta's unborn child. The concluding scene mirrors the opening of the book, including the "tall walls of the commercial heart" of a city, a little group of street preachers, and a pair of bystanders who remark upon Russell's youth and inquire "what kind of life is that for a kid?" (872). When the company ends their evening's singing, Russell asks his grandmother whether he might go for an ice-cream cone, which she allows with the admonition that "you are to come right back" (874). The scene is a call-back to her stewardship of Clyde, who as a boy hungered for pleasure, found employment as a soda jerk, and never returned to the straight and narrow. In light of her perceived mistakes in childrearing, Mrs. Griffiths has resolved to be "more liberal with [Russell]" and "not restrain him too much" (874). Yet the novel ends before the boy returns, and the final image is of the family disappearing into the "yellow, unprepossessing door," matching the portal the condemned Clyde enters, which "quickly closed … on all the earthly life he had ever known" (870). With that, Dreiser ends the book, suggesting that Russell, who displays a keen desire for pleasure at a young age, might follow the same tragic path as his late uncle.

"The compelling and corrosive power of the capitalist infrastructure"

I have made a number of allusions to *The Great Gatsby* throughout this essay, and for good reason. Published in the same year, featuring a pair of low-class, socially ascendant protagonists in Clyde Griffiths and James Gatz, the novels are on the surface a tandem; Charles Thomas Samuels writes that "*An American Tragedy* tells another part of the story Fitzgerald recorded in *The Great Gatsby*. Clyde and Gatsby pursue the same dream, the dream of an orgiastic future embodied in a beautiful girl with a voice like the sound of money; both pursue it passionately but illicitly, and with similarly disastrous results" (317). Lavelle, in turn, explores the sociological dimensions of the novels, arguing that Fitzgerald (like Dreiser, I might add) "shows class in America to be decidedly Weberian. The relationship to the means of production is not a factor; rather, class is defined through difference in social fields through language games—discourses and metanarratives in relation to power networks" (Lavelle 231). While they share the same basic theme and story arc, a crucial difference between the novels is that the reader of *An American Tragedy* has extensive access to Clyde's origin, backstory, and interior thought, whereas Gatsby is a cipher throughout, his history and motivation relayed secondhand, after the fact, by a speculative narrator. On account of Dreiser's painstaking naturalism, we witness the various influences that convert Clyde from a missionary's child to a social striver to a murderer, obliging the critic to conduct a postmortem accounting of the forces that transformed him.

Foremost is the power and pervasion of American ideology, which suffuses Clyde's consciousness and the story at large. The novel itself was based on the 1906 murder of Grace Brown by Chester Gillette, which Dreiser selected from a half-dozen like occurrences. As Joseph Flora reports, "Dreiser recognized something distinctly (and frighteningly) American about the nature of the murders, and he studied a group of these 'American tragedies' before he decided that the circumstances of the Gillette-Brown murder were ideally suited to the book he wanted to produce" (77). Dreiser's title telegraphs the novel's content, with "an" suggesting that Clyde's tragedy is merely one of many and "American" positing a uniquely national affair which does not translate to other cultures. Every critic can see that Clyde is addicted to what Dreiser termed "the common dope of success that is injected into all classes and conditions of people in this country" (*Interviews* 140), though they vary on the exact composition of this "dope." Flora calls it the "illusory but widely accepted American notion that an ambitious boy may rise to wealth with comparative ease" (78). Phipps refers to "a uniquely American ideal in which a 'poor' and 'nondescript' man can climb the socioeconomic ladder" (229). Orlov focuses on "the standard American rags-to-riches story in which a man deprived of material advantages (including access to educational institutions) is able to triumph against the odds" (230). I bundle these terms under the larger umbrella of the American Dream—the idea that there are no barriers, no limits, no excuses, not only to what one can achieve, but therefore to what one *should* achieve. As any American who grows from a youth to an adult realizes, such an outcome is far from assured. Though it is mathematically possible for anyone who buys a ticket to win the lottery, it is similarly impossible for everyone who hopes to win to do so.

Though the outside critic may easily suss out why Clyde has failed, he is gifted no such self-perception,[6] else he would have avoided the tragedy altogether. As Phipps notes, "it is evident that he lacks a clear conception of the links between his beliefs and the consequences of his actions. At the same time, the novel also presents a fearsome picture of the compelling and corrosive power of the capitalist infrastructure" (225), a strong factor in Clyde's self-alienation. The reason *An American Tragedy* resists a Marxist reading is because the American ideology upon which it subsists is incompatible with Marxist ideology and terminology. Then as now, it is difficult to instill class consciousness in a society avowedly without classes, wherein everyone purportedly has equal opportunity and the poor see themselves as (to borrow a phrase from John Steinbeck) "temporarily-embarrassed millionaires" rather than exploited proletariat. So consumed are Americans by pursuit of the Dream that purely economic concerns (whether minimum wages, organized labor, or income inequality) take a backseat to more visible and attainable markers of status, as recognized by Bourdieu, Veblen, and Weber.

In their dedication to preserving the caste system the Lycurgus Griffithses unwittingly diagnose the problem, for Clyde, Roberta, and Sondra may have been happier were they in a rigid yet transparent society where relationships between the proletariat, bourgeois, and capitalist classes were fixed and adversarial. *An American Tragedy* aligns with Lavelle's claim that above all, "what constitutes happiness is an ideological construct" and that many Americans believe happiness "stems from conspicuous consumption transferring into status and status groups in a straight hierarchy … the higher status position a person holds, the happier he or she will be" (143). Though commonly swallowed then as now, such a conviction is belied by the text, for the higher Clyde climbs, the more obsessive he becomes. For a brief moment after Roberta's death, he glimpses "a clear path! A marvelous future!" (578) with Sondra and her set, like Gatsby reaching for the green light across the bay. Then the law arrives, and the house of happiness he has constructed collapses. From the beginning, it was nothing more than a dream.

Notes

1. There is a reason Dreiser originally called the novel *Mirage*.
2. John Dale points out, "Dreiser deliberately transposed the story of Chester Gillette's 1906 murder of Grace Brown to the early post-war years, which were characterized by a massive rise in consumerism, fueled by mass production and easy credit" (142).
3. A textbook example of habitus is Clyde's fascination with the Green-Davidson, which others more accustomed to luxury find gauche.
4. Such self-policing is common practice enacted against marginalized communities, whether sexuality among women, intelligence among schoolgirls, or nativism among subalterns under colonialism.
5. The same is true for Roberta when a country doctor denies her access to an abortion on purportedly moral reasons, "although in several cases in the past ten years where family and other neighborhood and religious considerations had made it seem quite advisable, he had assisted in extricating from the consequences of their folly several young girls of good family who had fallen from grace and could not otherwise be rescued" (435).
6. Mason labels Clyde "clever in one sense, not so clever in another—just half clever, which is the worst of all" (749).

Works Cited

Blunden, Andy. "Bourdieu on Status, Class and Culture." *Ethical Politics Org.* May 2004.
Bourdieu, Pierre. *Distinction: A Social Critique of the Judgement of Taste.* Trans. by Richard Nice. Cambridge, MA: Harvard University Press, 1984.
Cassuto, Leonard. "Lacanian Equivocation in *Sister Carrie*, *The 'Genius,'* and *An American Tragedy*." *Theodore Dreiser: Beyond Naturalism.* Ed. Miriam Gogol. New York: New York University Press, 1995. 112–133.
Dale, John. "'…and not your famous Dreiser'; Jean-Paul Sartre Passes Too Lightly over the Travails of Clyde Griffiths." *Midwest Quarterly*, vol. 57, no. 2, 2016. 137–51.
Dreiser, Theodore. *An American Tragedy.* Cleveland: World Publishing Company, 1948.
_____. *Theodore Dreiser: Interviews.* Ed. Frederic E. Rusch and Donald Pizer. Champaign: University of Illinois Press, 2004.
Eby, Clare Virginia. *Dreiser and Veblen, Saboteurs of the Status Quo.* Columbia: University of Missouri Press, 1999.

Gerber, Phillip L. *Theodore Dreiser Revisited*. Woodbridge, CT: Twayne, 1992.
Hakutani, Yoshinobu. "Wright, Dreiser, and Spatial Narrative." *Theodore Dreiser and American Culture: New Readings*. Ed. Yoshinobu Hakutani. Newark: University of Delaware Press, 2000, pp. 248–273.
Lavelle, John F. *Blue Collar, Theoretically: A Post-Marxist Approach to Working Class Literature*. Jefferson, NC: McFarland, 2011.
Neel, Phillip. "The Doldrums, or Shadows of Revolution in Theodore Dreiser's Cold World." *Philosophy and Literature*, vol. 37, no. 1, 2013, pp. 164–78.
Orolv, Paul. *An American Tragedy Perils of the Self Seeking Success*. Lewisburg, PA: Bucknell University Press, 1998.
———. "Technique as Theme in 'An American Tragedy.'" *The Journal of Narrative Technique*, vol. 14, no. 2, 1984. 75–93.
Phipps, Gregory. "One Crime, Two Pragmatisms: The Philosophical Context of Theodore Dreiser's *An American Tragedy*." *Studies in American Naturalism*, vol. 10, no. 2, 2013. 214–35.
Pizer, Donald. "Theodore Dreiser's *An American Tragedy* and 1920s Flapper Culture." *Studies in American Naturalism*, vol. 10, no. 2, 2016. 123–32.
St. John, Shawn. *Pagan Dreiser: Songs from American Mythology*. Madison, NJ: Fairleigh Dickinson University Press, 2001.
Samuels, Charles Thomas. "Mr. Trilling, Mr. Warren, and *An American Tragedy*." *Yale Review* vol. 53, no. 1, 1964. 629–40.
Spindler, Michael. "Youth, Class, and Consumerism in Dreiser's *An American Tragedy*." *Journal of American Studies*, vol. 12, no. 1, 1978, pp. 63–79.
Veblen, Thorstein. *The Theory of the Leisure Class*. 1899. Rpt. Chelmsford, MA: Courier Corporation, 2012.
Weber, Max. *The Protestant Ethic and the Spirit of Capitalism*. 1930. Rpt. Chelmsford, MA: Courier Corporation, 2012.
Zanine, Louis J. *Mechanism and Mysticism: The Influence of Science on the Thought and Work of Theodore Dreiser*. Philadelphia: University of Pennsylvania Press, 1993.

The Sun Also Rises for Some
Hemingway's Exploration of the Ideologies of Social Class in The Sun Also Rises

JOHN F. LAVELLE *and* DEBBIE LELEKIS

When F. Scott Fitzgerald wrote in "The Rich Boy," "Let me tell you about the rich. They are different from you and me, ... that they are better than we are because we had to discover the compensations and refuges of life ourselves" (318), Ernest Hemingway responded in "The Snows of Kilimanjaro" with "...yes, they have more money" (53). It had been a critique of Fitzgerald's assumption, and those of the "privileged" class, that the rich were not held to the same moral codes as the rest of humanity just because they were rich. Although Hemingway was tweaking Fitzgerald's nose and the critique did bother Fitzgerald, Fitzgerald did critique this privileged ideology in *The Great Gatsby*, stating, "They were careless people, Tom and Daisy—they smashed up things and creatures and then retreated back into their money or their vast carelessness" (179).

Hemingway was decidedly middle class, the sort of middle class of Nick Carraway, not rich but landed or to be exact, well ensconced in the middle class gentry of his community. He should have, by all accounts, adhered to a privileged ideology not unlike Nick Carraway. "[A]s my father snobbishly suggested, and as I snobbishly repeat, a sense of the fundamental decencies is parceled out unequally at birth" (Fitzgerald 2).

In Mary V. Dearborn's biography of Hemingway, she describes his family as solidly middle-class people whose views on work and morality were shaped by religion and the belief that "material success was the just reward for their virtuous private lives" (11). Hemingway's maternal grandfather, Ernest Hall, was Episcopalian, while his paternal grandfather, Anson Hemingway, had ancestors that were Puritan and Congregationalist ministers. Dearborn contends that Anson Hemingway's health condition—a mitral valve prolapse and a deformity of the chest causing the sternum and rib cage to protrude—may have inspired his son Clarence "Ed" Hemingway (Ernest's father) to become a doctor. Before attending Rush Medical College in Chicago, Ed went to Oberlin, where he was involved with the Agassiz Club, which followed Louis Agassiz's teachings on nature. This interest in nature and the outdoors was passed on to Ernest and his siblings who were involved in the Oak Park chapter of the club, which was established by Ed Hemingway. Agassiz's concept was that learning about life and earth sciences was best undertaken by spending time outside and gaining first-hand experience studying nature. The Hemingway family further developed those interests during summers that were spent boating, swimming, fishing, and hunting at their cottage along Walloon Lake in Michigan, where Dr. Hemingway also provided medical care for the people in the area. Dearborn describes the ways in which Ed taught his children "how to survive in the wilderness, how to walk like an Indian, how to preserve and stuff animals after they were dead, [and] how to tie flies to catch trout" (21).

While his father's enthusiasm for the outdoors certainly made an impact on Ernest, the influence of his unique and talented mother may have influenced him in more profound, yet more subtle ways. Grace Hall Hemingway came from a family that contained several musicians, and her father Ernest Hall supported the musical education of his entire family. According to Dearborn, the family often sang together and attended the opera and musical performances in Chicago (15). Grace appears to have been the most talented, and she excelled in her piano and voice lessons. She suffered from poor vision due to childhood illnesses (both scarlet and rheumatic fevers), but she persevered despite her ailments. The Hall and Hemingway families lived across the street from each other, so Grace and Ed had known each other for a while before they began a romantic relationship. While Ed was finishing his medical training in Europe, Grace spent a year in New York where she made her singing debut at Madison Square Garden, followed by a brief European tour with her father, but she ended the pursuit of a singing career abruptly and returned to Oak Park to marry Ed Hemingway in 1896. Dearborn speculates that it was due to Ed's relentless courtship of Grace through letters, rather than Grace's complaint about the bright stage lights bothering her eyes, that caused her to return to life in Oak Park (16). Grace was able to shift her interest in music from performance to teaching (and occasionally composing songs that were published), and her financial contributions to the family were substantial.

However, Ernest saw his mother's financial success in a negative light. Dearborn describes Ernest's critique that his mother emasculated his father and suggests that it was linked to Grace's financial status; he also saw his mother as extravagant and seemed to feel a sense of resentment towards her when he recounted instances when she would spend money on herself for personal items like expensive hats, rather than spending money on the family (17). Despite his criticism of his mother, Ernest was said to be the most like her, according to his siblings. By all accounts, she was a devoted mother to her children when they were young, but in other ways, she was far from a conventional mother of her era. She did not perform typical domestic chores like sweeping and laundry, and she rarely cooked, a task that she left to her husband Ed, who had learned to prepare food when he was part of a government survey team in the Smoky Mountains (Dearborn 19). Grace also challenged gender boundaries in her treatment of Ernest and his older sister Marcelline as "twins" (even though they were 18 months apart) who she dressed alike as either girls or boys. As Dearborn asserts, the practice of dressing baby boys in girls' dresses with lace and bows, and the styling of their hair in long curls, was not uncommon during that time period as an "expression of a general sentimentalization of childhood, wherein innocence—associated with what was thought to be the gentler, fairer sex—was highly prized," but this was generally halted after the child's first year (22). This unusual practice of dressing Ernest in girly stockings, dresses, Mary Jane shoes, and flowered hats seems to be a sign of Grace's dominance in the household, and that combined with her own challenges to gender roles through her profession, created mixed feelings in her son, according to Dearborn (24). Ernest would later in life blame his mother's emasculating of his father, characterized as a wearing down "until he had no strength to weather crises of confidence," and this aspect of his parents' relationship is what Ernest believed led to his father's suicide in 1928 (Dearborn 27).

Hemingway, then was exposed to both an egalitarian ideology through his father and a privileged ideology through his mother. Of what we know of Hemingway and through his biographies and his writing both fiction and nonfiction, he seems to have sided with the egalitarian ideology for good reason. Ernest's influential high school teacher, Fannie Biggs, described the education provided at Oak Park and River Forest High School as one focused on the arts, and she identified the student population as coming from families who would usually attend private schools. Dearborn examines how the Hemingway family was removed from Oak Park society's "acute class-consciousness and its bourgeois respectability," even though they had an elevated status within their community (42). Biggs recounted to Hemingway scholar Charles Fenton that Ernest didn't have spending money, and his parents did not attend events at the Oak Park country clubs or social clubs. Michael Reynolds describes the Hemingways as living in a "respectable neighborhood of businessmen, salesmen, doctors, and dentists" (18). Ed and Grace Hemingway raised their large family in a nice, modern house, which also contained a music studio and Dr. Hemingway's medical office. As a classically-trained, professional musician, Grace was able to earn a respectable income from the music lessons she gave and royalties from the music she composed. Dearborn argues that it was because of the money that Grace made early in their marriage, when Dr. Hemingway was still growing his obstetrical practice, that the Hemingways were able to obtain a middle-class position within their community (17). Despite the fact that both parents worked and they had six children and an uncle who lived with them, Dearborn notes that previous Hemingway biographers have criticized the Hemingways as designing a house that was too grand. The blame seems to be focused on Grace, but Dearborn argues that this critique is misguided because there is no evidence that the family was financially strained by the building of their new house, even though their neighbors seemed to think otherwise. The neighbors also gossiped about Ed Hemingway's appearance and abilities as a doctor, describing him as unkempt and wretched (Dearborn 32). The Hemingway family, and Dr. Hemingway in particular, are allegedly the basis for John Dos Passos's Warner family in his novel *Chosen Country* (1951), which also contains a doctor who is described in less than flattering terms. Ed Hemingway required periods of rest away from his family, and Dearborn contends that Ed's behavior, which alternated between charming and stern, indicates an "underlying emotional struggle" that evolved into depression with symptoms of paranoia and psychosis and perhaps a manic-depressive illness later in life that might have been the root cause of his suicide (31–32). Clearly, the experiences of Hemingway's youth and the relationships that he had with both of his unconventional parents impacted his development and likely shaped his conception of class and its complexities. He must have seen the playing out of a social class struggle between his mother and father and may have come to understand innately the idea of asocial fields, power loci in these social fields, dominant people with dominant ideologies and the games that were played out with social fields. In particular, his attitude towards his mother seems to have influenced his creation of complicated female characters like Brett who is at the center of his examination of power and class in *The Sun Also Rises*.

There is little doubt that anyone who reads *The Great Gatsby* is confronted with it being predominantly concerned with class. Although *The Sun Also Rises*, at first, does not seem to be overly concerned with class, it is in its own way as invested in it as Fitzgerald's novel. Neither book, though, constructs class in a Marxist three-tiered economic configuration. Rather they construct class in the Weberian sense of *Strande* as social and mutable.

The Weberian idea of social class complicates a more simplistic reading of the interactions of the characters in *The Sun Also Rises*. Weber contends that rather than class being economic, it is social and a person's position within a social group *Strande* determines his or her access to life chances (opportunities), and thus a person's economic status. Pierre Bourdieu suggests in *Distinctions* that through taste and taste makers, people are in-grouped/out-grouped. He later develops his theory of social fields, fields of power or to say social groupings, which are inclusionary as well as exclusionary. "A field is a structured social space, a field of forces, a force field. It contains people who dominate and people who are dominated. Constant, permanent relationships of inequality operate inside this space, which at the same time becomes a space in which the various actors struggle for the transformation or preservation of the field" (Bourdieu, Homo Academicus 40). People exist within many social fields. "[W]ithin every society, each social agent is inscribed in a multiplicity of social relations [...]. All these social positions determine positionalities or subject positions and every social agent is therefore the locus of many subject positions" (Mouffe 90). These fields of power come into existence and defuse as society demands. In *The Sun Also Rises*, Jake exists in a multitude of social fields including the field of journalism, specifically foreign correspondents with Woolsey and Krum, the world of prostitutes having invited several to dinner, the social fields of the bullfight aficionado, and of the peasants, of people who fish and finally in the social fields of the Latin Quarter and the bars and night clubs around Paris. *The Sun Also Rises* is concerned mostly with the small groups of expats, those persons who dominated these fields and those who are dominated within those fields.

While *The Great Gatsby* seems more of a macro study of social class, *The Sun Also Rises* is a study in the micro workings of class within a social field specifically that of Lady Ashley, Jake, Mike, soon to be Robert Cohn and Bill Groton, and others such as Zizi and Count Mippipopolous. Jake seems at first to be the power locus of this field. This is an effect of first person narration and in fact, Lady Brett Ashley holds the position of power within their group. She is in this position not just because she is beautiful but because she is intelligent and exercises an ideology of privilege, which allows her to be manipulative, lie, insult people when necessary, and to do anything she must do to maintain her power including controlling the other ideologies, what might be said or done in the group. With just a few words she can exclude a person from the group—out-grouping. She is so powerful, she actually invades other groups, such as the group of gay men she is with when she first appears in the story, Jake and Bill's small field of fishermen, by insisting on going with them, although she never plans to fish, and most importantly the social field of the aficionados. Some readers see her as a survivor; however, it is more than just surviving it is exploitation and will to power.

> Life itself is essentially appropriation, injury, overpowering of what is alien and weaker; suppression, hardness, imposition of one's own forms, incorporation

and at least, at its mildest., exploitation—but why should one always use those words in which a slanderous intent has been imprinted for ages? ... Exploitation' does not belong to a corrupt or imperfect or primitive society: it belongs to the essence of what lives, as a basic organic function; it is a consequence of the will to power, which is after all the will of life [Nietzsche 393].

Friedrich Nietzsche claims in *The Genealogy of Morality* that morality has always had a historical function, a sort of practical reason d'etre, and that morality is not some universal constant. "Nietzsche purports to provide a genealogy of the value judgments 'good' and 'bad' and 'good' and 'evil.' He argues that the value judgments 'good' and 'bad' originated among the noble classes as a form of 'self-glorification'" (Owen 68). Nietzsche's critique on morals, other than being an apology for the conservative hegemony of the time, points out that two different core metanarratives exist, the privileged, Nietzsche's noble ideology (morality) and an egalitarian ideology based on the fundamentals of humanism. Where Nietzsche justifies the actions of these nobles and their self-righteous postulating, Thorstein Veblen names them the violent class and sees this postulating, including Nietzsche's apologies, as a weak justification for their violent and inhumane actions. Veblen contends that "...the scheme of life for the class is in large part a heritage from the past and embodies much of the habits and ideals of the earlier barbarian period ... the age of prowess and predatory life" (290–91). He goes on to say that this class "the leisure class claims the distinction as a matter of pride" (291). "These new values 'reactively' affirmed the poor, weak, and oppressed through the espousal of slavish virtues and qualities they embodied and the nobles abhorred, such as meekness and humility, which were actually just the opposite of the characteristics and virtues evident in the nobles" (Snelson 3). The nobles found humanism repugnant and believed that birth or position in society allowed for privilege, a sort of God given right and thus their actions were only to benefit themselves and if it benefited themselves it was moral and good. Brett states, "'I don't say it's right. It is right though for me. God knows'" (147).

The term "bitch" as it concerns Brett has been bandied about in more than several readings of *The Sun Also Rises*. "The British bitch for Hemingway is only a demi-bitch ... the Lilith of the 20s. No man embraces her without in some sense wanting to be castrated" (Fiedler 319). These discussions are usually concerned as to whether Brett is actually a self-professed "bitch" ["'I've never felt such a bitch'" (147)] or is misunderstood, suffers from the war or the death of her true love, or is another victim of the society of the time.

Critics quickly labeled Brett as a "bitch." Members of what Roger Whitlow terms the "Brett-the-bitch" (51) school of criticism include Leslie Fiedler, ... John

Aldridge, who calls her a "compulsive bitch" (24), and, more recently, Mimi Gladstein, who labels her as part "bitch-goddess" (61). Even those who shy away from the actual term "bitch" tend to delineate Brett in other destructive ways [Fulton 61].

In the beginning of the story, Brett first arrives on the scene and learns that Jake has brought a prostitute with him. "'It's wrong of you, Jake.... It's a restraint of trade'" (18). It may seem like Hemingway is commenting on women and that there is not much difference in the way they act between the lowest prostitute and a "Lady"; however, Brett is talking about power, specifically her power over Jake and other men. When Jake answers Brett's query stating that he did it because he was bored, Brett counters what seems to finally be a comment on her lack of attention, by suggesting they leave, taking Jake away from any temptation even though he is incapable of acting on it. Once alone, she allows him to kiss her and then tells him not to touch her and then that she must see him and tells him it isn't good to see him (22). Although one might say Brett is confused, or that because of her own psychic war wounds, she has a right to be as she is, her ideology allows her to say what she says and do what she does as a way to manipulate the power within their social field. She convinces Jake she loves him, but she has already accepted an invitation to San Sebastian with Robert Cohn. Once she returns and has a chance to tell him the truth, she still does not and only tells Jake the truth when she is hoping Jake will tell Robert not to come along to Pamplona. Whether she even bothers to lie to Mike, we don't know, and it seems as though she is brutally truthful to him while cuckolding him. Thus, she calls herself a bitch not as an admission, but as part of the language game of their social group, forcing Jake to assure her she is not one and to manipulate Jake into doing what she asks.

As Bourdieu suggests, within this social field is a power locus, some people being placed near, some farther away. Because Jake is a first person narrator he seems to be the center, the locus of the field, but he is actually placed away from the locus of power and in fact Brett could be said to be this locus of power within the field by her ability to manipulate the discourse within the field to her advantage. Peter L. Hayes states, "The imperial force in *The Sun Also Rises* is Brett" (239). He believes that "a spirit of rebellion from domination by exacting masters, a need to be free from the control of others, runs through the novel, as Jake seeks to separate himself from Brett's hold on him" (239).

Foucault constructs this social field within the idea of discourse. It is through discourse that a Subject/subject relationship is created. "There are two meanings of the word 'subject': subject to someone else by control and dependence and tied to his [or her] own identity by a conscious or self-knowledge" *(Essential* 130). Simply put, the Subject, what Derrida calls the transcendental signifier, is the locus of power in a social field created by the dominant ideological discourses within that field. "For Althusser, our entry into the symbolic order, and thus our constitution as subjects, is the work of ideology, which, he argues, hails or 'interpellates' concrete individuals as concrete subjects" (Baker). Brett is the Subject that constructs all others as subjects to her. She controls the discourse, what Wittgenstein calls the rules to the language game. "I am summarizing. Wittgenstein, ... he calls the various types of utterances he identifies along the way (a few of which I have listed) language games" (Lyotard 9). The rules of a language game allow for certain utterances while disallowing others. Within the field then, these discourses also construct subjects who derive their identities from the Subject/transcendental signifier, or the locus of power. "The autonomy of a field of restricted production can be measured by its power to define its own criteria" (Bourdieu *Field of Production* 113). Brett is constantly testing the loyalty of a subordinate within the field of power of which she is the locus, or to say she is testing as to whether or not she is still the locus of power in her social group. Thus the debate as to whether Brett is a bitch or as Adair states "in performative terms ... she seems a mother figure" (190) depends on whether she has the right to the power her position provides.

That she calls herself the "bitch" to elicit sympathy from Jake seems likely, and yet, one could say this is exactly what she strives to become and calls herself a bitch leaving Jake no choice but to deny the truth as her privileged position within the group allows her the right to include or exclude and since he is in love with her as most everyone else seems to be, he cannot afford to have her out-group him. This is no more evident than when comparing Montoya and Jake's conversation over whether or not to give Romero a note from an American woman who wants to meet him and later when Brett wants the same thing. When Montoya seeks Jake's advice as to whether he should give Romero the note from the American woman, Jake says, "All you have to do is not give him the message" (138). He is protecting Romero from "mix[ing] in that stuff" (138), and also doing what he believes is an honorable thing. Later Brett corners Jake and insists he do exactly what he told Montoya not to do, a dishonorable act, introduce Brett to Romero. She again calls herself a bitch and it is the closest Jake comes to telling her the truth.

"I do feel such a bitch."
"Well," I said [147].

Brett has hoped to put Jake into another untenable position, but instead of denying the self-accusation, he suggests, with the one word, that not only might she be, but she should know this and why. "'My God!' said Brett, 'the things a woman goes through'" (147). His answer is "'Yes?'" (147). Notably, he is not agreeing, but rather questioning her remark. Jake has called her bluff as to what she would do if he refused. He has weighed the consequences of her out-grouping him as she is attempting to do to Robert Cohn, against being dishonorable. Although if he refused, she would likely out-group him later in the future, right at that moment he is her only avenue to Romero and with nothing else to say she repeats her mantra. "'Oh, I do feel such a bitch.'" (147).

When her affair has run its short course and Romero has left her, Brett uses her same trigger phrase to elicit sympathy from Jake, not that she, sitting in bed looking abandoned, does not make her sympathetic. "'I'm not going to be one of those bitches that ruin children'" (195). Here, as before, Brett has put him in an untenable position. He cannot refuse her requests or admit to his true feelings without being dishonorable to a woman in need. There is also the real possibility of out-grouping as has happened to Cohn. Again the normal reading is that Jake denies that Brett is a "bitch" because he is in love with her, and like almost all the other men in her life is helpless around her, but rather, because he is in love with her he must deny any wrong doing on her part to remain within the field of power that is the social network of their Paris. When she says to him "'we could have had such a damn good time together'" (198), his reply is "'Isn't it pretty to think so'" (198). He is at best pragmatic about their relationship and seems to understand the truth as Mike does, that she will always demand to be the center of their world and the power in their social field.

The greatest testament to her domination over Jake and the others is when she forces Jake to give her Pedro Romero. Jake is forced to destroy his longtime friendship with Montoya but more so, to act in a shameful way by going against his ideological beliefs in that a man must act honorably to be a man as when he later takes a swing at Robert Cohn when Cohn calls him a pimp even though Jake knows quite well that Robert is much better than he at fighting. Mike has no such problem with honor and is only beaten by Robert because he gets in the way.

What is truly in play here are the rules of the social game within their in-group. Brett, since she is the locus of power, constructs the rules to the game, which ironically is one of the major narratives of the game.

> In the group we must account not only for the link between a person's identity and his or her behavior, but also for the maintenance of that link in the presence of other demands on the person's behavior; these other demands take the form of others' behavior and expectations, as well as the situational demands of the group in regard to attaining its goals [Riley, Burke 61].

Each person, as they are added to the group within the field of power, are given by the others, specifically Brett, a place within the field of power, a subject position, defining his (and it's always a male) place within the group. This is why Jake accepts his position and does not protest when asked to do favors like arrange the trip to Spain, buy double tapered leader for Cohn, and accepts that Mike and Brett say one thing and do another, and although may seem to apologize, they will never be apologetic.

Brett sets up the rules of the social game and has the power to change them at will, both the explicit rules and implicit rules of the game. The explicit rules, as seen in *The Sun Also Rises*, are that we're all the same—all equal. The implicit rules are that maybe some people are better than others. This is seen through the character of Robert Cohn. Although Cohn was "a member of one of the richest Jewish families in New York" (4) and has a successful novel published, he is still Jewish, thus should never be allowed a close place to the locus of the field of power, and yet is because of Brett's use of him allowing him access to this power locus. Brett, of course, assumes Cohn will take a more subordinate role once they are back in Paris, not unlike Jake and Mike, and can't understand why he does not. "'He was an ass, though. He came down to San Sebastian where he damn well wasn't wanted. He hung around Brett and just *looked* at her. It made me damned well sick'" (114). That Cohn refuses his place in the group raises anti–Semitic bias among the group, especially with Mike, a Jew usurping the power and changing the dynamics of the group, dynamics that the other men have long ago settled on. This, of course, upsets the equilibrium that has been established within the field. Cohn should manifest aspects of a privileged ideology, but being Jewish, he is normally out-grouped and the idea of who you are makes you better than what you do is undercut by him being Jewish. He should be in any in-group because of his money and education, Princeton, but cannot be because of his birth. Cohn has had to define himself in what he does and is at all points undercut by anti–Semitism. It is not clear that he wants Brett because he is in love with her or wants her because of his assumed position within this new field of power he has entered, one that is now in flux.

When Robert Cohn asks Jake about Lady Ashley, Jake gives the polite answer, "'She's very nice'" (31). When Cohn states he could "'very well be in love with her'" (31), Jake's reply is "'She's a drunk'" (31). Why Jake says this is never made clear. He might be angry that he is powerless to stop Cohn from pursuing her as Mike is angry not being able to stop Romero because of the rules of the game of their social field, all constructed by Brett. He might be being anti–Semitic, angry that a Jew does not seem to know his place, a larger discourse from a larger social field. He might also be warning a young man that he is in over his head and has no idea of the rules of this game. "'I'm just trying to give you the facts'" (32). Cohn's reply is "'I didn't ask you to insult her'" (32), which is one of the underlying narratives within this social group that Brett is a "lady" and thus needs protection and Cohn thinks he is defending Brett's honor. It is the honorable thing to do. Mike, being privileged, has no qualms about doing the honorable thing and, as Pedro Romero takes away his fiancé, he can only sit by and insult bulls. Jake tells Cohn "'to go to hell'" (32). Cohn stands up and insists on Jake taking the insult back. The insult demands that Cohn act in an honorable way and his standing is, of course, his suggesting that he means to find satisfaction. Jake, realizing he's pushed Cohn too far and them fighting would only make matters worse, apologizes.

Of course Cohn is unfamiliar with the rules of the game within this new field of power and never quite fits in because he refuses, unknowingly, his position within the field prescribed by those who are more established and have grasped and held on to the power, the old rich or not so rich, as Mike and Brett. Although Mike and Brett have little money, they are in the first group by virtue of their lineage or at least Mike's lineage. Because Cohn is not of old money and Jewish, he has not been inculcated by habitus into the rules of the game that state Brett and Mike can do no wrong even going to San Sebastian with a Jew and dumping him once she is back. Mike and Brett are the doppelgangers of Daisy and Tom, breaking things and hiding in their money or for Europeans hiding within their titles. They are Nietzsche's nobles and manifest a noble morality or to say privileged ideology.

Jake and Bill Groton, among others in the story, hold to an egalitarian ideology, one of humanism that believes good or evil are invested in what a person does—deeds and not their birth or position in the social field. Bill Groton sees a stuffed dog in the window of a taxidermist and tells Jake he would like to buy him the stuffed dog. "Mean everything in the world to you after you bought it. Simple exchange of values. You give them money. They give you a stuffed dog" (60). Hemingway who had more than likely seen more than one stuffed animal in his lifetime and was probably familiar with the process is critiquing a Marxist reading of the stuffed dog and of the idea of value. Groton is also not just questioning the exchange value of a stuffed dog, which is not a dog at all but the skin of a dog pulled over a molded form. He, in a way, is questioning the use value of a stuffed animal as he does when he says he will have a "horse-cab" stuffed to give to Jake for Christmas (61). A stuffed horse, especially one hooked to a cab has absolutely no use value at all. Thus any exchange value must be found in the item's social, cultural, or symbolic capital. The dog's value is no longer in what it does or is capable of doing, not in being a dog, nor is the horse's but in its value as a type of cultural or social capital, what Veblen considers "conspicuous consumption. Conspicuous consumption of valuable goods is a means of reputability" (91). People buy an item not for its use value—the function it performs, but rather to show that they have taste. The value of goods depends on taste and as Cook states taste is, "a hegemonic project, the making of a social world fit for the bourgeoisie class" (99). This hegemonic project "must have the means for inviting people to join in" and "ways of making them obey the rules" (100). Thus "this predisposes tastes to function as a marker of 'class'" (Bourdieu *Distinctions* 1–2). Bill's running joke about stuffed dogs and stuffed horses brings to light his and Jake's attitudes toward what makes an honorable person. As the horse's and dog's worth is in what they do or how they act, so acts/deeds, honorable or dishonorable, for Bill, Jake, and the peasants in Spain define good and evil. This is no more telling than the peasants' rejection of Jake's and Bill's bottled wine on the bus. "Everyone took a drink very politely, and then they made us cork it up and put it away. They all wanted us to drink from their leather wine-bottles" (83–4). The bottle seems to represent for them the bourgeois that buy it and its value for them as cultural capital and not so much use value as a drink. In a way the wine has lost its use value, but more so it represents the division of classes by taste allowing for not only exclusion but of criteria based on who you are, what you have, and the importance of knowing the rules within a closed social field, and not what you do.

In *The Sun Also Rises*, the character of Pedro Romero, is Hemingway's consummate representation of an egalitarian ideology manifesting itself in honorable acts. He is young, shy, and polite but also brave and proves himself in the ring by his actions. In *The Sun Also Rises*, Hemingway makes a comparison between Romero and Belmonte, an older toreador who has come out of retirement. "Belmonte imposed conditions and insisted that his bulls should not be too large, nor too dangerously armed with horns, … and the public, who wanted three times as much from Belmonte, who was sick with a fistula, as Belmonte had ever been able to give, felt defrauded and cheated" (171). Belmonte's fighting of the bulls is honorific. "A honorific act is in the last analysis little if anything else than a recognized successful act of aggression; … The naive, archaic habit of construing all manifestations of force in terms of personality or 'will power' greatly fortifies this conventional exaltation of the strong hand" (Veblen 24). Importantly it is a public "act" of aggression done to elicit praise and not necessarily a brave and honorable act. Belmonte is performing for praise and, of course, money. His act of aggression is mostly theater, a play at a successful act of aggression, but it is conspicuous which Veblen contends is the most important part. Notably, the audience, mostly peasants from the countryside, who, like Jake and Bill, judge most people by their deeds, honorable or dishonorable, see through the charade and judge Belmonte by his actions, not his reputation, finding him wanting and dishonorable. Romero's actions, whether fighting bulls or

Robert Cohn, are honorable. He does not seek praise but to prove himself to himself and others.

These major metanarratives within the group, as in most of society, are antithetical to each other. While Jake and Bill attempt to treat everyone as equals, Brett and Mike see themselves as privileged and it is both Brett and Mike insisting on decorum that allows for the uneven doling out of privilege within the group in which they manipulate people for their own advantages using the others' belief that honor is in what you do, not your position in society. In a sort of circular argument, they contend that because they are of a higher class, they must be better than the others, and thus what they do is honorable even when it is not.

Jake and Bill, being somewhat middle class, are chameleons, something typical to many middle class. They not only straddle the line between the middle class and the rich as we see in the small group of characters and the other rich in Paris, but manage to be comfortable with the peasants of Spain in differing situations. However, this does not mean they cannot tell the difference. For Bill and Jake it is just the correct thing to do. Several times, though, Jake breaks with decorum and acts in a way which is meant to reflect the way he feels about these people and his place within the groups or speaks his mind truthfully, which, of course, the rules of the game forbid as when he tells the truth about Brett when Cohn asks.

The story is full of dishonorable acts from Brett's lies to her affairs, to her using men, to Mike's allowing her to do it—not that he really thinks he's being honorable—we see this in how he treats Cohn especially after Brett wants to go off with Romero. He has no courage to attack Romero and Romero, although feigning not understanding English, knows well enough Mike is insulting him, but rather than be impressed by Mike's rank, he sees Mike as less than a man and refuses to bother with him. He could very well see his taking of Brett as an honorable thing to do as with his insistence she grow her hair out as a way to make her more of a traditional woman—an honorable woman in his eyes, and less the person she had been. Jake's most dishonorable act is, of course, capitulating to Brett's demand to be introduced to Romero. Where Jake does not act honorably and keeps belittling Cohn's insistence on honor not in his acts only but in the way he thinks, Cohn attempts to act honorably as does Romero. In fact, all the men are forced to act dishonorably due to the metanarratives that insist Brett is acting with honor when she has none.

A major question about the novel is why Jake does not leave Brett or at least straightforwardly admonish her for her lies and manipulations. His inability to end it with Brett is most times relegated to his unrequited love or that Jake has a lack of resolve, being sometimes compared to the steers of the bull ring. While Mike attempts to compare Robert Cohn to the steers,

"It's no life being a steer," Robert Cohn said.

"Don't you think so?" Mike said. "I would have thought you'd loved being a steer, Robert.... They lead such a quiet life. They never say anything and they're always hanging about so."

The obvious comparison is that both Jake and Mike are steers, Jake castrated by the war, to say the dominate hegemonies who orchestrated the genocide of a generation of young men and Mike by Brett who insists on sleeping around. Mike says to Cohn, "'What if Brett did sleep with you? She's slept with lots of better people than you'" (113). However, more is at stake than losing Brett for both Jake and Mike. Brett might very well out-group them both. It is a real danger for Mike. If he complains, she can replace him, maybe with Jake. If Jake does protest, Brett will certainly out-group him.

The first time he has a chance to end the one-sided affair is when Brett announces that she is ending the affair. The day before Brett leaves for San Sebastian she says to Jake, "'I'm going away from you, and then Michael's coming back.... Better for you. Better for me'" (47). She then says, "'Good night, darling. I won't see you again'" (53). She is going to San Sebastian with Cohn for a little holiday but makes it sound as though she is doing it for Jake.

However, leaving for San Sebastian with Robert Cohn takes her out of the social field and her effect on Jake is lessened. "Brett was gone. I wasn't bothered by Cohn's troubles" (57). Jake seems much happier. The moment she returns to Paris, though, she begins to reestablish herself as the dominant player in their social field. "'I say, I'm just back. Haven't bathed even'" (61). Jake is now with Bill Groton who invites Brett for a drink, thus not allowing Jake the opportunity to decline any invitation. Jake seems to understand the long social game Brett is playing and understands their differing positions within the social world they have created in Paris. Her ideology, his ideology, and his position within their social field give him little choice but to capitulate to her implicit demands. He must concede power to Brett or seem impolite to both Brett and Bill. The latter he loses face by acting, in a way Bill will interpret as dishonorable; for the former, Brett, he takes the chance of being out-grouped and even though he seems to contemplate it, now with Bill visiting, it would also seem dishonorable. By the evening, Jake has no choice but to capitulate to the demands of the group in his social field. That evening Bill and Jake are walking around almost as if they are attempting to avoid the inevitable. Bill is patient with Jake, waiting for him to make up his mind. On the Boulevard Port Royal Jake finally asks, "'What do you want to do? ... Go up to the café and see Brett and Mike?'" (64). Bill answers "'Why not?'" He has already ascertained some entanglement between his friend and Brett and is waiting to see exactly what Jake might do.

Jake has a second chance to end the relationship at the end of the story when Brett runs off to Madrid with Pedro Romero. Jake could have gone back to Paris or he could have ignored the telegrams that catch up to him in San Sebastian. Some critics suggest he stays in San Sebastian because he knows he will need to rescue Brett. He could have stayed there because he thought Brett would not be coming back to Paris and there was no longer any hurry to return. He could have also stayed away, hoping to miss the telegrams and escape her altogether. However, he travels to Madrid to rescue her once he receives the summons.

> "Oh, Jake," Brett said, "we could have had such a damned good time together."
> Ahead was a mounted policeman in khaki directing traffic. He raised his baton. The car slowed suddenly pressing Brett against me.
> "Yes," I said. "Isn't it pretty to think so?" [198]

The Sun Also Rises could be considered a discussion of these ideologies, specifically the set of beliefs which contend a person is honorable or dishonorable not through their inherited position in social class but through how they act and what they do. This ideology exists throughout much of Hemingway's writing, but *The Sun Also Rises* is a complex discussion of the interactions of two antithetical ideologies and the way they might play out within a social grouping brought together in Paris after World War I. Jake, the narrator, although seemingly the center of the group is actually one of the outliers and thus the novel is told from the point of view of an outlier, someone on the periphery of the social field and only close to the power locus, Lady Brett Ashley due to his usefulness to her. Brett is neither truthful nor honest to him knowing that those insults will be, if not ignored, and Jake does not ignore them, then met with impotence. Because of his own ideology and his love for Brett (everybody loves her), Jake must meet her dishonesty with impotence as must Mike. They are the steers, not Robert Cohn, who, although much in love with her, will not take a subordinate position within this social group. Maybe because he is Jewish or having come from a rich family, having gone to Princeton, Robert does not act immediately to win Brett but seems rather patient, although not understanding much of what is going on. Romero, however, does act and in a way that destroys the little social group. The meeting of the two, Cohn and Romero, can only end one way with a true straight-up confrontation, a deed/act that both deem honorable. The last scene of the story has Brett back together with Jake having lost Romero and beginning again to reform her power structure.

The Sun Also Rises is Hemingway's complex discussion of class in a Weberian sense. He has been privy to this type of class performance most of his life. Due to his relationship with his unconventional parents and their status within their middle-class community, Hemingway's concept of class evolved to include these notions of social fields and power loci within these social fields. This had a significant impact on the development of Brett and her central position of power within the novel.

Works Cited

Adair, William. "*The Sun Also Rises*: Mother Brett." *Journal of Narrative Theory* 40.2 (Summer 2010): 189–208.
Barker, Chris. "Ideological State Apparatus." *The Sage Dictionary of Cultural Studies*. London: Sage, 2004. 97.
Bourdieu, Pierre. *Distinctions*. Trans. Richard Nice. Cambridge, MA: Harvard University Press, 1884.
―――. *The Field of Cultural Production*. Ed. Randal Johnson. New York: Columbia University Press. 1993.
Cook, John. "Culture, Class and Taste." *Cultural Studies and the Working Class: Subject to Change*. Ed. Sally Munt. London: Cassell, 2000. 97–112.
Dearborn, Mary V. *Ernest Hemingway: A Biography*. New York: Alfred A. Knopf, 2017.
Fiedler, Leslie, A. *Love and Death in the American Novel*. Champaign, IL: Dalkey Archive Press, 2003.
Fitzgerald, F. Scott. *The Great Gatsby*. Ed. Matthew J. Bruccoli. New York: Macmillan, 1992.
―――. "The Rich Boy." *The Short Stories of F. Scott Fitzgerald: A New Collection*. Ed. Matthew J. Bruccoli. New York: Scribner's, 1989, 317–49.
Hayes, Peter, L. "Imperial Brett in *The Sun Also Rises*." *ANQ* 58.2 (1995) 61–73.
Hemingway, Ernest. "The Snows of Kilimanjaro" *The Complete Short Stories of Ernest Hemingway*. New York: Scribner's, 1987. 39–55.
―――. *The Sun Also Rises: The Hemingway Library Edition*. Ed. Sean Hemingway. New York: Scribner, 2016.
Lyotard, Jean-François. *The Postmodern Condition: A Report on Knowledge*. Trans. Geoff Bennington and Brian Massumi. Minneapolis: University of Minnesota Press, 1984.
Mouffe, Chantal. "Hegemony and New Political Subjects: Toward a New Concept of Democracy." *Marxism and the Interpretation of Culture*. Eds. Cary Nelson and Lawrence Grossberg. Champaign: University of Illinois Press,1988. 89–104.
Nietzsche, Friedrich. *Basic Writing of Nietzsche*. Trans. Walter Kaufmann. New York: Modern Library, 2000.
Owen, David. *Nietzsche's Genealogy of Morality*. New York: Routledge, 2007.
Reynolds, Michael. "Ernest Hemingway, 1988–1961." *A Historical Guide to Ernest Hemingway*. Ed. Linda Wagner-Martin. Oxford: Oxford University Press, 2000.
Riley, Anna, and Peter J. Burke. "Identities and Self-verification in the Small Group." *Social Psychology Quarterly* 58.2 (1995) 61–73.
Veblen, Thorstein. *The Theory of the Leisure Class*. Auckland, New Zealand: The Floating Press, 2009.
Watkins-Fulton, Lori. "Reading Around Jake's Narration: Brett Ashley and *The Sun Also Rises*." *The Hemingway Review* 24.1 (Fall 2004) 61–80.

Accidents of Birth
A Class Study of Faulkner's Colonel John Satoris, Emily Grierson and Abner Snopes

Michael J. Finnegan

In *Life on the Mississippi* Mark Twain clearly places the blame for the American Civil War on Sir Walter Scott for "Sir Walter had so large a hand in making Southern character, as it existed before the war, that he is in great measure responsible for the war" (250). By "Southern" character, Twain accused most of the land-owning class of the antebellum and post-war South of constructing, if not a society, then a belief system that placed them at the top of a hierarchy not unlike feudal lords. This belief system was deeply rooted in the ideology of privilege, blood ties, and honorific acts. John F. Lavelle explores this idea of privilege as "an ideology allowing (morally) for the positioning of oneself in a hierarchy of power" in which "one has not only the right to do so but also the birthright"(198). In the character of Colonel John Sartoris, William Faulkner carefully crafted a feudal lord of mythical proportions whose ideology was based on this birthright and it is in this creation of Sartoris that we clearly see Faulkner's ambivalence toward the old antebellum ideology of privilege in contrast to the new post-war order of equality.

This ambivalence toward the character of John Sartoris is apparent in Edmund Volpe's comment that Faulkner "created around the Sartoris family an aura of romanticism that he could not and probably did not want to shake off" and that Faulkner "was clearly aware that these legendary figures whom he cherished and admired did not share his own moral position" (86). The most significant moral position that Faulkner did not share with his character was John Sartoris' belief in the morality of a social hierarchy that allowed for the institution of slavery, a belief which leads Sartoris to be seen as one of the legendary figures of the Confederacy. Matthew Speiser clearly articulates that "this glorification of the slave past fit into a veneration of the southern past generally," a past which created the dominate ideology of the antebellum South and compelled men of privilege, like Sartoris, to act on what he saw as a threat to his birthright (147). Speiser then goes on to explain how these men became "Lost Causers," men who had "adapted their approaches to slavery and race to the new reality of emancipation" so that they were able to sustain "the efforts of earlier white southern advocates to defend slavery, and more fundamentally, the South's white supremacist racial hierarchy" (146–47). These men saw themselves as the epitome of what Twain calls Southern character, feudal lords who saw it as their birthright to own not only land but people and to govern this land and people as their birthright demanded. The Civil War prompted them to take action to defend this same birthright from what they saw as insults to their honor throughout the war and the post-war years.[1]

William Faulkner may have had his own great-grandfather in mind when he created Colonel John Sartoris and like his character, Colonel William C. Falkner was a Civil War hero and a builder of railroads (Tuck 213). Colonel Sartoris was a romantic hero who believed firmly in all that was good about the ideology of the antebellum South. He appears in several of Faulkner's works as either a character or a symbol, although Faulkner never develops him as a fully realized character. However, in "An Odor of Verbena," the last tale of Faulkner's loosely constructed Civil War Novel, *The Unvanquished*, Faulkner fleshes out the character more so than in any other work. Here we see Sartoris in a rare moment of introspection as he makes a conscious decision to go unarmed into a pistol duel with his business partner, Ben Redmond.

Feudal lord that he was, John Sartoris had enforced his birthright by both ridiculing and killing those who opposed him, and at this point in his life, he feels the need to atone for his many wrongs. We assume that he had killed many Yankee soldiers during the war, and in its aftermath, he is guilty of killing the northern abolitionists, the Burdens, in order to ensure that Cash Benbow, the Benbow's Black coachman, was not elected U.S. Marshall. Furthermore, he humiliated his business partner, Ben Redmond, both by cheating him out of his share of the ownership of the railroad and then defeating him in the election for a State legislative seat. The evening before his death, John Sartoris admits to Bayard that "I am tired of killing men" and "Tomorrow when I go to town and meet Ben Redmond, I shall be unarmed" (Faulkner 175). He tells Bayard that it is his time now and that "you, trained in the law, can hold your own—our own" (175). The reason he gives Bayard for this suicidal mission is to do some "moral housecleaning" (175). This is a crucial scene that shows Sartoris has finally abandoned the feudal belief system of blood ties and blood vengeance as he abdicates the role of "The Sartoris" to Bayard.

This story is about the will of Bayard who chooses an entirely novel way of avenging his father's death. More significantly, however, it is a tale about the death of the privileged ideology and class. While Bayard's choice to confront his father's killer unarmed mirrors the Colonel's same choice, the fact that he walks into Ben Redmond's law office not out of guilt as we assume that his father had done, but out of a desire to break the old feudal tradition of blood revenge that had characterized the Colonel long before the Civil War and through the first few years of Reconstruction.

Colonel John Sartoris is the literary embodiment of Friedrich Nietzsche's ideology of the master and Bayard Sartoris would be what Nietzsche saw as the slave. In his commentary on Nietzsche's ideology, John F. Lavelle explains that these "two core ideologies exist, the first, his noble or master, privileged or elitist ideology contends virtue is held within the person and not within the person's actions. The other insists virtue is within actions, the altruistic, unprivileged or equalitarian ideology" (175). In this sense then, Nietzsche would support the master John Sartoris' justification that "I acted as the land and the time demanded" (Faulkner 174–75) and it also explains his bestowing of his title of "The Sartoris" on Bayard since the "land and the time" are changing (175). Therefore, Bayard sees his action of confronting Redmond unarmed as that of a man committed to the new post-war order of altruism and equality.

In Dorothy Tuck's view, Colonel John Sartoris was "a mixture of nobility and arrogance, honor and intolerance, courage and braggadocio, in short, a mixture of good and evil" (70). Bayard Sartoris, by contrast, is simply a noble, courageous, and honorable man whose will compels him to watch the two orange flashes and smoke appear from the foreshortened barrel of Redmond's pistol as the bullets deliberately miss him. Bayard's choice represents one of the few moments in Faulkner's saga where his ambivalence toward the old ideology is resolved in favor of the new order of "love and honor and pity and pride and compassion and sacrifice" (Faulkner 723).

At the age of twelve, Bayard, along with his boyhood companion, Ringo, a black slave family's son who is raised as a brother to Bayard in the Sartoris home, shoot at a Yankee soldier, and at the age of fifteen, kill Grumby, a Confederate Raider who had murdered Rosa Millard, Bayard's maternal grandmother. The irony of Ringo's character in "Odor of Verbena" is that he, like most of the other characters, expects Bayard to kill Redmond, thus fulfilling the old antebellum ideology of blood privilege through honorific acts. Despite his skin color and his position at the bottom of the class hierarchy, Faulkner portrays Ringo as a firm believer of the feudal order as he is constantly asking Bayard to remember how they had killed Grumby, nailed his carcass to the door of an old cotton compress, cut off his right hand and nailed it to the headboard of Granny's grave. Ringo's actions in this tale place him firmly with those who believed that Bayard had not only the right, but the responsibility to avenge his father's death. Ironically, Bayard's black brother, Ringo, sees Redmond as one who had offended both Bayard's and the Colonel's name and blood.

Bayard's choice is clearly delineated by the contrast of the two major women characters in the tale. Drusilla Hawk is his father's wife who in every way characterizes the vengeful feudal order of the South while Aunt Jenny, the colonel's sister, represents a new ideology of compassion and sacrifice. Natasha Klancar states that Drusilla "wants to take his [John Sartoris'] authoritative role and act according to the [old] code of honor still very much present in 1874" (54). Aunt Jenny, however, understands Bayard's dilemma as she "shows a calm poise, her composure, sincerity and obedience fit into the Southern belle description perfectly" (55).

The twenty-four-year-old Bayard feels a strong attraction toward Drusilla, the thirty-two-year-old wife of his father who rode at the Colonel's side throughout the Civil War. On the evening before Sartoris' death, Drusilla demanded that Bayard kiss her. He does kiss her and immediately confesses to his father who chooses to ignore Bayard's admission in favor of telling Bayard of his plan to meet Redmond unarmed. This attraction complicates Bayard's decision to face his father's killer unarmed because it is Drusilla's expectation that Bayard will avenge his father's death in a pistol duel with Redmond. Bayard is strongly drawn to this beautiful young woman and is torn between his desire to please her and his plan to confront Redmond.

The evening after his father's death Bayard returns home from his study of law at Ole Miss to find Drusilla waiting for him "the two hands shoulder high, the two identical dueling pistols lying upon, not clutched in, one to each: the Greek amphora priestess of a succinct and formal violence" (Faulkner 165). She is poised with a sprig of verbena behind each ear for "she said verbena was the only scent you could smell above the smell of horses and courage" (166). When Drusilla discovers that Bayard is rejecting her offer of the pistols, she breaks down in a fit of uncontrollable laughter, lamenting the fact that she had blessed Bayard's action by kissing his hand. As a loyal representative of the old feudal system, Drusilla is expecting Bayard to defend the honor of the Sartoris name with the honorific act of the pistol duel and, simultaneously, with the sprigs of verbena, she is acknowledging Bayard's coronation as the head of the family. She may even be offering herself to Bayard as long as he follows the expectations of the old order. Edmond Volpe sees Drusilla as "a personification of the forces that Bayard must defy; to retain his integrity and individuality he must uphold his belief in the sanctity of the human being" (85).

Aunt Jenny resembles her brother in many ways, but as Bayard sees, she has not the same look of intolerance that dominates the Colonel's eyes. She is Bayard's confident and after Drusilla's breakdown, she is the only character who knows what Bayard is planning. Aunt Jenny tells Bayard to ignore both the hysterical young woman and the group of old soldiers who rode with his father's cavalry. With Aunt Jenny's compassionate blessing replacing the blood vengeance of Drusilla, Bayard is at last able to meet Redmond on his own terms. We are told that Ben Redmond is no coward and by choosing to spare Bayard's life, he too rises above the feudal order of blood vengeance.

Like Redmond, Drusilla's character is elevated at the end. Before she leaves the Sartoris home, she places a sprig of verbena on Bayard's pillow, perhaps as an acknowledgment of Bayard's choice of a higher moral code. Finally, it may be that by developing the character of Bayard Sartoris, William Faulkner is offering the reader his own acknowledgment of a new way to see courage.

Like Drusilla Hawk, Emily Grierson from Faulkner's story, "A Rose for Emily" is a character who, as Ruth Sullivan notes, is an august representative of "the Old South contending with the New Order of the Post-Civil War era" (159). Emily is a woman who clings so tenaciously to the old ideology of the antebellum South that she drives herself insane. This is true especially in her pathological inability to accept death, whether it be the death of her father, the death of her lover, or the death of the Old South.

Near the conclusion of the tale, Faulkner uses five adjectives to summarize the town's eye view of Emily Grierson's seventy-four years in Jefferson, Mississippi. "Thus she passed from generation to generation—dear, inescapable, impervious, tranquil, and perverse" (Faulkner 442). It is in these adjectives that we see not only the town's eye view of their "fallen monument" (433), but Faulkner's own revulsion toward the old antebellum ideology that allows a hierarchy of people who justify the perversion of slavery. Perhaps it is this revulsion which led him to the creation of the characters of Colonel Sartoris, Drusilla Hawk, and Emily Grierson. In Emily, we see both Faulkner's love of the old southern nobility and his revulsion at the feudal ideology of owning both land and people.

The perversion, however, does not end with Emily's death and it is in her relationship with her father that we are given a suggestion that can help explain her homicidal necrophilia. Early in the tale, Emily refuses to accept the fact that her father is dead and when she finally breaks down three days later, the reader is told that "We remembered all the young men her father had driven away, and we knew that with nothing left, she would cling to that which had robbed her, as people will" (437). It is Faulkner's use of the verb "robbed" which gives us a clue that the origin of Emily's psychosis may well be the result of a type of rape and incest caused by an ideology that saw women as property too, a common occurrence both before and after the Civil War. It may be that Faulkner is using Emily and other female characters like Drusilla Hawk as metaphors for the incestual South. Thus, we have William Faulkner hinting at an explanation of just how pervasive and perverse the ideology of ownership was for the landed gentry. Seen in this light, Emily is a victim every bit as much as her lover.

Colonel John Sartoris never physically appears in Emily's tale, but we learn that as mayor in 1894, he did remit her taxes "dating from the death of her father and on into perpetuity" (433–34). Emily first uses this special edict when a young Board of Aldermen confront her ten years after the Colonel's death about her unpaid taxes since 1894. We are told that "she vanquished them, horse and foot, just as she had vanquished their fathers thirty years before about the smell" (435). Here the new ideology of the young Aldermen is powerless in the face of the old ideology of Colonel Sartoris, a feudal ideology that only a man of his generation could have used to invent such an edict.

Emily had vanquished their fathers about the smell as a young woman. As a daughter of privilege, Emily believed that her actions were justified, including her sexual relationship with the northerner, Homer Barron. With Barron's character, Faulkner introduces us to a man of no class, the northern white day laborer who arrives as the foreman of a road crew building new sidewalks in Jefferson. As a member of Nietzche's noble class, Emily believes that good comes from who she is rather than what she does. Thus, we see her defy the town's condemnation by flaunting her affair with this Northerner on Sunday afternoon buggy rides into the country. In the town's eye view, Emily was a fallen woman and the town wants to believe that Emily intends to marry Barron. Barron leaves Jefferson while Emily's cousins are visiting from Alabama, and it is during this time that Emily buys a monogrammed men's silver set, a complete outfit of men's clothing and finally, a package of arsenic labeled as rat poison by the druggist. Faulkner's use of the adjective "inescapable" is appropriate since a neighbor saw Tobe, Emily's black manservant, admit Barron to Emily's home three days after the cousins leave. Barron is never seen again as it becomes clear to the reader that by poisoning Barron and keeping his body in her bed for forty years, Emily has found a way to assert her southern aristocratic will over this day laborer from the North. Faulkner is again characterizing Emily's "impervious" nature during this period at the turn of the century when the ideology of the southern aristocracy was near death. Emily is fighting her own civil war, which can only end with her death. She vanquishes the old Alderman about the smell, she vanquishes the new Alderman about her taxes and she vanquishes all with the murder of her lover.

Faulkner's last two adjectives, "tranquil" and "perverse," dominate the final scene of the tale. The "two mute shoes" emphasize the tranquility of the bridal scene with its "pervading dust" and "thin acrid pall of the tomb" as the horror of Emily's necrophilia is revealed (443). The perversity of the scene is detailed by the indentation of Emily's head on the second pillow and the "long strand of iron-gray hair" (444). This is where the reader discovers what Faulkner has hinted at since the opening of the story. In his creation of Emily Grierson, Faulkner has given us the one character who represented all that was good and all that was bad about the ideology of her class. She is indeed dear, inescapable, impervious and tranquil, but it is her perversity which condemns the notion of the ownership of human beings. Thus, Faulkner's ambivalence toward the old order of the aristocratic South is understood. Faulkner admires Emily's will of iron as he abhors her perversion.

With the creation of Emily, Faulkner appears to be again showing us his ambivalence toward the feudal order of the antebellum South. While revolted by her perversion, Faulkner may also be asking the reader to have some compassion for this woman trapped by the expectations of both her father and the town. She is desperately trying to keep up appearances of the old order despite both her moral and actual poverty. Natasha Klancar states that it "is via Emily and other heroines that Faulkner wanted to show criticism of the antebellum Southern Society that interfered with women's lives and destinies" (56). Faulkner is highly critical of the antebellum South but, it may be possible to read "A Rose for Emily" with an odd sense of hope for the young women who, without the stereotyped constraints of the feudal order, may have found some meaning in their lives following the war.

Another possibility of hope amid the final horrific scene of the tale should also be contemplated when we consider Faulkner's enigmatic and much-interpreted title, "A Rose for Emily." It is Emily's bridal chamber after all and the fact that the faded rose color of the curtains and the rose shaded lights along with the carefully arranged placement of Barron's suit, shoes and monogrammed toilet articles suggest that Emily regarded this room as a symbol of love and the man in the bed as her ever-faithful husband. Faulkner's ambivalence toward Emily is again prevalent as he offers this story as his faded rose, a final gesture to both the dignity and the death of the old South.

"Barn Burning" is also a story wherein the character of Colonel John Sartoris plays a role in the history of the Snopes clan every bit as much as the landowning post-war patrician, Major de Spain, plays his role as the victim of Abner Snopes' rage. Lionel Trilling describes both Sartoris and de Spain as men whose "mode of life is established and affluent; their bearing is dignified and benign; their military titles suggest a heroic past …

and their sonorous and 'romantic' surnames imply their patrician connection with still further reaches of the past" (321–22). In other words, Sartoris and de Spain were men of honor, but only as they represent the aristocratic and privileged land owners of the antebellum South. Faulkner's ambivalence toward the old ideology of the South is no more clearly drawn than in his creation of Abner Snopes, a poor white sharecropper who, in the years following the Civil War, regards Sartoris as his hero and at the same time, de Spain as his enemy. The story opens with Snopes' hungry, poor and illiterate ten-year-old son Sarty (Colonel Sartoris Snopes) crouching on a nail keg in a southern Mississippi country store during the 1890s as his father is on trial for the burning of a landowner's barn. This is a tale of class consciousness as we see Sarty troubled by Snopes' maniacal need to burn the barns of all landed gentry who employ him as a sharecropper. It is also a tale of a young boy's idea of justice in conflict with the blood allegiance that he feels for his father. Because of Sarty's age, the Justice of the Peace refuses to question the boy about his father's actions as he quickly rules that they have no proof to convict Snopes and orders him to leave the town before sunset.

At the evening campfire after the trial and the Snopes moving away, we first see Snopes' ideology in his warped notion of integrity and power. Snopes makes Sarty follow him away from the campfire and then hits him across the face because he knew that Sarty would have told the truth of the barn burning at the trial had the judge questioned him. He tells Sarty that he has to "stick to his own blood" and that the men in the store "knew I had them beat" (Faulkner 312). In this sense then Snopes, while being at the bottom of the class ladder for whites, sees himself, like Ringo, as a representative of the feudal order of men like John Sartoris, especially as he honors blood ties and blood vengeance.

Snopes' nature is such that he sees fire as the only weapon that he has in which to take his share of recompense. Abner Snopes, like many of the landless white men of the post Civil War South, felt abandoned and forced to wander literally between the new class of freed slaves and the reestablished order of the old southern aristocracy. Abner Snopes sees himself cheated by both classes and he is desperate to find his place in post-war Mississippi. In his article, "Farmers Without Land: The Plight of White Tenant Farmers and Sharecroppers," Professor Charles C. Bolton offers historical evidence of Abner's plight with his observation that in postbellum Mississippi both freed African American slaves and poor white sharecroppers were trapped in "an endless cycle of landlessness, debt, and poverty" (3). To understand the pervasiveness of this hopeless situation, Bolton goes on to state that by the turn of the century in Mississippi 36 percent of all white farmers were sharecroppers like Snopes compared to 85 percent of all black farmers (3). Bolton's research elucidates the existence of an entrenched set of ideologies leading to "in-grouping" and "out-grouping" of people into social classes allowing and restricting access to life chances whether they be occupation or education. What enrages Snopes is that because of skin color alone he sees himself as in a higher social class than the freed slaves, but in all other outward manifestations of class, whether it be language, clothing, food, education, housing or transportation, he is no better off than the black farmers who are his competition for the same sharecropping contracts.

Abner Snopes is obsessed with fire. "the element of fire spoke to some deep mainspring of his father's being, as the element of steel or powder spoke to other men, as the one weapon for the preservation of integrity" (Faulkner 312). Fire is Snopes' only weapon; he defines himself by his power to inflict economic harm on men with more possessions and respect than he is ever granted. Thus, his statement to Sarty that the men in the courtroom "knew I had them beat." Snopes sees life as a social class struggle defined by the ideologies of men like Sartoris and de Spain where honor comes through violent honorific acts of revenge. His pathological need to "beat" other men comes from his misunderstanding and distrust of this same ideology that the rich landowners have established. Abner Snopes does not have the cultural, social, or symbolic capital necessary to be allowed into the landowners "in group" and therefore, his only recourse to regain his honor is destruction of their property. In fact, this hatred of the "in group" may well explain his Civil War compulsion to steal from both sides. It was a rich man's war, not his.

Again, Trilling offers an especially comprehensive look into the very essence of this patriarch of the Snopes Clan. "They [Snopes] find an especial satisfaction in succeeding at the expense of others, for they are consumed by resentment of those who are better off than they, and they cherish their malice and ruthlessness as Major de Spain and Colonel Sartoris cherish their honor" (322). It is this "malice and ruthlessness" which Abner Snopes shows in his attitude toward the de Spain home.

When Sarty first sees the house of De Spain he feels certain that the house itself was so big that these people must be safe from his father's "ravening and jealous rage" and that these folk must be *impervious to the puny flames he might contrive*" (Faulkner 313). Perhaps Faulkner is offering the reader a bit of false hope here for, as if to prove Sarty wrong, his father deliberately soils his booted foot as he drags it through a pile of fresh horse droppings on his way to the portico. Snopes then proceeds to barge inside and with the same deliberation, stands rigid on the pale rug in the vestibule and then slowly drags his stiff foot in an arc, leaving a long smear of filth as he turns to leave. In Snopes' remark to Sarty as they leave that the house "ain't white enough yet to suit him" (Major de Spain) and that "he wants to mix some white sweat with it" we see clearly that Snopes' uncontrollable rage consumes him with his jealousy of being out-grouped (314).

Of course, the rug becomes all the excuse that Snopes needs in order for him to exercise his own form of class justice. Major de Spain makes his first appearance in the story two hours after the soiling of the rug as he gallops up to the Snopes' cabin dressed in a linen suit and saddled on a beautiful sorrel mare. He has ordered the Negro youth following him on a lesser mount to drop the rolled rug on the ground with the implication that Snopes must clean the soiled area. The fact that Snopes' first encounter with Major de Spain is one in which the Major appears dressed in an expensive linen suit riding a horse that Snopes could never possess only serves to galvanize Snopes' hatred of a man who is treating him like the servant that he is.

Snopes then rejects his wife's plea to clean the rug herself as he demands that Sarty's two lazy sisters scrub the rug with harsh homemade lye. When the sisters can do no more, Snopes finishes the job by grinding a large flat field stone into the rug through the tracks that he made with his soiled boot leaving only "long water-cloudy scoriations" (315). To complete his act of defiance early the next morning, Snopes demands that Sarty go with him both riding on one mule back to de Spain's house where Snopes again mounts the stairs of the portico and with "wooden and clocklike deliberation" drops the rug against the wall with loud bang (316).

It is no wonder that the one-hundred-dollar Parisian rug then becomes the symbol of Snopes' fury as it further drives Snopes to challenge de Spain in court over the Major's demand that Snopes pay him twenty bushels of corn over his contractual amount for ruining the rug.

In this second courtroom scene of the story, the Justice of the Peace decides to find against Snopes, but lowers the payment for damage to the rug to ten bushels of corn at harvest time. By lowering the fine, the Justice unknowingly insults Snopes by telling him that "twenty bushels of corn seems a little high for a man of your circumstances to have to pay" (318). Once again, Snopes feels humiliated by this class-conscious comment of the Justice delineating him to a lesser class and this serves to cement Snopes' pyromaniacal decision to burn Major de Spain's barn.

At this point in the tale, we begin to understand the significance of Sarty's full name, Colonel Sartoris Snopes. By naming Sarty after the legendary Colonel Satoris, Snopes is subconsciously trying to achieve an aristocratic status for himself. In his "Nobel Prize Acceptance Speech," Faulkner says that the only thing worth writing about is "the human heart in conflict with itself" (723). Sarty is clearly in conflict with his Snopes blood as he feels *"pulled two ways like between two teams of horses*" (317). He feels torn between the power of the blood bond with his father and the larger truth of the new ideology of compassion and sacrifice. Sarty's dilemma is magnified as his father tries to force him to help with the preparation for the fire by topping off the kerosene can with the oil used for lubricating the wagon. In Sarty's final action of running to the de Spain home and waking the Major in order to warn him of the barn burning, he finally breaks free of the "old fierce pull of blood" that has trapped him since the opening scene in the country store.

Sarty is not only literally breaking away from his father, but he is severing his ties to the feudal ideology of Colonel John Sartoris. However, Abner Snopes equates property with the ruling class and since he is not allowed into the ruling class, he will destroy its symbols, the rug and the barn. This seems to satisfy some pathological need for Abner Snopes, but not for his ten-year-old son who chooses a new ideology where one's values of integrity and justice take precedence over the feudal values of blood and vengeance. The tale ends in ambiguity as we do not know if de Spain's shots strike Snopes, but we are told that Sarty "did not look back" (321). Sarty has made his choice and perhaps it is young men and women like him who will shape the future of this new ideology. Like the new Board of Aldermen in "A Rose for Emily," and Bayard Sartoris in "An Odor of Verbena," this boy's choice for Faulkner may well signal the beginning of a new era for the South, an era in which the value of one's character is not based on ownership of barns and people, or blood and revenge, but on a class ideology of stewardship which espouses "love and honor and pity and pride and compassion and sacrifice" (724).

Through the accident of birth Colonel John Sartoris, Emily Grierson, and Abner Snopes all came of age in a time when the ownership of land and people was considered to be a birthright and proof of certain rights and privileges. All three characters suffered through a war which left them both financially and morally bankrupt. In the development of these characters, William Faulkner has shown us how they are all so completely trapped by their individual class identity that they cannot escape the inevitability of their own actions. It seems that perversions like murder, necrophilia, and pyromania are their only choices. Finally, the fact that we do see some hope with characters like Bayard Sartoris, Aunt Jenny Sartoris, and Sarty Snopes suggest that, while Faulkner may be making his final bow to the values of the Old South, he is also welcoming a new class of men and women who will understand that the ownership of people is a perversion and that the only way to live fully is by embracing the new values of understanding and compassion.

"An Odor of Verbena," "A Rose for Emily," and "Barn Burning" all take their appropriate place in the larger Yoknapatawpha Saga and all contribute to what Malcolm Cowley spoke of as a mythical kingdom:

> There in Oxford, Faulkner performed a labor of imagination that has not been equaled in our time, and a double labor: first, to invent a Mississippi county that was like a mythical kingdom, but was complete and living in all its details; second, to make his story of Yoknapatawpha County stand as a parable or legend for all of the Deep South [viii].

It is this effort of Faulkner's to make these tales stand as parables for both the antebellum South and the post-war South that concerns this study, and it also shows us a way to understand the author's love of the old ideology and his hatred of its perversions.

NOTE

1. For a similar take on Sartoris, see Elizabeth Margaret Kerr's *William Faulkner's Gothic Domain* (1979).

WORKS CITED

Bolton, Charles. "Farmers Without Land: The Plight of the Tenant Farmers and Sharecroppers." *MSHistorynow*. Mississippi Historical Society 2004, Web. 15 Aug. 2017.
Cowley, Malcolm, ed. "Introduction." *The Portable Faulkner*. New York: Viking Penguin, 1974.
Faulkner, William. "Address Upon Receiving the Nobel Prize for Literature." *The Portable Faulkner*. New York: Viking Penguin, 1974.
_____. "Barn Burning." *The Experience of Literature*. Ed. Lionel Trilling. New York: Holt, Rinehart and Winston, 1967.
_____. "An Odor of Verbena." *The Portable Faulkner*. New York: Viking Penguin, 1974.
_____. "A Rose for Emily." *The Portable Faulkner*. New York: Viking Penguin, 1974.
Kerr, Elizabeth Margaret. *William Faulkner's Gothic Domain*. New York: Kennikat Press, 1979.
Klancar, Nastsa. "Faulkner's Southern Belle—Myth or Realty?" *Acta Neophilologica*. 44 (2011): 47–57.
Lavelle, John. *Blue Collar, Theoretically*. Jefferson, NC: McFarland, 2012.
Speiser, Matthew. *Seeking the Roots of the Lost Cause*. 2008. University of Virginia, PhD dissertation.
Sullivan, Ruth. "The Narrator in 'A Rose for Emily.'" *The Journal of Narrative Technique*. Vol, No. 3, Sep 1971: 159–78.
Trilling, Lionel. "Commentary on 'Barn Burning.'" *The Experience of Literature*, New York: Holt, Rinehart and Winston, 1967.
Tuck, Dorothy. *Appolo Handbook of Faulkner*. New York: Crowell, 1964.
Twain, Mark. *Life on the Mississippi*. New York: New American Library, 1961.
Volpe, Edmund. *A Reader's Guide to William Faulkner*. New York: Farrar, Straus and Giroux, 1964.

The Root and the Link
Talismans of Class-Consciousness in Douglass' Narrative *and Ellison's* Invisible Man[1]

MARK HENDERSON

Frederick Douglass' *Narrative of the Life of Frederick Douglass, An American Slave, Written by Himself* (1845) and Ralph Ellison's *Invisible Man* (1952) were written over a century apart, the former being the representative American slave narrative and the latter being an important work of twentieth-century American modernism. Both are indispensable not only to African American literature but to the general American literary canon. Style provides a key point of difference between the two: Douglass combines Romanticism's sentimentality with the brutally realistic depictions of the horrors of slavery experienced by both himself and his friends and family (torture, rape, murder, denial of education, denial of healthcare, and dehumanization), all to inspire sympathy and human connection on the part of the reader; Ellison's non-autobiographical, purely fictional depiction of a nameless young black man negotiating the nightmarish Jim-Crow landscape of continued oppression in the twentieth century is more surreal and darkly comical (moving roughly from a literal battle royal for a white scholarship to a southern black college and a problematic attendance of that college to being expelled, sent North, becoming employed at a painting plant that literally adds a touch of black to its most popular white paint, receiving something of an electro-lobotomy from mad white scientists, and falling into the exploitative hands of a white Communist group called the Brotherhood before escaping them).

What is most astonishing, however, is how similar the plotlines and the protagonists of these two works are despite their being historically separated by the Emancipation Proclamation and Reconstruction. Both works, however, involve protagonists who must use highly unconventional means to realize both their freedom and their individuality. Ellison's *Invisible Man*, in fact, establishes itself as something of a neo-slave narrative through linking itself to Douglass' *Narrative*. The reference is explicit and deliberate: Brother Tarp, an elder black member of the Brotherhood, a northern and white-founded Communist organization, hangs a portrait of Douglass on a wall in front of the titular "invisible" narrator, saying, "He belongs to all of us" (378). Shortly after, Tarp further reinforces the connection to Douglass' *Narrative* by giving the narrator a broken chain link as a gift—one that plays a large part in the narrator's ultimate escape to safety, calling to mind a similarly enigmatic and talismanic object: the supposedly magical root that plays a part in Douglass' successful stand against the slave-breaker Edward Covey. Tarp, then, acts as the new Sandy Jenkins, the fellow slave who tells Douglass about the root, thus establishing the continued need for Douglass-esque, pre–Emancipation tricksterism in the middle of the twentieth century.

Brother Tarp's own story attests to the Emancipation Proclamation's failure to magically and instantly repair African American grievances—how a black man from the South could be unjustly imprisoned and put on a chain gang just for saying no to a white man, losing his wife, children, and land in the process (387). After finally breaking the chain that bound him (the source of the link given as a gift) and escaping to the North, and having lived there for nineteen years, six months, and two days, Tarp tells the invisible man how he's been "looking for freedom ever since" (388). The chain link, then, is the magical root for the twentieth century's new slave narrative, as provided by Ellison through his demonstration of the African American urban migration narrative's potential to be that new narrative. What defines this potential is the return to and renewal of a *successful* strategy against the new and updated forces of white oppression, the twentieth-century version of what Douglass had achieved against Covey with the help of the root.

But the chain link given by Brother Tarp is only one of the weapons used by the invisible man to fight his way past the white police officers and the followers of the militant Ras the Exhorter (who sees the invisible man as a treacherous Uncle Tom) during the Harlem riot—the other being the briefcase given to him by white people as part of a scholarship prize for winning the battle royal at the beginning of the novel. He thus reappropriates both black *and* white gifts (with the "gift" of the briefcase perhaps more deserving of sarcastic quotation marks) to make his way toward the fortunate, accidental discovery of the underground space.

The key to each object's (the link's and the root's) influence upon the success of its possessor is a shrewd awareness of the complexities pertaining to *class*—particularly, those complexities that present themselves when class intersects with and is problematized by *race*. An understanding of the true, ironically master-slave relationship of the overseer/slave-breaker to the plantation owner proves crucial to a young Douglass' stand against Covey's violent discipline and surveillance strategies; and the young, "invisible" man's gradual realization of the power of his own black individuality results from his incremental discovery of the ultimate failure of the Brotherhood's simplistic Marxism to foster and protect that individuality. "Class" in the abstract, metaphysical, and monolithic sense of Marxism, after all, tends to conveniently ignore intra-class divisions (based on race, gender, sexuality, nationality, history, etc.) which threaten to undo Marxism's mechanistic neatness—its view of the history "of all hitherto existing society" as one purely of class struggles (*The Communist Manifesto* 219). *Invisible Man* is arguably part of a mid-twentieth-century, African American literary trinity, including (working chronologically backward) itself, Ann Petry's *The Street* (1946), and Richard Wright's *Native Son* (1940). All involve a black protagonist malevolently affected by overwhelming, white panoptic forces. However, Ellison's invisible man, like Douglass in the nineteenth century, is a *successful* example of negotiating overarching systems of *white panopticism* (a widespread and seemingly omnipresent surveillance system perpetrated by the dominant white culture upon minorities, theoretically based upon Michel Foucault's discussions of panopticism in *Discipline and Punish*) that, in large part, works upon its respective victims by disseminating an oversimplified version of class based on race prejudice and a social investment in whiteness. These successes are the result of each protagonist's gradual acquisition of a more nuanced class-consciousness that goes against the dominant white culture's indoctrination. Also, Ellison's novel has the added importance of demonstrating the continuing need for such awareness and tricksterism just over a century after Douglass demonstrates this in his *Narrative*.

The fate of Ellison's protagonist is more ironic, humorous, and ambiguously optimistic than those of Wright's Bigger Thomas (who is executed) and Petry's Lutie Johnson (who lives, but pays a heavy price for her escape by having to abandon her young son). Key to this relative hopefulness is the invisible man's growing, explicit awareness of white panopticism and its connections to pre–Emancipation slavery—the seed of this awareness planted during the aforementioned reference of Brother Tarp to Douglass. Furthermore, his realization of individuality as a strategy against white panopticism's enforced "invisibility" proves essential to the invisible man apparently succeeding where Wright's and Petry's protagonists fail. And, remarkably, this realization echoes that of Douglass, as evidenced through his *Narrative*, over a hundred years before. Also, this realization of individuality, even within one's own minority group, echoes that of Douglass as portrayed through his *Narrative*.

Class, Complicated

Key to the invisible man's and Douglass' ultimate successes is the acquisition of a class consciousnessthat goes beyond the perhaps oversimplifying scope of orthodox Marxism, and both of these acquisitions involve a more nuanced awareness of the white panoptic strategies that are working against them. The case for Douglass might seem more surprising given his earlier historical placement, but a less sophisticated form of white panopticism certainly existed within actual, pre–Emancipation slavery, as evidenced by nineteenth-century slave narratives. Consider what is perhaps Covey's most oppressive psychological strategy in Douglass' *Narrative*: Covey creates an atmosphere of paranoia and panic among the slaves through creating the illusion of constant, omnipresent surveillance by randomly sneaking up on them, even crawling on his hands and knees to avoid detection and pretending to ride away on his horse only to actually hide close by and spy. Because of this, as Douglass recounts, Covey's work continued "in his absence almost as well as in his presence" (71). Such strategies call to mind Foucault's description of the major effect of panopticism: to create in the surveilled subject a state of "conscious and permanent visibility" assuring the "automatic functioning of power" (201)—a state of constant, unrelenting, and exhausting discipline induced by the dominant power.

What Douglass comes to realize, however, as perhaps enigmatically signified by the talismanic, folk-magic root given to him by Sandy, is how Covey's strategies do not ultimately signify him as the apex of the white panoptic power within the system of slavery. Covey, hardly a god, must *answer* to someone—namely, the actual slave-owners who send their problematic slaves to Covey to be "broken." It turns out that, within this panoptic regime, whiteness is not monolithic, because race is not the only form of inequality. (Race, in fact, plays an important role in diverting attention away from tensions born of class difference.) Therein lies a loophole in the panoptic regime. In realizing Covey's true position as a peon within the larger system of slavery, Douglass discovers just how cripplingly dependent Covey is on his own *reputation* as a slave-breaker—a reputation that would be immediately and irrevocably ruined should he even call for help against or turn in the then sixteen-year-old Douglass. This epiphany leads to an unspoken understanding between the two during the remainder of Douglass' stay with Covey—during which Douglass' confidence, sense of manhood, and sense of individuality increase dramatically.

A class-blindness on the part of Covey thus works in tandem with a corresponding race-blindness; Covey's apparent denial of his true lower-class position within the dominant white culture (within which it is clear that all white people are not equally dominant, if dominant at all) leads to an underestimation of his own dependence on Douglass so severe that it arguably *reverses* the master-slave relationship! Similarly, Douglass' new awareness will go on to teach him other lessons concerning the tumultuous relationship between race and class, even in the North, when he is harassed and beaten by resentful poor whites who see his working alongside them as a ship-calking apprentice as a potential danger to their job opportunities.

Even before they are confronted with the daunting urban setting and the more sophisticated mechanisms that the modern era's technological advances would afford white panopticism, the would-be urban migrants of the nineteenth-century slave narratives thus feel the Foucauldian effects of the institution of slavery none the less. Through the less sophisticated system of night patrols and unevenly scheduled visits by the slave owner and/or his overseers, the actual slaves of pre–Emancipation America are not spared the oppressive power of white panopticism. Their experiences, in fact, foreshadow what is perhaps the further horror of the more subtle, intricate, and technologically and bureaucratically advanced systems to be confronted in the North—not only by themselves, but by their twentieth century, Great-Migration descendants as well.

The narrow views of orthodox Marxism corresponds with the literary trend of *naturalism*, still in vogue during Ellison's early career, and which Ellison viewed as far too limiting for his goals as a writer. Particularly for what he had in mind with *Invisible Man*, the free-floating and non-human nature of naturalistic forces inevitably led to a "final and unrelieved despair" and ran counter to the images of "hope, human fraternity and individual self-realization" that he saw as integral to the American identity and American ingenuity (*Shadow and Act* 105). Also, naturalism ran the risk of masking many of the true, *human* sources of the forces acting upon an African American migrant. The individual, then, is what Ellison decided to make his focus. As demonstrated through the "invisible" narrator, individualism proves to be an effective strategy against white panopticism, whose strategies of segregation and surveillance assume that all members of the black population it seeks to manipulate are the same. Such essentializing pressures also find their way, via internalization, into the black population itself, creating a form of unconscious self-policing that further adds to individual marginalization within communities and further ensures the success of the white panoptic strategy to label, isolate, and control.

Accordingly, Brother Jack and the Brotherhood's insistence upon history over the individual is not as naïve as it may seem. Their neglect and seeming ignorance of race as a real component of social inequality in the grander scheme of their Marxist worldview proves, in fact, a convenient means of perpetuating the sufferings resulting from racial inequality. The

Brotherhood is assuming a pseudo-objective pose, with their seeming embracing of the "norm of color-blindness" actually helping to achieve the "protection of the property interest in whiteness" (Harris 60). The Brotherhood's willful color-blindness, then, reflects Ellison's problems with naturalism, calling to mind Ian Haney Lopez's observations on the "perversity" of color-blindness—how racism, when left unchallenged and embedded in society, can appear "seemingly natural" rather than the product of hegemonic choices (177). Race-blindness, then, ironically does not target the harmful effects of racism, but the very efforts to do something against such harms through willful and convenient ignorance and neglect. The invisible man gets an early sense of these sinister contradictions within Brother Jack—of Jack's supposedly being an agent working *against* social oppression while also expressing a desire to control and manipulate the masses.

Brother Jack's cynical, dehumanizing, and de-individualizing use of African American recruits such as the narrator and Tod Clifton reveal him to be just another agent of white panopticism—perhaps even against his conscious knowledge, as hinted by the narrator's discovery of Jack's obviously symbolic glass eye. The very us-against-them lure of the Brotherhood's initial offer to recruits is attractive and immediately gratifying in its simplicity, and it reflects Marx's own essentializing summation of the working man's and the minority's enemy as the "individual bourgeois manufacturer" (227). Also, Marx saw the ultimate fall of such bourgeois individuals as inevitable by design (233). However, Brother Jack's inclusion in the very regime that he claims to be working against undermines Marx's simplicity; the panoptic mechanism that is the regime's *modus operandi* requires a network of *myriad* individuals, not all of whom are even consciously recruited, rendering the notion of a dominant white individual inapplicable.

For Ellison's narrator, a further complication concerning race presents itself with, obviously, Dr. Bledsoe, thus demonstrating how the white panoptic pressures acting upon the narrator are not always so obviously, well, *white*. However, even the case of Dr. Bledsoe shows how even the most supposedly covert act of only showing and telling white people like the rich patrons from the North what they want to see and hear nonetheless internalizes play-acting African Americans within the system of white panopticism through indoctrination and recruitment. Even the narrator himself realizes how, upon seeing the Harlem riot, even in his dishonesty toward the Brotherhood, he was nonetheless working for the interests of the organization. This trap, which consumes Bledsoe and which the invisible man barely avoids, follows Foucault's description of panopticism's internalizing mechanism—of those who are subjected to a field of visibility's becoming the "principle of [their] own subjection" through their complicit knowledge of that very subjection (203).

Ellison also understood the sinister willingness of the white panoptic regime to exploit self-defensive and communal anti-individualism and how *collective* rebellion has often played right into the hands of white panopticism. The Harlem riot near the conclusion of *Invisible Man* provides the ultimate diversion strategy of white panopticism in the text, making clear to the narrator the Brotherhood's intentional absence in Harlem and its cold-blooded willingness to sacrifice individuals for what it sees as the greater good of its political aims. The riot thus confirms for the invisible man how collective action can be a trap. Ellison stresses the importance of individuality by focusing on the Brotherhood's specific use of *mob* violence as a hegemonic strategy of fulfillment of stereotypical black criminality through anger-baiting. In surveying the nightmarish chaos of the riot, the invisible man understands how Brother Jack had stumbled upon a collectively angry black population and used them "to prepare a sacrifice" (564).

Outright deception, then, is not the answer (even the invisible man's initial attempt to assume the identity of the enigmatic Rinehart, with whom he is confused, in order to evade both the Brotherhood and the followers of Ras); it is not a matter of picking a side, but negotiating the very boundaries that define the separation between black and white, good and bad. Such ambiguous measures—the aim of which is to baffle both the direct forces of white panoptic power and fellow members of the black community who have been unwittingly recruited by it—call for the subtlety of archetypal tricksterism, the "masking," discussed by Ellison in "An Extravagance of Laughter," through which the individual makes himself a "work of art" through projecting his self-elected identity (629). Similar to how Douglass had used both the folk traditions of his fellow black slaves (the root given by Sandy) *and* the tools acquired from white people (reading and writing), Ellison's narrator must discover and realize his true, hybrid, individual American identity in ways that break with the status quo—that is, in true trickster fashion.

Invisible, Individual

Douglass and the invisible man both make their way through a period of ostensible insanity—or, rather, a period of mental collapse in which the status quo has apparently broken them as individuals. Douglass' victory over Covey takes him to being a "man" (75) from the insensible "brute" (73) to which he was reduced under Covey's previous treatment and all of the other mistreatments he had experienced leading up to this point. Similarly, the invisible man must gradually recover himself after a surreal, personality-numbing electro-shock therapy performed on him by a group of white doctors after the explosion at the Liberty Paints factory where he had been working. Each protagonist's breakdown is a result of the abject incompatibility between their individuality and the systems that are working against them. They are "schizophrenic," according to how Gilles Deleuze and Felix Guattari describe the individual trapped within capitalism, in how producer and product become fused (7); the producer becomes his own product through his very perpetuating involvement within the system that has recruited and entrapped him. The agony and numbness of each protagonist's "insanity" is, in fact, the *sane* reaction to an insane system—when every sound and movement of the "machine" becomes unbearable to what Gilles and Guattari call the "body without organs" (9), the self-discovering, nonproductive individual. Just as the invisible man was, at Liberty Paints, a black man symbolically in charge of adding just the right amount of blackness to the whiteness of the company's Optic White paint, Douglass' involvement within the system of chattel slavery is that of both victim and perpetuator through his own labor, his part in the great economic machine of the dominant white culture.

By definition, Gilles and Guattari's "body without organs" is invisibility—the body that, having escaped and forsaken production, is image-less, having no product-image to any longer reflect. And such a lack can be advantageous. As opposed to how Richard Wright renders the underground space in "The Man Who Lived Underground"—as a hell, in which the sense of squalor and inferiority instilled upon protagonist Fred Daniels by the white world prove to be so internalized that he finally, and lethally, resurfaces—the underground space for Ellison represents a means of *evading* the white panoptic gaze. The uncovered manhole into which the invisible man serendipitously falls acts as a kind of wormhole to a space lying off the white panoptic map. Given that Brother Tarp's chain link is one of the defensive weapons used by the invisible man to make his way through the perilous and apocalyptic landscape of the Harlem riot—and how, as previously mentioned, this chain link is the new magic root given to Douglass by Sandy—one is reminded of Paul Gilroy's punning of "rooted" and "routed" in *The Black Atlantic* (3); Ellison's narrator finds the individualistic self-realization gained by Douglass via Sandy's *root* through the alternative *route* of the underground space.

In "Change the Joke and Slip the Yoke," Ellison reveals how, early on, he became just as familiar with "Ulysses" (the ancient Roman name for Homer's Odysseus) as with the "wily rabbit of Negro American lore" as archetypal tricksters (112), thus pointing out his equal knowledge of such figures from both canonical western literature *and* African American folklore—the point being the actual cultural plurality of the *American* identity. Such a deliberate and unashamed owning of every facet of one's individuality and Americanness provides the means for the narrator to, as Franz Fanon would say, to liberate the black subject from himself by escaping the "zone of nonbeing" (xii) and the "double narcissism" of white people's feeling of superiority and black people's need to prove themselves (xiv). Rather than lament his sense of dislocation for having to negotiate the margins of the absurd American landscape, the invisible man learns to embrace it, to slip the rigid prescriptions of both the dominant culture and his own minority community through accepting contradiction and complexity.

White panopticism, after all, stifles the subject's true, American multiplicity, something that Marx appears to historically disregard, writing of America's discovery as merely an opening up of "fresh ground for the rising bourgeoisie" (219). The invisible man ultimately decides to remain underground because "only in division is there true health" (576), and the aboveground norms of the dominant white culture make such division maddeningly impossible. The trick is to side-step white panopticism's indoctrinating notions of cultural exclusivity by freely borrowing and reappropriating the past which is every individual's common inheritance. To do so is the only means of escaping detection by white panopticism as well as avoiding white panopticism's psychological consequences. Like Douglass, the invisible man recognizes how he has no conceivable stake in obeying the rules and norms set by the dominant white culture whose interests are against his very existence. As a black migrant from the South confronting this uncanny new slavery in the North, the invisible man too is a paradoxical "free slave" (Hyde 227), left with the marginal pits and crevices within and outside of white panopticism's rigid definitions as his only resort.

Ellison's protagonist therefore comes to, as an advantage, the "invisibility" which he had at first lamented; he has transformed it, underground, according to Marjorie Pryse, from a "symptom of personal disorder" to a "symbol of social rebellion" (12). "Invisibility" as defined by white panoptic power involves a denial of humanity and individuality through an essentializing and opportunistic exploitation based on race; it means an erasure of personhood and being seen as a mere means or a tool rather than a human being. The invisible man's strategic reappropriation of invisibility comes closer to the word's literal meaning, for it allows him to actually *hide*, to drop off the white panoptic grid. Invisibility, for the narrator, is thus a strategy against the enforced visibility of white panopticism.

Invisibility goes hand in hand with Ellison's definition of "nowhere"-ness as the black subject's being left wandering in a "ghetto maze" as a "displaced person" of American society ("Harlem Is Nowhere" 325). This is consistent with Guy Debord's notion of the *spectacle* and how its seeming omnipresence leaves both subject and spectator feeling "at home nowhere" (30); within the spectacular regime of white panopticism, the black subject, whose individual existence is both denied and exploited to perpetuate the status quo, experiences a self-detachment and a feeling that his actions and perhaps even thoughts are not his own. And yet his further description of invisibility as reflecting the "great formlessness" of African American life "wherein all values are in flux" lends a more positive note ("Working Notes" 343). Therein lies the contradiction that is central to the invisible man's trickster strategy.

As Ellison's invisible man ultimately used both his black-given (the talismanic chain link) and white-given (the briefcase) gifts to find his way to the fortunate sanctuary of the underground space, Douglass too negotiated the fraught boundary between black subjection and white subjugation by taking advantage of white prejudice and turning it against itself. Even before his life-defining encounter with Covey, an even younger Douglass demonstrates (though perhaps less consciously) an understanding of how to artfully manipulate notions of white supremacy; he supplements his secret, piecemeal learning of how to read and write by playing upon young white kids' condescending racism to correct his mistakes and misunderstandings. He uses one education—a lifelong examination of the nuances of the dominant white psyche—to gain another, literacy, which becomes his prime mover not only to freedom but to self-realization. Such a realization, of course, evades both the notions of supremacy left by his white oppressors *and* the notions of inferiority and self-loathing experienced by black subjects oppressed by and recruited into the white panoptic regime.

Another, earlier underground space in *Invisible Man*, the subway, provides an epiphany running counter to the narrator's attempts at survival through conformity to the norms of both the dominant white culture and his own self-preserving community. While in the subway, he spots three boys in zoot suits whose stark individuality both impresses and inspires him. They do not appear concerned with belonging altogether to one or the other world (black/white, North/South, urban/rural) but rather celebrate their "transitional" cultural status (441). Pondering these boys' potential toward future generations, the invisible man entertains a trickster version of history, one counter to the more rigid and scientific version central to the Brotherhood's ideology—and, by extension, counter to Marx's pessimistic (and, in this case, rather gothic) view of social existence as a "world-historical necromancy" in which the living, individual subject is hopelessly tormented by the "incubus" of "dead generations" (*The Eighteenth* 287–288). Such a gloomily one-dimensional attitude towards history and one's past threatens both the present and the future with a vicious, unbreakable cycle—one against which the usual, traditional strategies are inevitably powerless.

There is something, however, to Marx's equally problematic view of proletarian revolutions (vs. bourgeois revolutions) as somewhat doomed given their propensity to "constantly criticize themselves" and "continually interrupt their own progress" (291); and central to the problem is a blindness toward individual humanity, diversity, and fluidity. If the frozen state in which Marx's proletarian subjects finds themselves is because of the false self-conceptions—the "phantoms of their brains" (*The German Ideology* 162)—born of the discrepancy between individual and system, then the homogenizing mob mentality that induces this state begs for an alternative. For the invisible man, the most tangible and potentially prophetic casualty of the *lack* of such an alternative is the Brotherhood's previous, exploited black star, Tod Clifton—who, out of his ultimate disillusionment with the Brotherhood, disappears, only to resurface on the streets selling grotesquely stereotyped Sambo dolls, a tragic testament to his own baffled surrender to the dominant white culture and white panopticism. Just as Douglass was confronted with his "brute," broken self during the first half of his stay with Covey, Clifton's presence on the street interrogates the invisible man like an uncanny mirror, shocking him toward the beginnings of fleeing a similar living death.

Ellison's narrator concludes *Invisible Man* in the epilogue with: "Who knows but that, on the lower frequencies, I speak for you?" (581) His realized individuality, then, is not as selfish as it might seem initially. At the heart of his success is a redeeming paradox: an individual, through his example, hoping to both represent and encourage other individuals toward a *collective*. But this collective is no mob or monolith; it celebrates difference through its stark demonstration of difference, its dark warning against the suppression of difference. Also, the invisible man's ultimate plan is for *action*; he strongly hints that his stay underground is merely a hibernation—a period to decompress and to further self-discover and self-refine, away from white panoptic pressures—and that resurfacing is imminent. The lack of plot beyond this point ends the novel on an ambiguously hopeful note.

Similarly, Douglass concludes his *Narrative* optimistic toward the future, having left it off only shortly after the moment of his escape. And his deliberate vagueness concerning the details of his escape also reflect the same paradoxical collective solidarity expressed by the invisible man. For though the *Narrative* is a celebration of individual ingenuity and triumph, Douglass hopes to, through his omission of details such as crucial people's names and the means and routes of his escape, help others—a greater collective—to achieve their freedom (and thus realize their individuality) in similar fashion. More is certainly known, after all, about the nonfictional Douglass than the fictional invisible man after their narratives conclude—particularly through his expansion on the *Narrative*, *My Bondage and My Freedom* (1855), in which he documents the continuing perils of the northern cities, his abolitionist work, his further acquisition of illuminating worldly knowledge through trips to such places as England,

and his tumultuous relationship with abolitionist William Lloyd Garrison. Through its ups, downs, and ultimate success and legacy, Douglass' story certainly reflects optimistically, if by nonfictional example, upon the potential of Ellison's protagonist.

Through their tricksterisms—their slipping of the darkly ingenious intricacies of white panopticism through realizing their individualities, neither Douglass nor the invisible man are thus forsaking their communities, their cultures, or their countries; they are, in fact, *reclaiming* them. For what was being taken for granted as the social reality was a dishonest and perverse system of rigged inequality. And at the heart of that system's dishonesty and perversity is an advantageous oversimplifying and homogenizing of identity based on *either* race *or* class (not to mention the many other points of inequality outside the scope of this essay), with a willful ignorance and/or neglect of the real complications arising from their inevitable intersections. For in such complications lies the fact of *humanity*, which is chiefly seen and acknowledged only on the individual level. And the ultimate celebration of collective individuality put forth by both Douglass and Ellison is undeniably paradoxical, but it is also undeniably American. And undeniably human.

NOTE

1. This essay is adapted from work done on Mark Henderson's dissertation. See Works Cited for full citation.

WORKS CITED

Debord, Guy. *Society of the Spectacle*. Trans. Donald Nicholson-Smith. Detroit: Black & Red, 1983.
Deleuze, Gilles, and Felix Guattari. *Anti-Oedipus: Capitalism and Schizophrenia*. Trans. Robert Hurley, Helen R. Lane, and Mark Seem. Minneapolis: University of Minnesota Press, 1983.
Douglass, Frederick. *My Bondage and My Freedom*. New York: Penguin, 2003.
_____. *Narrative of the Life of Frederick Douglass, An American Slave, Written by Himself*. New York: Signet Classic, 1997.
Ellison, Ralph. "Change the Joke and Slip the Yoke." *The Collected Essays of Ralph Ellison*. New York: The Modern Library, 1994. 100–112.
_____. "An Extravagance of Laughter." *The Collected Essays of Ralph Ellison*. New York: The Modern Library, 1994. 613–658.
_____. "Harlem is Nowhere." *The Collected Essays of Ralph Ellison*. New York: The Modern Library, 1994. 320–327.
_____. *Invisible Man*. New York: Vintage, 1980.
_____. *Shadow and Act*. New York: Random House, 1964.
_____. "Working Notes for *Invisible Man*." *The Collected Essays of Ralph Ellison*. New York: The Modern Library, 1994. 341–346.
Engels, Friedrich, and Karl Marx. *The Communist Manifesto*. Trans. Samuel Moore. New York: Penguin, 2002.
Fanon, Franz. *Black Skin, White Masks*. New York: Grove Press, 2008.

Foucault, Michel. *Discipline and Punish: The Birth of the Prison.* Trans. Alan Sheridan. New York, Vintage: 1995.
Gilroy, Paul. *The Black Atlantic: Modernity and Double Consciousness.* Cambridge, MA: Harvard University Press, 1993.
Harris, Cheryl. "Whiteness as Property." *Critical Race Theory: The Key Writings That Formed the Movement.* Ed. Kimberle Crenshaw, Neil Gotanda, Gary Peller, and Kendall Thomas. New York: New Press, 1995.
Henderson, Mark. *Striking Back at the New Overseer: Response to White Panopticism in the Works of Richard Wright, Ann Petry, and Ralph Ellison.* 2013. Auburn University, PhD dissertation.
Hyde, Lewis. *Trickster Makes This World: Mischief, Myth, and Art.* New York: Farrar, Strauss and Giroux, 1998.
Lopez, Ian Haney. *White by Law: The Legal Construction of Race.* New York: New York University Press, 1996.
Marx, Karl. From "The Eighteenth Brumaire of Louis Bonaparte." *The Portable Karl Marx.* Trans. Eugene Kamenka. New York: Penguin, 1983. 287–323.
_____. From *The German Ideology* Vol. 1 [excerpt]. *The Portable Karl Marx.* Trans. Eugene Kamenka. New York: Penguin, 1983. 162-195.
Petry, Ann. *The Street.* Boston: Mariner, 1974.
Pryse, Marjorie. "Ralph Ellison's Heroic Fugitive." *American Literature* 46:1 (March 1974): 1- 15.
Wright, Richard. "The Man Who Lived Underground." *The Norton Anthology of African American Literature.* Ed. Henry Louis Gates, Jr., and Nellie Y. McKay. New York: W.W. Norton, 1997. 1414–1450.
_____. *Native Son.* New York: Harper Perennial, 1993.

Haunted Privilege
Uncanny Estates in Flannery O'Connor and Shirley Jackson

Jason Marc Harris

Although readers of American Gothic may be most familiar with the haunting presence of the degraded aristocracy in the form of the progressively fouler looking and smelling house in Faulkner's "A Rose for Emily" or the gloomy mansion with its "decayed trees" and "bleak walls" in Poe's "The Fall of the House of Usher," the uncanny estate also figures prominently in Flannery O'Connor's short story, "Everything That Rises Must Converge" and Shirley Jackson's novel, *We Have Always Lived in the Castle*. Despite the lack of apparitions and clanking chains, there are doppelgangers, deaths, a black cat, and catastrophes that intensify the gothic nature of aristocratic privilege. The uncanny and ambivalent burden of the past—and the privileges that their inherited elite ideologies confer—psychologically dominate the actions and beliefs of the protagonists of each narrative: Julian Chestny and Mary Katherine Blackwood.

Aristocratic identity in these texts is "ghostly" because there is no overt feudal structure or other social institution to prop up the class hierarchy and give a consistent rationale for the actions and ideologies of the protagonists. Nevertheless, the "longing" that Julian has for "that decayed mansion" shapes his sense of class identity and privilege despite his current socio-economic impotence (485). The "decayed mansion" ties Julian to a golden age of propertied entitlement much like the Blackwood legacy of Mary Katherine defines her, though she is even more isolated and misanthropic than Julian: "our house was built up with layers of Blackwood property weighting it, and keeping it steady against the world" (1). Yet, the world both within and without "Blackwood property" violates Mary Katherine's fabled stability. The narratives' radical reversals resemble the emotive dynamics of the literary fantastic because of the hesitation and shock they arouse.[1] Because they lack the supernatural, both texts do not strictly qualify as examples of the literary fantastic, but they conduct the charge of supernatural disconcertion and disrupt socio-economic complacency through gothic motifs, including uncanny eruptions of violence by the less privileged—burdened by labor and antagonized by those who dwell in mansions. These disruptive acts challenge the gap between ghostly aristocratic identity and a new world that resents pretensions to privilege.

These decaying mansions are familiar motifs of American Gothic, which often features an isolated, obsessive, and narcissistic character in settings of faded grandeur representing past traditions, deviant morals, and asymmetrical class relations.[2] These mansions in Jackson and O'Connor are fading on the horizon of history yet cast long shadows of discontent. Attempts in both narratives to chronicle the aristocratic past compete with the volatility and urgency of present survival in a world that depends upon labor. The identities of these protagonists defy Marxist assumptions about class, where aristocratic identity relies upon feudalism. Rather than demanding services from serfs or exacting transactional labor from the proletariat, these protagonists manifest multiple layers of class identity—while their deteriorating domiciles collapse around them—partly participate in, identify with, and perform the rage of the oppressed.

Julian is aware of his diminished status, but he inwardly maintains a tie to the ghostly aristocratic fabric while outwardly he celebrates the awakening egalitarian class and racial consciousness against his bigoted mother. As for Mary Katherine, her hostility against her Blackwood family exceeds that of the townspeople, who yet manifest vestiges of feudal allegiance after many of them have participated in a mob attack on the mansion. Rather than only reassert aristocratic privilege, Mary Katherine seeks an alternative solution. Her desire to live "on the moon" with her sister is a utopian and misanthropic retreat—defined by the absence of other people, as well as their commerce, except for her sister. Their retreat sterilizes and renders obsolescent the Blackwood legacy. While "Everything That Rises Must Converge" explores the torment and cruelty of hypocritical pretensions towards socio-economic equality, *We Have Always Lived on the Castle* evades contemporary social institutions: rejecting a generational legacy, civil community, and legal authority by ultimately choosing secluded self-determination.

In "Everything That Rises Must Converge" readers only engage the hereditary estate as an idea; the main point-of-view character, Julian Chestny, has never been to the family estate when it was intact, for it is before his time. Thus, he is haunted by its removal from his grasp:

> He never spoke of it without contempt or thought of it without longing.
> He had seen it once when he was a child before it had been sold. The double stairways had rotted and been torn down. Negroes were living in it. But it

> remained in his mind as his mother had known it. It appeared in his dreams regularly. He would stand on the wide porch, listening to the rustle of oak leaves, then wander through the high-ceilinged hall into the parlor that opened onto it and gaze at the worn rugs and faded draperies. It occurred to him that it was he, not she, who could have appreciated it [488].

The contrast between Julian's pretense of "contempt" for the "decayed mansion" and his reoccurring dreams where he enjoys both the porch and parlor demonstrate the deep-seated bitterness and identification with the vanished estate. The assumption of Julian that he is the true arbiter of taste for the family estate, although his mother had visited it several times as a little girl, further emphasizes his arrogance and appetite for the absent mansion, which is a ghost of a receding golden age whose glamour was brutally built upon slavery. As Peter A. Smith argues in "The Domestic Dynamics of O'Connor," Julian himself is partly to blame for the loss of the house, which likely financed his education while his mother's teeth never got fixed: "whatever legacy there was to his mother from its sale went to augment the funds scraped together by her in the struggle to better her son's welfare, as her own was largely neglected" (231). It is an added irony that the estate never qualified strictly as patrimony for the Chestnys: "the place belonged to the Godhighs but your grandfather Chestny paid the mortgage and saved it for them" (488). Even the possession of the estate then was a slippery phantom since the Godhighs were the maternal grandmother's family. A matter of matrilineal pride while masculine bankers and mortgages patronized the pompously named "Godhigh" family. The ostentatious religious name marks the Chestnys by association for a further fall.

Unlike the Blackwood sisters in Jackson's novel, Julian and his mother only carry with them this internal phantom estate rather than any material property of significance. Julian and his mother have no wealth. Their pretensions rely on past socio-economic conditions. The sun has set on the world that once enabled their privilege: "The sky was a dying violet and the houses stood out darkly against it, bulbous liver-colored monstrosities of a uniform ugliness though no two were alike. Since this had been a fashionable neighborhood forty years ago, his mother persisted in thinking they did well to have an apartment in it" (486). They have no house but an apartment in a neighborhood whose aesthetics Julian despises more than he appreciates how Mrs. Chestny works hard as "a widow who had struggled fiercely to feed and clothe and put him through school and who was supporting him still" (485). Julian has no faith in his ability to earn money, so there will be no recovery for the Chestnys.

Despite their diminished status, Mrs. Chestny continues to view herself as a lady of distinction and urges Julian to recall that his "great-grandfather was a former governor of this state [...]. Your grandfather was a prosperous landowner. Your grandmother was a Godhigh" (487). Since they were also slave owners, it is a karmic socio-reversal of space and status that "Negroes were living" in the estate they once occupied. Mrs. Chestny's assertion of maintaining the same status despite "reduced circumstances" (488) is typical of class identity, as John Lavelle describes in *Blue Collar, Theoretically*: "As Dickens and Austin have recounted, people from differing classes, when a turn of events casts them into poverty, still retain their class ideologies and do not suddenly switch to a working-class ideology" (131). Thus, instead of emphasizing to Julian the need for him to work, and her own monetary sacrifices and labor, she encourages him to be inspired by hereditary and the haunting privilege of phantoms that evoke vanished elite familial status.

Unlike his mother, Julian feels the absence of the estate so bitterly that it haunts his dreams and leads him to mock and rebuke his mother for her memories and gestures of gentility. He makes fun of the "decayed mansion" (488) and despises the hat she has purchased as "jaunty and pathetic" (485). Widely analyzed by critics, the fact that Mrs. Chestny and the black woman on the bus have the same hat is often identified as "convergence of the rising classes" (Rubin 214). The hat's social value is more complicated than symmetrical convergence since race and class both shape the hat's perceived value. As Lavelle explains, outwards signs of class membership depend upon interpretative acts: "if the person is able to produce signs consistent with what, for the group, are middle-class signs, that person will take on the identity of a middle-class person, whether positive (the group is middle class) or negative (the group is working class)" (192). The hat while marking the ascension of the black woman indicates the diminishment of Mrs. Chestny's status, who attends the "reducing class at the Y" partly because it is *"free,"* had hesitated to buy the hat due to its price, and also "the illusion of Julian's mother that she belongs in a separate class is subtly destroyed and publicly exposed" (70). Such a judgment also relies upon the bigotry that contributes to the low social status African Americans held in the South during the 1960s when O'Connor wrote the story. Stephen R. Watkins observes that both the African American mother and Mrs. Chestny both "share their common affliction, obesity" (71) and is part of the "diminishment" that allows for "the opportunity to find God hidden in the inside and outside forces of life" according to the precepts of the Catholic thinker, Teilhard de Chardin, who influenced Flannery O'Connor's thinking regarding grace and social communities (72). The proverbial roof is gone from Mrs. Chestny's and Julian's legacy, and it is up to God to sort out the merits and justice of their eternal reward, but that does little for helping to address how they proceed in terms of their class identity in the material world.

Besides the infamous penny that Julian's mother attempts to thrill the black child with, the house and hat together are the most consequential objects in the story related to their class identity, and in both cases, Black Americans have gained the objects that the Chestny family had prized for their markers of class identity. With regard to the hat, the marker is not an agreed upon sign of status, since Julian despises the hat based on his sense of taste—a luxury of his acculturation. "Taste finds its social expression hierarchically," as Jon Cooke observes in "Culture, Class and Taste"; however, as is the case with this family, taste is also often a source of contention within a familial community. With his higher education, which contributed to his mother's reduced circumstances, Julian's mother has in effect literally paid for her son's contempt enabled by what Bourdieu terms "'educational capital'" (106).

Mrs. Chestny's lack of knowledge about the social capital of the taste she might aspire to partly condemns her to mere materialism. Ignorant of her son's disdain about her hat, Julian's mother worries over the price of the hat she bought. Shortly thereafter she encounters a woman on the bus, who is her "black double," as Julian puts it. Not only is her "black double" wearing the same costly hat but she also hits Julian's mother with her purse when she offers that penny to the black woman's young boy (499). As Julian lambasts his mother with what he considers insightful and even "funny" explication, he thinks again of the family estate and projects onto his mother his own crisis of identity: "'What all this means,' he said, 'is that the old world is gone. The old manners are obsolete and your graciousness is not worth a damn.' He thought bitterly of the house that had been lost for him. 'You aren't who you think you are,' he said" (499). Julian also is not what he thinks he is. Julian relishes his mother's comeuppance, but the result is that she dies of heart trouble or a stroke, and he is left to a vision of indefinite bleakness without the shelter of his mother's stories of their erstwhile estate or any companionship with the past.

Unlike the Blackwood sisters, Julian now has no meaningful home in which to return. Although the black woman's family may be rising—given the Civil Rights era and the marker of the purple hat as sign of growing wealth—his family is in full decline. His failure to find employment or another identity other than nostalgic bitterness defines his legacy as empty. His lack of a job is not a sign of his privilege to contemn labor. He is outcast and betwixt and between. Unlike Mary Katherine, he cannot stomach the death of his mother, nor his vanished ancestral privilege. His isolation and failure is a torment, not a retreat to a macabre utopian otherworld. He enters a gloomy absence beyond even the margins of gentile decay. Far from the phantom estate, he becomes a phantom himself. Dispossessed, Julian enters the "world of guilt and sorrow" (500).

Julian's callous and self-righteous haranguing of his bigoted mother reveals, instead of his fancied progressive and large-minded socio-political sophistication, the selfish core of his motivation. If he could still have an estate, he would not be so interested in provoking his mother by lecturing her about how the world has changed or purposely sitting next to a Black man on the bus to show off his broad-minded views of race relations and badgering him with intrusive attempts at communication. Julian's phantom house is empty, and he must speak for himself, not his mother, who from the outset of the story, is sanctified by O'Connor's narrative attention to her eyes: "sky-blue [...] innocent and untouched by experience as they must have been when she was ten" (485). Those eyes, despite looking out from a mind that has nostalgia for slavery and the leisure and wealth it brought white people, only become physically distorted when Julian's mother asks to return "home": "One eye, large and staring, moved slightly to the left as if it had become unmoored. The other remained fixed on him, raked his face again, found nothing and closed" (500). It is no coincidence that this physical distortion includes the disconcerting alteration of those beautiful eyes that we learned about in the outset of the story. Nor that she calls upon "the old darky who was my nurse, Caroline" who lived in that estate that Julian so bitterly longs for and which his mother feels was her spiritual home. Julian's mother had praised the nurse earlier when recalling the house: "There was no better person in the world. I've always had a great respect for my colored friends," she said. "I'd do anything in the world for them and they'd..." (488). Julian had interrupted this reminiscence, and it is then that he "made it a point to sit down beside a Negro, in reparation as it were for his mother's sins" (489). We transfer from the memories of the phantom estate to the public domain of the bus. Julian's actions are to punish his mother, but despite his mother's bigotry, her sentiments for Caroline come across as earnest, and her death scene validates the core of her praise for Caroline.

Julian's mother's final human attachment to Caroline, the guardian black angel of their dispossessed estate, may seem condescending or offensively sentimentalized. However, the connection of human intimacy, class identity, and hereditary domesticity is telling: "'Tell Caroline to come get me'" (500) are her last words after she first asks in vain for her grandfather. The old man would have been the proprietor—even if merely by proxy and mortgage—of that estate, which clearly haunted the dreams of Mrs. Chestny as much as Julian's own. More compelling than an expression of personal intimacy, the final words of Julian's mother mark her as one who looks out from the past with the eyes and heart of that child who lived with "double stairways" that "had rotted and been torn down" by Julian's time but preserved something like a paradise of nostalgic beatification for the dying woman and by extension the estate itself (488). She has turned inward and to the past, and she has left Julian to rush into the future darkness alone. And in that darkness when Julian realizes his mother has died is the horrific sense of his own dissolution of identity: separation from his ancestral past and any familial tie to class distinction. In the same way that the Black woman violently reminds Julian's mother that race and class are connected through condescension with currency in the form of charity (she knocks her with her purse after Mrs. Chestny brought forth one of her own pennies), Julian is reminded that he has been emptied out of any real market value or meaningful class identity: he is suspended in the void of nonbeing as he imagines those years ahead.[3]

Determining class identity is also a challenge for the characters in Shirley Jackson's *We Have Always Lived in the Castle* because like in William Faulkner's "A Rose for Emily" the Blackwood family's status has deteriorated along with its moldering mansion. The family has lost the means of increasing wealth since the youngest daughter murdered all her relatives except for her older sister Constance, her Uncle Julian (who survived the poisoning due to not taking a lot of the arsenic-laced sugar), and a disreputable cousin Charles, who arrives late in the novel and then departs before he suffers the full revenge of Mary Katherine, the eighteen-year-old psychopathic protagonist of the novel.[4] Jackson's novel speaks with Mary Katherine's voice, and readers are immersed in her superstitions, arrogance, vengeance, pique, and misanthropy.[5]

Mary Katherine's sense of class is arguably Weberian, as Lavelle explicates, "The relationship to the means of production is not a factor; rather, class is defined through difference in social fields through language games—discourses and metanarratives in relation to power networks" (231). Although Mary Katherine's isolation and obsessive nature renders her socially inept when it comes to social "power networks," she does engage in language games via not only her public threats of poisonous herbs to the villagers and her hated cousin Charles, but also via her private magical formula for protection of the estate: "I thought of using *digitalis* as my third magic word, but it was too easy for someone to say, and at last I decided on *Pegasus*" (46). Her "educational capital" gifts her a vocabulary that helps to reinforce her sense of being high class—imagining the flying horse highlights her sense of transcending the baser elements of the despised community of the villagers—while simultaneously disdaining the less fortunate (Bourdieu 106). A casual reader might think the choice of Pegasus is fanciful, but by the conclusion of the narrative, we recognize that Mary Katherine is megalomaniacal and believes in her own semi-divinity. She, as Bourdieu remarks about habitus, enjoys the "self-assurance given by the certain knowledge of one's own value" (206). Thus, a mythic steed is a fit reminder of her sense of elevation and apartness that entitles her in a mystical hierarchy to a place far above the working and middle class villagers.

In the outset of the novel, Mary Katherine (nicknamed "Merricat") detests the villagers and craves solitude in the Blackwood estate. However, to survive, she must interact with the villagers by participating in commerce, such as purchasing groceries. In addition, occasional services must be rendered, or at least requested. Thus, the exigencies of socio-economic forces keeps the Blackwood family's surviving members in contact with the outside world, although the interactions between the Blackwoods and the villagers do not often run smoothly.

The villagers do not always fulfill their obligations to socio-economic expectations of work roles, and the Blackwood estate provides the locus for these revelations of defiance. There are two notable examples in the novel of this dereliction of duty: one is the loose step and the second is the handling of the fire. The matter of the loose step reveals some of the tensions between the Blackwood family and the villagers. We learn that the wonky step is viewed differently by the villagers and the Blackwood household. When Mary Katherine does her usual bi-weekly trip to the market, she is harassed by Jim Donell (the fire chief) and Dunham, the carpenter. They insist they have heard rumors that the Blackwoods are moving away and Jim sarcastically refers to how he was "thinking the town would be losing one of its fine old families. That would be really too bad" (13). Dunham volunteers later during the harassment that "I can always tell people I fixed their broken step once and never got paid for it" (14). His grievance is undercut by the other side of the story, provided by Mary Katherine's internal narration:

> That was true. Constance had sent me out to tell him that we wouldn't pay carpenter's prices for a raw board nailed crookedly across the step when what he was supposed to do was build it trim and new. When I went out and told him we wouldn't pay he grinned at me and spat, and picked up his hammer and pried the board loose and threw it on the ground. "Do it yourself," he said to me, and got into his truck and drove away. "Never did get paid for it," he said now [14].

Here we have a mutual grievance characterized by each side as a breach of contract. The hostile reaction of Dunham and the air of a condescending critique of Constance—delivered not by the twenty-eight-year-old mistress of the house herself but her eighteen-year-old quixotic sister—exemplifies the antipathy between the Blackwood family and much of the village. Dunham's sloppy handiwork with the broken step and his petulant response to being reprimanded and denied his money by the high-and-mighty well-heeled Blackwood family not only sets the tone for the novel's community relations but serves to construct a framework of deep resentment and smoldering hostility that contributes to later conflict and violence.

However, class resentment is not the whole motivation of villager antipathy towards the Blackwoods. After all, the community's belief that Constance poisoned her family—a crime for which she was acquitted in court—earned the family such notoriety that sightseers have heckled and vandalized the property in minor ways since the court case, as Mary Katherine describes:

> the stubborn ones, the ones I wished would die and lie there dead on the driveway, went around and around the house, trying every door and tapping on the windows. "We got a *right* to see her," [...] "she killed all those people, didn't she?" [...]. Most of them locked their cars carefully, making sure all the windows were shut, before they came to pound at the house [...]. They wrote their names on the walls and on the front door [56–57].

From this clash of private and public property and private and public identity, we see the entitled access that the villagers feel they deserve: since Constance Blackwood is believed to be a murderer, she loses the right to privacy, and the Blackwood estate becomes a site for public entertainment where this notorious murderer can be mocked. The public deserves nothing less.

The way villagers respond to the fire is where their resentment and hostility against the Blackwood family explodes—a conflagration of class tensions and self-righteous rage. While the firefighters perform their duties, some villagers encourage the fire chief and his employees to "let it burn" (104). Jim Donell, the fire chief, first laughs off the exhortation, asserting his professional identity: "We're the firemen," he called back, "we *got* to put it out." However, after the fire is put out, Jim takes "off his hat saying CHIEF" and "while everyone watched, he took up a rock" (105). When Jim throws that rock, the crowd behind him—young and old—joins in a vandalistic orgy of annihilation and theft of spoiling the Blackwood estate.

This scene is the climax of the novel where the suppressed feelings erupt and the villagers regale the hidden sisters with the opening folk rhyme that memorializes the poisonings: "Then, through the laughter, someone began, 'Merricat, said Constance, would you like a cup of tea?'" (106). Merricat's response is to tell herself that she is "on the moon" even plaintively repeating inwardly "please let me be on the moon," but the vandalism continues, penetrating the house with violence and the ridicule of the popular regional chant:

> Then I heard the sound of dishes smashing [...] from just inside the dining-room window a shout went up: "Merricat, said Constance, would you like to go to sleep?" and I pulled Constance away a second before the window went; I thought a chair had been thrown through it, perhaps the dining-room chair where our father used to sit and Charles used to sit [106].

Merricat's words highlight the house's role as the embodiment of the lineage of Blackwoods. Although Merricat found something in her family to hate—motivating her to kill them except for her sister—she values the house and identifies with its components as a representation of the Blackwood legacy. Her ambivalence towards her family is a prime example of the nuanced range of identity that people have about a sense of class from the range of institutional influence—including familial—and how a writer can offer something of that complex construct of identity:

> A person has many complex identities, both personal and social, derived from both self-categorization and social categorization—in-group/out-group interpellation in a complex play of signifiers including, sometimes, forms of resistance. These signs are garnered through narratives passed down through habitus existing throughout social fields suggesting schemas and prototypes of objects, ideas, and beliefs [Lavelle 210].

With Mary Katherine, we see her "self-categorization" partly depends upon her "social categorization" as one of the Blackwoods, who are at odds with the villagers, but she also defies the authority of her family. Nevertheless, the habitus of her upbringing to identify herself as superior is powerful and lasting. Certainly her habitus produces far more confidence in her own powers of discrimination and right to act than the bitterness occasioned in Julian, whose sense of lineage alienates him and inspires his anti-maternal theatrics of racial enlightenment. Perhaps this is due to Julian's greater distance from the "material conditions" of his habitus, for he did not enjoy the daily visual reminder of the power of his family that Mary Katherine did by inhabiting the actual estate. As Omar Lizardo notes, one critique of Bourdieu's theory of habitus is that it is "'shamelessly deterministic' in the strict sense of positing a one-to-one correspondence at the point of genesis between habitual systems of dispositions, conscious preferences, the cognitive-emotive schemes constitutive of habitus, and the material conditions under which the habitus develops" (344). However, although Julian did not experience the physical environment that could reinforce the conviction of privilege, the mental environment that his mother inculcated in him, arguably serves as an ideological substitute for the "material conditions" per se. Regardless, both characters' "cognitive emotive schemes" do depend upon their familial patterns of historical privilege, and their mothers emphasizing of that privilege.

In particular, Mary Katherine's mother's attitude dominates much of Mary Katherine's classist reflections about the despicable villagers and the sanctity of private property to defend against the unruly common public: "'The highway's built for common people,' our mother said, 'and my front door is private'" (18). Mary Katherine's antipathy against the villagers also depends upon her awareness of their own hostility, which she seems to recognize partly comes from the economic privilege of the Blackwoods: "The people of the village have always hated us [...]. The people of the village disliked the fact that we have always had plenty of money to pay for whatever we wanted [...]" (7). That envy of Blackwood wealth, however, is also mixed with a relish of contempt for the land, which one of the villagers derides as undependable: "'Man could get rich, farming the Blackwood land. If he had a million years and three heads, and didn't care what grew [...]'" (10). This attention to the chaotic yield of the Blackwood land emphasizes its quality as an uncanny site and also not socio-economically fruitful. Mary Katherine's father had also realized the land was unpredictable: "The path was dark, because once our father had given up any idea of putting his land to profitable use he had let the trees and bushes and small flowers grow as they chose [...] our land was heavily wooded, and no one knew its secret ways but me" (19). Mary Katherine cherishes this wild rebuke of nature against utility, so she is not then contradicting the simultaneous esteem and disdain by the villagers for the property. This village ambivalence towards Blackwood property parallels Mary Katherine's own unacknowledged ambivalence towards her heritage. After all, why else kill the familial goose that lays the golden eggs if she cared more about being able to "pay for whatever we wanted" than keeping "secret ways"?

The riot against the house during the fire, which Mary Katherine started, only ends when representatives of the petit bourgeoisie—the doctor and Jim Clark, the husband of the gentile Helen Clark (who used to regularly visit the sisters in honor of knowing their mother)—announce the death of Uncle Julian Blackwood: an account of a heart attack likely caused by the stress of trying to recover his notes on the Blackwood poisonings during the fire. Before this intervention, calls came from the mob to "'Put them back in the house and start the fire all over again'" (108), and these words seem more than hyperbolic rhetoric, given the vandalism and explicit hostility. It is at this dispersal of the rioters—banished by the presence of death and the authority of Jim Clark—that Merricat makes a threat similar to what she did to her family:

> One of our mother's Dresden figurines is broken, I thought, and I said aloud to Constance, "I am going to put death in all their food and watch them die."
>
> Constance stirred, and the leaves rustled. "The way you did before?" she asked.
>
> It had never been spoken of between us, not once in six years.
>
> "Yes," I said after a minute, " the way I did before" [110].

It is not the death of Uncle Julian but the destruction of one of the "figurines" that arouses Merricat's most direct utterance of hate. This recalls her earlier thought when she considers her sister's preoccupation with the need for cleaning after the riot: "I was pleased that she thought of the house and forgot the people outside" (103). Merricat wants her sister to join her in amnesiac existence, a barrenness outside of the world of commerce, socialization, and community where they wander as caretakers of the ruined museum of Blackwood artifacts.

Mary Katherine's ambivalence towards her family—long before the revelation of the poisonings—is evident when she makes an implicit separation of identity from her family (except for Constance) in the first paragraph of the novel's first chapter where she boldly states her identity: "My name is Mary Katherine Blackwood. I am eighteen years old, and I live with my sister Constance. I have often thought with any luck at all I could have been born a werewolf, because the two middle fingers on both my hands are the same length, but I have had to be content with what I had. I dislike washing myself, and dogs, and noise. I like my sister Constance, and Richard Plantagenet, and *Amanita phalloides*, the death-cap mushroom. Everyone else in my family is dead." Not only do readers receive an obvious hint that Mary Katherine with her penchant for a poisonous mushroom might be responsible for her dead family but also her words broadcast a peculiar and sinister sense of lineage. Her notion that her birthright would have been improved if she'd "been born a werewolf" as her middle fingers superstitiously suggest, underscores both a sense of essential derivation—genetic identity via ancestry—but also sense of pragmatic deprivation. That she has to be "content with what I had" evokes an almost stereotypical proud working class mentality which is quite to the contrary of the inherited privilege of Mary Katherine. After all, the Blackwoods are well known in her community—the last aristocratic family in the area.

Mary Katherine's rhetoric highlights a puzzling sense of deprivation and disgruntled alienation from that family. The supernaturalism of her lycanthropic birth-wish rather than some mere child's fantasy conveys focused ferocity. She contains monstrosity and she owns it. She's a poisoner, and she's proud of that. Her poison allows her to break from the legacy of the Blackwoods and to set up her utopian community with her sister "on the moon." And the vandalism against the Blackwood estate, as well as the death of their Uncle Julian, serves Mary Katherine's goal to insulate her sister and herself in a perpetual lunar sorority. It is this younger murderous sister who comforts her elder with the example of Robinson Crusoe in their deprivation after they have to clothe themselves in tablecloths and the leftover clothes of their uncle: "Listen to me, Constance. We are going to be very happy" (136).

Mary Katherine's utopian vision of living on the moon is an intimate but far from innocent isolation where ultimately Merricat is the ruler of all and Constance—loyal and affectionate as she may be—is a subject. Mary Katherine's desire for Constance to forget the outside world is an expression of solipsism. The contracted realm of the house is Merricat's domain of ego, and she is a merciless ruler. Even though she had aimed to treat her Uncle Julian well, after his death, she reflects that he had—because of his mental difficulties—thought that she, Merricat, had died in an orphanage, and she approves what she takes as the karmic metaphysics of the world according to severe dictatorial terms that are in her favor: "I sat by the creek, wishing that I had been kinder to Uncle Julian. Uncle Julian had believed that I was dead, and now he was dead himself; bow your heads to our beloved Mary Katherine, I thought, or you will be dead" (111).

We are reminded again with Mary Katherine's morbid reflection of just desserts that she considers herself to occupy the highest seat in a great chain of being where she is elevated above mere mortals, even beyond her own very privileged family and elders. Her authoritarian megalomania—"bow your heads to our beloved Mary Katherine or you will be dead"—explicitly marks her character-based ethics as absolute and exemplifies Nietzsche's belief that "individual human beings or characters are the ultimate telos or value" as Thomas H. Brobjer articulates in "Nietzsche's Affirmative Morality: An Ethics of Virtue." Her superlative self-conception of rank also epitomizes Nietzsche's description of the self-consciousness of nobility: "'the noble soul […] *knows itself to be at a height*'" (Nietzsche qtd. in Acampora 202). Mary Katherine's narcissistic dictatorial thinking embodies the dangerous egoistic tendencies of Nietzsche's "character-oriented perspective" of ethics; Hitler is often cited as another negative exemplum.[6] Certainly, Mary Katherine's actions and consciousness underscores her conviction in her character as the cornerstone of ethics. Nietzsche claims, "'an action in itself is perfectly devoid of value: it all depends on who performs it'"—Mary Katherine murderous actions follow this dictum, and her lack of guilt over the murders reveals assurance of her rectitude (Nietzsche qtd. in Brobjer 73). Even if she takes a moment to mourn what other small acts of kindness she might have done for Uncle Julian, she does not regret poisoning him and the rest of her family, nor does she question that he deserved to die for even coming to the senile belief in her own death as a child. She believes the very cosmos expresses the essential confirmation of her impeccable rightness.

Mary Katherine's arrogant and radical elitism relies upon a combination of fairy-tale fantasizing and overall upbringing of privilege. As Lavelle explains, such privilege has been ingrained historically and philosophically—and championed by Nietzsche:

> inherited character comes down through history, as Nietzsche suggests, from those believing they were of the elite, bolstered by the major disseminator of the major metanarratives—the church through the "great chain of being," which posits, similar to Greek and Roman myth, that differing levels of humans exist, some more divine than others [200].

When the villagers rise up to vandalize the Blackwood estate, they are arguably recapitulating historical defiance of such privilege, which—in their eyes—was glaringly manifested by the fact Constance was acquitted for her alleged murder of the Blackwood family and that the privileged family had economically exploited the community for a very long time.

Although the revolt of the villagers against the privilege of the Blackwoods is arguably a righteous act of vigilantism—a violent assertion crying out against the injustice of a murder acquittal within a wealthy family—the irony of the vandalism is that the destruction helps to create the ideal sisterly utopia "on the moon" that Merricat craved. After the sisters retreat to full reclusion within the ruins of their shattered estate, several neighbors come by—hesitantly at first, but then with more frequency—and offer food and supplies at the doorstep. Notes accompany some gifts; these missives seek redemption—not only for guilty consciences but for restitution of vandalized property. It is as if having failed to conventionally uphold capitalistic standards of respect for property, some of the villagers return to a communal exchange of goods and services, but instead of providing goods in exchange for services rendered by the Blackwoods, the villagers are offering their goods to atone for the violence and dereliction of conventional duties. Like Mary Katherine, their focus is on objects—the house and its contents—rather than the individuals within it: "'This is for the dishes,' or 'We apologize about the curtains,' or 'Sorry for your harp'" (139). The vandalized objects were not goods that were acquired merely by the wealth of the Blackwoods. What the villagers destroyed was partly the labor of Blackwood women: the objects that they created or maintained:

> Drawers of silverware and cooking ware had been pulled out and broken against the table and the walls, and silverware that had been in the house for generations of Blackwood wives was lying bent and scattered on the floor. Tablecloths and napkins hemmed by Blackwood women, and washed and ironed again and again, mended and cherished, had been ripped from the dining-room sideboard and dragged across the kitchen. It seemed that all the wealth and hidden treasure of our house had been found out and torn and soiled [...] [114].

The attack on the Blackwood household is partly an attack on the matrilineal line of Blackwoods. The house's essence is—as Samuel Finegan observes in "Adolescent Occultism and the Philosophy of Things in Three Novels"—"though now reduced to only Merrikat, her older sister Constance and the disabled Uncle Julian, ... an accretion of family history" (4). And indeed it is as well as an archive of the objects acquired and modified by Blackwood women. Women who had worked in domestic roles, and whose labor had been consecrated by "generations" of stored and used place settings. When the interloper, Cousin Charles, shows up, it's revealing that Mary Katherine assumes his only mode of satisfactory work is making his bed, and she concludes a woman is responsible: "his mother must have taught him" (76)

It is important to stress that the Blackwood sisters value the labor of their relatives, which was not contemned despite Veblen's insistence in his *Theory of the Leisure Class* on the debasement of labor as a criteria for the privileged classes: "During the predatory culture labour comes to be associated in men's habits of thought with weakness and subjection to a master. It is therefore a mark of inferiority, and therefore comes to be accounted unworthy of man in his best estate. By virtue of this tradition labour is felt to be debasing, and this tradition has never died out" (27). In fact, Merricat and Constance clearly value the work their female forebearers did, and after the vandalism, while Constance busies herself with domestic duties, Merricat fortifies the remains of their estate and reveals knowledge of her own lack of skill with construction, but her very hesitation belies the importance of that craft: "I had found some boards around the tool shed, and nailed them rudely across the glass of the kitchen door, but I disliked putting them across the sides of the house as a barricade, where anyone might see them and know how clumsily I built" (133). Despite her self-consciousness about how the barricades could look unseemly, Mary Katherine is not daunted from contemplating additional labor: "I might try my hand at mending the broken step" (133). However, we do not see her pursue that infamous step, and none of her physical labor reaches the larger market of pecuniary exchange; this physical effort contributes solely to the welfare of the two Blackwood sisters. Merricat's work—if it can be called that—is intended to resecure the division between their household and the villagers. In other words, this is labor subordinated by the same elitist presumptions that fostered the tensions to begin with between the estate and the villagers. Nevertheless, something has changed. The Blackwoods have become on the one hand more self-sufficient, and need not pay anyone for anything ever again; on the other hand, their sufficiency now depends upon a kind of feudal pantomime. The villagers arrive quietly and make their offerings of food to keep these two princesses alive. The sisters live like shadows contained in their ruined mansion. But this is no diminishment, as far as Merricat and Constance are concerned. And the villagers gain the status of fostering living legends in their community. Ultimately, the villagers' offerings to the violated Blackwood household and legacy serve as votives for the sisters, validating the domineering power that Mary Katherine cherishes.

The sororal utopian community that Mary Katherine and Constance develop is both a repudiation of masculine primogeniture and an evasion of typical capitalist interactions, but Mary Katherine's identity predominantly relies upon her aristocratic advantages. She recognizes the family's "layers of Blackwood property [...] [kept] it steady against the world" (1).

Mary Katherine's desire for further stability is a continuation of the legacy of Blackwoods. Her very shoes are her mother's that she walks in (5). But even those layers of property do not keep body and soul together, so Mary Katherine earlier in the novel has to go to the grocery as well as the library. Books and food then are the necessary staples of the reduced Blackwood community. As is pride, hatred, and fear. Mary Katherine's days for village interactions are "terrible days" because she loathes the mingling with villagers (1). Mary Katherine insists on picking up coffee simply because she can't stand the idea that Stella, the shop-keeper, might think her afraid to stop in, given the antipathy of the village against the Blackwoods. Her desire for stability competes with her pronounced classist misanthropy, particularly against the harassing male villagers.

However, it is reductive to conclude that the struggle between the sisters, their Blackwood relatives, and the villagers is solely subversion of patriarchal oppression, as Lynette Carpenter concludes, when she asserts that the novel offers "a self-contained community of women, however small—one that shuts out the violence of the surrounding patriarchal society but accepts the support of its women" (Carpenter 38). Carpenter applauds Mary Katherine's "raging rebellion, culminating in her overthrow of the Blackwood patriarchy" (33). But Mary Katherine's murder of her relatives and manipulation of her sister to ensure seclusion is not based merely on a desire for liberty; she wants to freeze time and preserve what she believes it means to be a Blackwood, not simply to make the Blackwood family a commune of women.

She wants fixity and things to be kept in their places like in a museum where objects of Blackwood history are aestheticized and sterilized from interaction with living things. This emphasis on fixity and sterility achieves a formidable expression in the description of the Blackwood preserves in the cellar: "All the Blackwood women had taken the food that came from the ground and preserved it, and the deeply colored rows of jellies and pickles [...] stood side by side in our cellar and would stand there forever, a poem by the Blackwood women" (42). Thus, the female bonds between the two sisters are part of the narrative's function but to accept the novel as representing an ideal subversion of patriarchy too reductively misses the dark side of the moon and neglects the full dimensions of the "poem by the Blackwood women."

Although Carpenter convincingly tracks how female autonomy "threatens a society in which men hold primary power and leads inevitably to confrontation" the source of that confrontation also depends upon socio-economic tensions that are not accounted for by gender roles alone (36). While Carpenter argues that Mary Katherine's "rage against the villagers is justified. Within the context of feminist psychology, rage is the most appropriate response to oppression," Carpenter dismisses the rage of the villagers altogether (38). This tendency by some critics to rationalize Mary Katherine's poisonings of her family and hatred of the villagers appears to be contagious. Darryl Hattenhauer's comments about the symbolism of the destruction of the upper story of the Blackwood House are apropos: "the burning away of the storey of their house figures the loss of their rational minds; and their descent in the lower regions of the house suggest that they live only in rationalizations of base motives" (185). One can acknowledge the dynamics of subversion in the acts of Mary Katherine without insisting on exonerating her destructiveness.

But exoneration and psychological determinism has been a common approach with some critical responses to the Blackwood sisters and their sinister house. Karen Hall argues that the Blackwood family has indications of incestual abuse against the sisters and that "Merricat's and Constance's behaviors are reasonable" (116) and that the psychological dysfunction of Merricat is a "coping mechanism" (113). Hall insists that throughout the narrative the sisters' quest is for "a safe home" and that itself is "a transgression against patriarchal structures" and ultimately this subversive act is contained "in the castle" and the sisters are transformed (by local opinion) into "haunted, monstrous beings" (118). Honor Wallace also diminishes the role of Mary Katherine's agency based on an assumption of victimhood in "'The Hero Is Married and Ascends the Throne': The Economics of Narrative End in Shirley Jackson's 'We Have Always Lived in the Castle.'" Wallace argues that it is Mary Katherine's fear of her sister leaving the house with Charles that drives her to sacrifice the building: "Merricat is so terrified of the change and the disorder this would represent that she sets the house on fire" (667). It is true that Mary Katherine mentions being "chilled" at various points in the narrative when she senses the possibility that Constance might be taking an interest in the outside world, but to frame Mary Katherine's choices deterministically based on her fear is to ignore that she has seized the opportunity of both expelling Charles and shackling her sister to her perpetually. Charles is the poison that Mary Katherine uses on her sister to coerce her to renounce the world and be contained within the ruined Blackwood estate. Wallace derides the ending of the novel—where Mary Katherine acknowledges her choice of putting arsenic in her family's sugar because she knew that her sister did not take sugar—partly because Wallace misses the subtler power dynamics of the sorority: "The final revelation of the novel is maybe its weakest moment. The reader is well ahead of things by this time" (667). The exposure to the reader that Mary Katherine—not Constance—poisoned her family is not the real revelation. (After all, the first page of the novel stresses Mary Katherine's interest in poisonous mushrooms). The significant disclosure is the finality of the bond between the sisters that clarifies Constance's mental subordination to her younger sister's manipulative psychopathy. Constance may not have chosen to cleave herself to a demon lover or cousin, but she has succumbed to a narcissistic controlling sister. Like the preserves in the cellar, she's stuck in that house away from living beings, forever.

Preoccupied with the marginalized status of the sisters and the dynamics of feminist subversion against patriarchy, Wallace, Hall, and Carpenter do not address either the selfish obsessiveness and dictatorial nature of Mary Katherine or the oppression of those outside the castle. It is reductive to argue that the sisters are contained by the patriarchal structure of the town when it is Mary Katherine who has been so intent on keeping to her "castle" and convincing her sister to dwell with her forever "on the moon."

Like Mary Katherine herself, Carpenter and Hall miss the consequential sense of social injustice due to "the fact that the object of the proletarians' wrath is not the sisters but their property. The villagers do not harm the sisters; what they destroy is the sisters' store of commodities" (Hattenhauer 188). Although one might argue that the property itself embodies the living spirit of the Blackwoods, he is correct that no physical harm comes to the sisters' bodies. In fact, one might argue the sisters have exacted by their positional socio-economic exploitation a degree of bodily harm on the villagers. As Hattenhauer explains, Mary Katherine "is oblivious to the fact that she has never had to work, that she lives on wealth that her forefathers extracted from the locals" (188). The Blackwood's power of extraction is vampiric, reminiscent of Dracula or the elitist and visceral extractions of Carmilla upon the peasants in Le Fanu's "Carmilla."

The gothic motif of predation on the villagers is evoked by Mary Katherine's use of her father's accounting book of what people owed her as a magical tool of protection to keep out the unwashed. Elitist separation more than mere safety is part of her ethos. She may wish to live on the moon, but she wishes to be mistress of all she surveys of the lunar regions. Although she has an aristocratic identity, her mode of thinking is also mystical:

> On Sunday mornings I examined my safeguards, the box of silver dollars I had buried by the creek, and the doll buried in the long field, and the book nailed to the tree in the pine woods; so long as they were where I had put them nothing could get in to harm us. I had always buried things, even when I was small; I remember that once I quartered the long field and buried something in each quarter to make the grass grow higher as I grew taller [...] [41].

Readers familiar with Shirley Jackson's "The Lottery" may recognize a comparable attitude with the traditional belief uttered in that story that "Lottery in June, corn be heavy soon." Mary Katherine acts as the priestess of the Blackwood family. Although her sister Constance is far older, Mary

Katherine wields the real power in the family. And it is her vision of what the Blackwood estate is and can be that ultimately controls the course of the relationship between the sisters, and the future of the Blackwood family, which is to retreat into legendary seclusion after the fire and riot. When the sightseers come they speak of the past in terms of the house, not only the crimes: "'It used to be a lovely old house, I hear […].' […] 'No one knows for sure if there's anyone inside or not. The local people tell some tall tales'" (140–141). The two sisters become "the ladies"—and it is significant that we see a term reminding us of their elevated class status despite the decayed monument they now inhabit—who serve as local bogeymen to frighten children. By sealing herself away with Mary Katherine, Constance becomes the witch in the gingerbread house that her sister claimed she was, but she also remains coveted by her cousin for the legacy of the family. When Charles shows up one last time to appeal to them to speak with him (and of course locate some of that money in the safe), she ignores him, and together the sisters overhear how, although he's partly remorseful for his role in the destruction of the house and their greater seclusion, he's arrived with a journalist—once again angling for some compensation for his exploitation of the Blackwood sisters. There may be a touch of irony with Constance's vision of their sisterly seclusion, but she willingly participates in Mary Katherine's gothic fantasy by the end of the narrative: "'I wonder if I could eat a child if I had the chance.' 'I doubt if I could cook one,' said Constance" (146). This playful participation in their legendary status evokes not a sense of oppression but delight in their power. If they are contained, it is a containment that continues to benefit them, not unlike gated communities for which safety and seclusion the wealthy pay a pretty penny.

Reducing all the villagers into a monolith of patriarchal repression also diminishes the role of class hierarchy in the dispersal of the vandalistic riot, and the sense of responsibility that Jim Clark and Dr. Levy manifest. Carpenter insists that regarding the riot, "The crowd leaves not out of respect for the sisters but out of respect for Uncle Julian, whom they perceive to have been the sisters' last surviving victim" (36) and after the sisters have retreated to full seclusion, Hall describes a solicitous visit by Dr. Levy later at the doorstep as a mission "to threaten and coerce" them (117). Both descriptions are imprecise because it was Jim Clark's initiative and using the death of Uncle Julian as a rhetorical strategy that broke up the riot, not the mere fact of a death. First Jim tries to silence the mob by saying "'That's enough'" but he has to add the death and it is Dr. Levy who counters the question "'Did she kill him?'" (109). Far from predatory patriarchs, Jim Clarke and Dr. Levy do their best to use diplomacy and shame to defuse the crowd's fervor, and although the doctor does later grow frustrated trying to communicate with the sisters after they have secluded themselves ("one of these days you're going to *need* help. You'll be sick, or hurt. You'll *need* help. *Then* you'll be quick enough to—"), one could argue that the doctor resents what he believes is the sisters' refusal to accept him as part of their community and their likelihood to value only his utility rather than his humanity (129). He may be resentful, but he recognizes his duty to be altruistic even while reclusive privileged sisters spurn him. Jim Clarke ends the visit telling Dr. Levy to "'Leave them be [...]'" (129). In other words, the petit bourgeois attempt a rescue, but they are ultimately rejected by the Blackwood sisters, who have withdrawn permanently after witnessing the unruly uprising of the disgruntled villagers.

Mary Katherine's first-person narration features a set of contradictory sensibilities, which shape the fate of the Blackwood estate. Her identity is an intriguing example of the multiple levels of interpellation, highlighted in Lavelle's analysis of class identity—"A person has many complex identities, both personal and social, derived from both self-categorization and social categorization—in-group/out-group interpellation in a complex play of signifiers including, sometimes, forms of resistance" (210). We learn from Mary Katherine that she is apart from the villagers but also not wholly partaking of the familial ethos of the Blackwoods, although she was brought up to feel safe in the Blackwood estate and that those who entered their domicile were worthy people while those that did not—and looked dirty—were the base villagers. Darryl Hattenauer asserts that Mary Katherine's "interpellation prevents her from perceiving her class privilege" (188). Having never learned alternative perspectives to what she felt entitled to, Mary Katherine has no sense of anything other than self-righteousness. However, she is rebellious. Murderously so. She was reprimanded periodically by family members; in fact, her alibi for poisoning the family is that she'd been sent to bed without supper (34). We see from her mystical approach to family heirlooms that her identity partly relies upon her family, but that integration of personality is far from respectful for conventional socio-economic markers of status in her familial power group.

In fact, her ultimate sense of authority is mystified; although we're led to believe that perhaps her sister instructed her with certain limits after Mary Katherine poisoned her relatives, we learn near the end of the novel that only Mary Katherine intuits these rules from a source never identified beyond her own sense of prohibitions. Even when Constance tries to give her permission to break some taboos, such as to wear Uncle Julian's clothes after the fire has decimated their own belongings, Mary Katherine is adamant about her sense of limits: "'I am not allowed to touch Uncle Julian's things [...].' 'But you are allowed. I tell you that you are allowed' (135). 'No.'" (136). Constance's status as older sister constitutes no leverage against the mystical certainty of her younger sister's inscrutable and narcissistic gnosis.

As a veritable hierophant, Mary Katherine excludes her sister from access and authority to the inner sanctum of determining Blackwood knowledge of what is and what is not a taboo.

Mary Katherine's words reveal an identity that amalgamates adolescent alienation, fairy tale fantasies, atavistic paganism, hierophantic intuition, aggrieved defiance, aristocratic elitism, and economic privilege. Most strikingly, she—as Hattenhauer articulates—"sees herself as disadvantaged" (188). Despite Mary Katherine's sense of deprivation and entitlement, she is not a tenderfoot who only inhabits drawing rooms and drinks (and poisons) tea. Her personality offers an active mixture of hostility and reflection: she misanthropically despises the ugliness of the more disadvantaged villagers, eschews companionship beyond that of her sister and Uncle Julian, prizes her ancestry largely only as an abstraction (after all, she killed most of her family, and chooses to burn up much of the mansion), and rather than depending upon luxury, often dwells—even sleeping—outdoors with her black cat amid nature (53).[7] Her affinity for the natural world also highlights her aversion to conventional morality and domestic passivity, and this attraction to natural settings resonates with Nietzsche's "belief that man is part of nature, and that in the natural world there is no morality" (Brobjer 65). Mary Katherine as a figure of the woods challenges the ethics of civilization even as she upholds the order of Blackwood conventions, storing their cultural legacy in her magical caches around the premises and helping her sister to secure food and household wares in the cellar.

Beyond these evocative ties to nature and its chaotic potential, Mary Katherine's attachment to her cat is most obviously reminiscent of a witch and its familiar. Whether her belief that her cat actually speaks to her is hyperbolic imagination or schizophrenia ("All cats stories start with the statement: 'My mother, who was the first cat, told me this'" [53]), the tradition of animal companionship for a fairy tale heroine is well known. One thinks of Puss and Boots, in addition to the commonplace depictions of witches and their feline familiars. Mary Katherine's storytelling emphasis on the mother cat relates to her sense of matriarchal decorum.

Mary Katherine's conception of authority is egotistically filtered through her own vision of rightness in the world, and that vision integrates a sense of family standards, especially her mother. Mary Katherine's identification with her mother's sensibilities even connects implicitly to her choice to start the fire: "When I stood near the summerhouse and looked at it I thought it the ugliest place I had ever seen; I remembered that our mother had quite seriously asked to have it burned down" (95). There is no direct acknowledgment from Mary Katherine that her mother's words elicited her later choice to toss Charles's smoldering pipe in the waste basket in the following chapter (99), but the spatial and temporal proximity of this reflection about burning down the "summerhouse" and the subsequent act of arson combined with the repeated statements that cite her mother as an influence of taste and sensibility corroborate the notion that Mary Katherine views herself as acting in line with maternal propriety when she commits arson upon the Blackwood legacy. As the self-appointed guardian of taste in the Blackwood household, Mary Katherine condemns Charles's crass materialism, but her actions at times belie her principles, since her behavior led to the fire that destroyed much of the Blackwood legacy.

Yet, if Mary Katherine's attitude is ambivalence, it still largely relies upon her sense of familial identity; she is haunted psychologically by the mother that she poisoned. On the same page where she contemplates her mother's destructive words about the summerhouse, Mary Katherine also imagines in her secret hiding place in the abandoned summerhouse a family meeting where her relatives mutually assert that "Mary Katherine is never punished" and that punishment does not apply to her since she "will never allow herself to do anything inviting punishment" (95–96). The summerhouse is an uncanny liminal space because as a relic of the past that also attaches to Mary Katherine's memory of her mother's disapproval of the building, it is a negative excrescence of debased Blackwood property. On the other hand, in its marginal location, the summer house occupies a zone of security: no one will disturb Mary Katherine there because no one even knows about its existence, or if they do—as Constance does—they will not enter its derelict interior. She is safe then from punishment within this edifice of a rejected Blackwood past. Within its space, she can imagine an alternative world where instead of being condemned for the murders of her relatives, she is adored. This reversal of standard morality reinforces her immunity from consequences external to her psyche. We also learn thereafter that the rules that Mary Katherine asserts—such as not being allowed to "handle teacups" (112) or "touch Uncle Julian's things" are set by herself, not her older sister, who even tells her she is "allowed" (135–136). Mary Katherine is her own chaperone. The judge of her own soul. Who else would have the discernment?

Although she killed her mother with the rest of the Blackwoods she poisoned (Uncle Julian survived because he didn't like much sugar, and Mary Katherine knew Constance took no sugar at all), she remembers her mother as a paragon of good housekeeping and high standards:

> I was shocked when we came into the drawing room to see our mother's portrait looking down on us graciously while her drawing room lay destroyed around her. The white wedding cake trim was blackened with smoke and soot and would never be clean again; I disliked seeing the drawing room even more than the kitchen or the dining room, because we had always kept it so tidy, and our mother had loved this room. I wondered which of them had pushed over Constance's harp and I remembered that I had heard it cry out as it fell [119].

The final sentence in this passage mentioning the harp evokes the folk tale of "Jack and the Beanstalk" where the magical harp famously cries out for its master—the giant—when Jack runs off with it. This echo of that folk tale underscores Mary Katherine's sense of essential order in the household that has been violated by the uprising of the villagers.

Similarly Merricat calls Constance an "Old Witch" and says she has "a gingerbread house" (75). Not an insult, this is another testimony to Merricat's identification with her sister in a world of fairy tales where they are supernatural beings that stand in solidarity; their house a fortress or castle to protect them from the rude and violent intruders of the outside world. More materially, the fact that Constance has a harp at all to play upon reminds the reader of the great privilege and cultural opportunities that this family has enjoyed. In the earlier sentence concerning the "wedding cake trim" a reader might sense something of the lonely and bitter legacy of Miss Havisham from Dickens's gothic jilted manipulator in *Great Expectations*. And this passage reinforces Mary Katherine's affinity for objects, which she prizes—not for monetary value as Charles does—but for their familial associations. This may seem perverse, since she killed her family, but her vision of her home expresses her notion of Blackwood heritage. That heritage—that sense of neatness, order, and elegance—constitutes her habitus of class identity, as does the framing of her family estate in terms of supernaturalism, particularly the domains of malicious supernatural power like that of the giant or a witch. Her imagination, upbringing, and property confirm her sense of superiority.

Although Mary Katherine's imaginative engagement with superstition and fairy tales might make her appear naïve, even her ritualistic measures for protection enlist the aura of socio-economic power: "My book nailed to a tree in the pine woods had fallen down. I decided that the nail had rusted away and the book—it was a little notebook of our father's, where he used to record the names of people who owed him money, and people who ought, he thought, to do favors for him—was useless now as protection" (53). It is likely that her deceased father's notebook is one of the reasons the villagers resented the Blackwood family.

Nor is it only the villagers who threaten the Blackwood sorority. Their own cousin, Charles Blackwood, when he comes to visit after the death of his father, seeks to claim for himself the command and wealth of Constance and Mary Katherine. Beyond his patriarchal pretentions, Charles also is confused and outraged by his discovery of what he considers the lack of appreciation for wealth. While Mary Katherine and Constance treat the Blackwood possessions as though they are sacred objects (Mary Katherine even goes so far as to perform intuitive and superstitious rituals with Blackwood artifacts), Charles sees only monetary value. In this respect, he demonstrates—rather than any vestiges of aristocratic cultural taste—the "naked self interest" of the bourgeoisie, which "has resolved personal worth into exchange value," that Marx critiques in his *Communist Manifesto* (43).[8] He angrily confronts the sisters and Uncle Julian when he discovers the gold watch chain of the sisters' deceased father "nailed to a tree, for God's sake. What kind of house *is* this?" (77). He whines to Constance that the watch could have been sold and lectures her how "This is a gold watch chain, worthy possibly a good deal of money. Sensible people don't go around nailing this kind of valuable thing to trees" (77). However, as Darryl Hattenhauer points out, Mary Katherine's disregard of monetary value partly depends upon her monetary privilege: "Merricat is so rich that she can destroy wealth [...]" (187). This is a sign of her security in property rather than childish fancy. In fact, Mary Katherine is so secure in what she possesses, that Cousin Charles's almost hysterical reactions to the destruction and cavalier handling of monetary property appear to her as absurd. Their diverse reactions to markers of wealth show a surprisingly complicated view of cultural capital where more typically an object or behavior will in one context have more stability of value and become more "attractive by associating it with supposedly familial and other 'agreeable' values" (Webb et al. 22). In the case of Mary Katherine her sense of the value of the coins and watch is solely as items imbued with protective powers because of the family legacy, not their market value because of their status as currency or their social value because of their status as signs of prestige and wealth. Her disdain for Charles's obsession over monetary value and prestige relates to what Bourdieu described as the "illusio"; he alludes to the conflict over court etiquette involving bowing and hats as an example: "if the structures of the game are not also in your mind, the quarrel will seem ridiculous and futile to you" (Webb et al. 26). She comes to recognize Charles's dependence on wealth, and she despises him for it: "I would like to have seen Charles on the ground, scrabling after my silver dollars" (88). What makes Charles's fixation on silver coins and pocket watches so intense is his own state of deprivation; his father died without leaving him much—or perhaps any—inheritance. However, Mary Katherine enjoys the benefit of the entirety of her parents' estate and wealth.

Mary Katherine's elaborate rituals of protection are, of course, utterly unknown in their meaning to Charles, and his insistence on monetary value is as alien to Mary Katherine as are her methods of magical thinking for aiming to expel her chauvinistic cousin whom she considers a demon and a ghost. Although Charles is not in the least supernatural according to the metaphysical criteria for the fantastic—a challenge to consensus reality—he does produce the emotional angst of an irrational disruption in the Blackwood home which is akin to the sense of alienation and fear the fantastic may cause, as Maria Tatar explains, "The fantastic [...] shatters the stability of the world to create a condition of radical homelessness" (181). Charles is an uncanny intrusion into the stability of the Blackwood household—albeit a stability that was only achieved by Mary Katherine's purge of poison. It's a notable reversal that the intrusion of capitalist values and masculine privilege serves the function of supernatural disruption in a household where a belief in the supernatural is the underlying organizing structure of Mary Katherine's method of protecting that household. The best laid plans and belief systems go awry when covetous cousins show up, and Charles literally threatens Mary Katherine with homelessness when he taunts her with the possibility of what her fate might be if both he and Constance align against her. Having incurred the death of his father, Charles is a circling vulture hoping to get money from these two sisters, and he's there to play hardball. To expel him takes a particular sort of exorcism: fire. Before he is exorcised, his materialism clashes with Mary Katherine's mystical valuations. To some degree this emphasis on subjective rather than objective value also applies to Constance, who when interrogated by Charles about the value of one of her mother's "Dresden figurines" explains it's not of significant monetary value but her "mother liked them" (85). Mary Katherine even "hoped that the house, injured, would reject him [Charles] by itself" (78). She ascribes an agency to the house where it is more than the sum of its parts—far more than economic measure. The house shares agency with her own vigilant consciousness: "I looked at the house with all the richness of love I contained [...]" (97). Her love does not include room for Charles, and Mary Katherine and the house conspire against him.

However, the house does not expel Charles "by itself"; that is left to the machinations of Mary Katherine, who first befouls her father's room, which fails to scare Charles away (87), so she places Charles's lit pipe in a waste basket, and thereby starts the fire. Mary Katherine, although some outside authority might dismiss her as a psychotic poisoner and pyromaniac, internalizes an intriguing set of competing identities with regard to class that are not reducible to ideology alone. She views herself as marginalized yet rigidly celebrates her entitlement. After the fire that guts their house, she wonders if time might reverse, and she and Constance would stand in the presence of their family again and those relatives would be "waiting for Constance to bring them their dinner" (111). This mention of servitude might partially relate to Mary Katherine's motivation to murder her family, as well as that they had dared to send her to her room for some offense: "'sent to bed without her supper'" as her Uncle Julian reported from his account of the night of the poisonings (34). Given that she poisoned her own family rather than the villagers—though she fantasizes and threatens about that as well—her rage and resentment is not solely that of misanthropic and elitist disdain.

Her anger appears to partly stem from any disruption of her fanatical vision of her mystical role as guardian of the Blackwood legacy. She obsessively identifies with the property and projects her own feelings onto the house: "When I opened the kitchen door to go inside I could feel at once that the house still held anger, and I wondered that anyone could keep one emotion so long" (97). Even though she willingly destroys her Blackwood family and sacrifices much of the house to fire to expel her cousin, Charles, she still jealousy claims the ruined property as her domain: a secluded domain only to be ruled by herself and only in companionship with her sister and cat.

There is a sterility to Mary Katherine's insistence on seclusion and her lunar fantasy. Aside from her penchant for poisoning her family and the fact that the moon itself is lifeless, she lacks an interest in reproduction. Whether this disinclination suggests immaturity, homosexuality, or perhaps incestual fixation on her sister, her sister, Constance, notes the abnormality: "You should have boy friends" (82). However, Constance laughs at her own idea, and that line of discussion is not pursued. Mary Katherine is not wholly a misanthrope since she does value her sister, and throughout the novel her thoughts tend towards how she could be nicer to her Uncle Julian, whom she is aware will die—and he was the only surviving victim of the poisoning. Not only does Mary Katherine have room for Uncle Julian in her view of community, but she alters her sense of what constitutes "safeguards" to the Blackwood home. After the vandalism and fire, she declares, "My new magical safeguards were the lock on the front door, and the boards over the windows, and the barricades along the sides [...]" (145). Although she does not disavow the power of magical thinking, she reifies the notion, contracting the metaphysical to the material. These dynamic elements of Mary Katherine's character suggest she has had an evolution of consciousness from condemning others for collective guilt to a more individual assessment of power and judgment, but that is not to say she becomes altruistic or disavows elitism. Rather, she becomes convinced of her own rightful vision that seclusion and material protections are the best choice for continued stability in their home. She never questions her right to maintain that reign.

Both Mary Katherine and Julian Chestny wander the corridors of their obsessive minds, haunted by the privilege they are either clutching after while their ancestral mansions either crumble around them, have already vanished, or passed into other hands. Although Mary Katherine is able to largely expel the outside world from her doorstep, the price she pays is the virtual imprisonment of her sister, the ruin of much of her inheritance, and the perpetual insularity of their psyches. While Julian ventures heartbroken and displaced into the darkness of a marginal existence where he lacks the resolve to earn his own money, O'Connor's narrative suggests the possibility of a more earnest soul emerging from the layers of arrogance and bitterness.

Two classics of American Gothic, these narratives offer readers engagement with the disruptions of evolving identities and changing power dynamics in a country where race, gender, and class converge, clash, dissolve, and reform in new configurations. Both texts engage competing models of valuation of property—based on material well-being and social identification with inherited status. The role of violence in these narratives—from assault and a stroke in O'Connor to mass murder by poison, vandalism, and a fire in Jackson—helps to articulate the high stakes of class identity, where frustrations over oppression and interpellation result in outrage at institutional and individual methods of containment. Far from models of ideal conduct, these protagonists do offer authenticity in their bewilderment, obsession, and tenacity. Whether it is the nostalgic, hypocritical, and jealous despair of Julian at his diminished heritage or the hallucinatory but perspicacious vigilance of Mary Katherine against the male proletariat, petit-bourgeois, and familial incursions into her domain, these protagonists exhibit fierce psychological and social critiques in their reflections and behavior in the face of the maze of class tensions that they must navigate through to pursue a semblance of coherent identity.

Ambivalence marks the tension between these protagonists' outward behavior and inward feelings and thoughts because they are inhabiting multiple liminal worlds in their material and ideal castles of entitlement. Their vanishing and porous estates have been supplanted or vandalized, and their sense of selves lacks stability. Julian wails under a veil of darkness, where neither his assumed sympathy for the rising African American population nor his economic impotence and bitter arrogance over loss of ancestral status will afford him relief. After clashing with the proletariat, disdaining the petit bourgeoisie, and expelling (and murdering) the rest of her wealthy landowning family, Mary Katherine secludes herself and her sister in a surreal utopia of semi-feudal privilege among the shadows of their ruined estate, doomed but content to dwell only in memory and legend rather the vital moment.

Both texts cocoon their protagonists amid the cobwebs of their ghostly estates which are emptied of meaningful social authority but still haunt the minds of their tenants—past and present—with desires and terrors of an elite order which can sustain them against the rise of equality and its unaesthetic and vociferous discontents. This rise has occasioned a greater connection of public and private spaces. In this nexus we find the decayed mansion of the Chestnys has passed into the hands of African Americans, and the Chestnys themselves have entered the public space of the bus. As for the Blackwoods, the mob literally penetrates and defiles the Blackwood estate through acts of vandalism, and although the sisters withdraw into seclusion, they must then depend upon the villagers' acts of charity—receiving not a mere patronizing penny or nickel—but fresh food that the Blackwoods require for survival. These gothic mansions in Jackson and O'Connor are permeable structures that while presenting views of fading privilege also incubate new communities; they offer readers a vision of the intersections of wealth, power, flux, oppression, entitlement, and entropy that provide a matrix for multitudes sharing space with conflicting class identities in worlds still struggling to be born.

Notes

1. Tzvetan Todorov's definition emphasizes not only the importance of the supernatural but also that reaction of "hesitation": "The fantastic is that hesitation experienced by a person who knows only the laws of nature, confronting an apparently supernatural event" (25).

2. For some of the convergences and disparities between American Gothic and Southern Gothic in particular for O'Connor see Louis H. Palmer III, "Southern Gothic and Appalachian Gothic: A Comparative Look at Flannery O'Connor and Cormac McCarthy." *Journal of the Appalachian Studies Association*. vol 3, 1991, pp. 166–176. For a more contemporary analysis—the same year as publication in January 1965 of the collection, *Everything that Rises Must Converge*—see Olive Tyne Snow's "The Functional Gothic of Flannery O'Connor." *Southwest Review*. vol 50, 1965, 286–299.

3. Many critics of the works of Flannery O'Connor see in her sinister depictions of human life not only a motif of Southern Gothic but also her vision of relying upon religion for the transfiguration of human and natural darkness into redemptive spiritual light. O'Connor is thought to present a "universe whose existential emptiness offers nothing unless those who live in it accept and recognize the need for a faith, an acceptance of innocence and a coming to peace with one's self in the realization that unquestioning love is all important" (Pappril 53). Arguably, one can see in Julian's final words of affection for his dying mother the underlying value of that love.

4. Insane characters are a common feature of gothic literature, which parallels the typical atmosphere of deterioration created by decaying mansions and wild landscape: "Another key marker of Gothic literature, as proclaimed by Andrew Smith, is the theme of 'insanity' (Smith 4), the term for the absence or the deterioration of the rational mental state" (Lathom 18).

5. It is also no surprise that we find a female adolescent protagonist at the core of a gothic narrative. As Deborah Martin observes, "Young or adolescent femininity is at the heart of many gothic and horror narrative" (1).

6. See, for example, Alexander Nehamas, "Nietzsche and 'Hitler.'" *The Southern Journal of Philosophy*. March 1999 vol 37 issue S1, pp. 1–17.

7. That Mary Katherine prizes her secret spaces in the more natural micro-environments available in the larger setting of the Blackwood estate is another common feature of American Gothic where wild settings articulate mental disorder: "nature in American Gothic owes Kant's philosophy one more fundamental favour—it is the reflection of individual consciousness and an insight into the mind—a haunted one" (Sawczuk 10).

8. In his apt analysis of the novel, Hattenhauer considers both aristocratic and bourgeois features of the Blackwoods: "a case study in the neo-aristocratic haute bourgeois exploitation of the petit bourgeois and the lower class" (187).

Works Cited

Acampora, Christa Davis, and Keith Ansell Pearson. *Nietzsche's Beyond Good and Evil: A Reader's Guide*. New York: Continuum Press, 2011.

Bourdieu, Pierre. *Distinction: A Social Critique of the Judgment of Taste*. Trans. Richard Nice. New York: Routledge, 1979.
Brobjer, Thomas. "Nietzsche's Affirmative Morality: An Ethics of Virtue." *Journal of Nietzsche Studies* vol. 26, 2003. 64–78.
Carpenter, Lynette. "The Establishment and Preservation of Female Power in Shirley Jackson's *We Have Always Lived in the Castle*." *Shirley Jackson: Essays on the Literary Legacy*, Ed. Bernice M. Murphy. 199–212.
Cook, Jon. "Culture, Class and Taste." *Cultural Studies and the Working Class*. Ed. Sally Munt. Cassell, 2000. 97–112.
Finegan, Samuel. "Adolescent Occultism and the Philosophy of Things in Three Novels." *Transnational Literature*. vol 8, no. 1, 2015. 1–11.
Hall, Karen J. "Sisters in Collusion: Safety and Revolt in Shirley Jackson's *We Have Always Lived in the Castle*." *The Significance of Sibling Relationships in Literature*. Eds. JoAnna Stephens Mink and Janet Doubler Ward. Bowling Green: Bowling Green University Press, 1993. 110–119.
Hattenhauer, Darryl. *Shirley Jackson's American Gothic*. New York: State University of New York Press, 2003.
Jackson, Shirley. *We Have Always Lived in the Castle*. 1962. New York: Penguin, 2006.
Lathom, Brandon. "Cobblestones and Doppelgängers: How Gothic Literature Contributed to the Dawn of Film Noir." *Film Matters*. vol 7, issue 2, Fall 2016. 17–21.
Lavelle, John. *Blue Collar Theoretically: A Post-Marxist Approach to Working Class Literature*. Jefferson, NC: McFarland, 2011.
Lizardo, Omar. "Taste and the Logic of Practice in Distinction." *Czech Sociological Review*. vol. 50, issue 3, 2014. 335–364.
Martin, Deborah. "Feminine Adolescence as Uncanny: Masculinity, Haunting and Self-Estrangement." *Forum for Modern Language Studies*. vol 49, issue 2, 2013. 139–144.
Marx, Karl, and Frederick Engels. *The Communist Manifesto: A Roadmap to History's Most Important Document*. Chicago: Haymarket Books, 2005.
Nehamas, Alexander. "Nietzsche and 'Hitler.'" *The Southern Journal of Philosophy*. March 1999, vol. 37 issue S1, pp. 1–17.
O'Connor, Flannery. *Collected Works*. New York: The Library of America, 1988.
Pappril, Alan. "The American Gothic." *English in Aotearoa*. issue 57, Oct. 2005, pp. 48–53.
Rubin, Charles T., and Leslie G. Rubin. "Flannery O'Connor's Religious Vision of Regime Change." *Perspectives on Political Science*. vol 31, no. 4, 2002. 213–225.
Sawczuk, Tomasz. "The Use of Nature in American Gothic." *Americana: E-journal of American Studies in Hungary*. Vol. 6, issue 2, Fall 2010. 10–10.
Smith, Peter A. "The Domestic Dynamics of Flannery O'Connor: Everything that Rises Must Converge." *Critical Insights: Flannery O'Connor*. Ed. Charles E. May. Pasadena: Salem Press, 2012.
Tatar, Maria. "House of Fiction: Toward a Definition of the Uncanny." *Comparative Literature*. vol 33, March 1981. 167–182.
Todorov, Tzvetan. *The Literary Fantastic: A Structural Approach to a Literary Genre*. Ithaca, NY: Cornell University Press, 1975.
Veblen, Thorstein. "Chapter Three." *Theory of the Leisure Class by Thorstein Veblen*. Project Gutenberg Literary Archive Foundation. 19–32.
Wallace, Honor McKitrick. "'The Hero Is Married and Ascends the Throne': The Economics of Narrative End in Shirley Jackson's 'We Have Always Lived in the Castle.'" *Tulsa Studies in Women's Literature*. vol. 22, no. 1, 2003. 173–191.
Watkins, Steven R. *Flannery O'Connor and Teilhard de Chardin: A Journey Together Towards Hope and Understanding About Life*. New York: Peter Lang, 2009.
Webb, Jen, Tony Shirato, and Geoff Danher. *Understanding Bourdieu*. Thousand Oaks, CA: Sage Publications, 2002.

About the Contributors

Teresa M. **Coronado** earned her MA at Eastern New Mexico University and her Ph.D. at the University of Oregon. While in academia, she attained tenure and was promoted to associate professor at the University of Wisconsin–Parkside. Since 2019 she has been the program director at the Milwaukee Community Sailing Center.

Charlene Taylor **Evans** is a tenured professor of English at Texas Southern University in Houston, Texas. She served as chair of the Department of English. She is a member of the graduate faculty and teaches a course in research methods as well as the American novel. She has published articles on nineteenth and twentieth century American writers, concentrating on issues related to miscegenation and the intersectionality of race, gender, and class.

Michael J. **Finnegan** taught composition and literature at the University of Rhode Island, Roger Williams University and Bryant University. He hold his Ph.D. in literature from the University of Rhode Island and his MAT degree is from Colgate University.

Deborah **Giggle** is a postgraduate research student at the University of East Anglia in the UK. She began her academic study after spending 35 years working as a public relations consultant, freelance journalist and TV screenwriter. Her Ph.D. focuses on literary representations of class, and she has a particular interest in texts by socially marginalized authors.

Jason Marc **Harris** earned his Ph.D. in English literature from the University of Washington, and his MFA in fiction from Bowling Green State University. He teaches creative writing, folklore, and literature at Texas A&M University. He is the author of *Folklore and the Fantastic in Nineteenth-Century British Fiction*, has articles in the *Journal of Popular Culture*, among others, and fiction in the *Arroyo Literary Review* and *Midwestern Gothic*.

Kailey **Havelock** is a writer, editor and scholar based in Toronto. She earned an SSHRC-funded MA in literatures of modernity from Ryerson University. She holds editorial positions at *The Puritan*, *The Town Crier*, and as a manuscript editor, while also working as an agency assistant at the Cooke Agency.

Mark **Henderson** earned his MA in English from the University of Louisiana at Monroe and his Ph.D. in English, with concentrations in nineteenth and twentieth century American literature and psychoanalytic theory, from Auburn University. He is an assistant professor at Tuskegee University. His research and publication interests include American modernism, the American Gothic, and American film.

John F. **Lavelle** is an associate professor at Florida Tech where he teaches English, literature, and creative writing. His book *Blue Collar, Theoretically: A Post-Marxist Approach to Working-Class Literature* was published by McFarland. He has published articles and papers in academic journals on the interception of class and literature. He has also published a novel as well as several short stories in diverse literary journals.

Debbie **Lelekis** received her Ph.D. in English from the University of Missouri. She is an associate professor teaching literature and writing classes at Florida Tech. Her scholarly research focuses on the notion of community in nineteenth and early twentieth century American fiction. In her book, *American Literature, Lynching, and the Spectator in the Crowd: Spectacular Violence*, published in 2015, she examines literary depictions of the witnessing and reporting of racial violence.

Adam **Nemmers** is an assistant professor of literature at Lamar University in Beaumont, Texas. His research interests include modernism, multi-ethnic literature, radicalism, and the New Woman. His publications include essays on Faulkner and reviews of *Popular Modernism*; *Revisiting Harper Lee*; *Representing Rural Women*; and *Hoodoo, Voodoo, and Conjure in African American Literature*.

Index

Adventures of Huckleberry Finn (Twain) 9, 28–45, 115
The Adventures of Tom Sawyer (Twain) 9, 28–45
Althusser, Louis 6, 11, 32, 45, 148
American Dream 82, 123, 126, 128, 135, 138
American Gothic motifs 182–183, 199, 208–209
An American Tragedy (Dreiser) 121–122, 133, 137–139
Anderson, Sherwood 10, 80–99

Blue Collar, Theoretically (Lavelle) 1, 5, 51, 96, 124, 185
Bourdieu, Pierre 1, 6, 130, 138, 145, 147–152, 186, 188, 205
bourgeoisie 7, 22, 68, 109, 111, 117, 122, 129, 139, 143, 152, 174, 177–178, 192, 201, 205, 208

Cane (Toomer) 10, 100–120
capitalism 3–4, 22–23, 32, 51, 56, 90, 95, 113, 121–123, 125–126, 129, 137–139, 176, 195–196, 206
caste 10, 100–117, 121–123, 130, 134, 139
class mobility 122, 129
class/social hierarchy 3, 19, 73, 81, 83, 111, 122, 139, 157–159, 182, 200
communism 3–4, 95, 169–171, 205
conspicuous consumption 8, 127, 139, 151
Crane, Stephen 52, 63–79

Darwin, Charles 4, 122
Derrida, Jacques 31, 147
Dickens, Charles 88, 185, 204
Douglass, Frederick 10, 169–181
Dreiser, Theodore 47, 59, 121–140
Du Bois, W.E.B. 102–104, 106–107, 117

Ellison, Ralph 10, 169–181

Faulkner, William 9, 43, 97–98, 110, 157–168, 182, 188
Fitzgerald, F. Scott 137, 141
flâneur 48–50, 52, 57
Foucault, Michel 8, 33, 42, 90, 147

The Great Gatsby (Fitzgerald) 135, 137, 139, 141, 144–145

habitus 41, 133, 139, 188, 191, 204
Harlem Renaissance 101, 109, 111
Harlem riot 170, 174–176
Haymarket Square riot 10, 51, 54–55, 58, 61
A Hazard of New Fortunes (Howells) 10, 47–62
Hemingway, Ernest 10, 97, 141–156
How the Other Half Lives (Riis) 71
Howells, William Dean 10, 47–62
Hughes, Langston 102, 109, 117

in-group / out-group discourse 1, 8, 10, 30, 33, 37–38, 123, 145, 149–150, 165, 191, 201
The Incorporation of America (Trachtenberg) 56
invidious comparison 125, 131
Invisible Man (Ellison) 169–181

Jackson, Shirley 10, 182–209
James, Henry 84
The Journal of Madame Knight 9, 13–25

Knight, Sarah Kemble 9, 13–25

Larsen, Nella 101
Lyotard, Jean-Francois 1, 8, 29, 33, 35, 148

Maggie, A Girl of the Streets (Crane) 9, 63–79
Marxism 1–10, 51, 55, 95–97, 122–123, 127–133, 138, 144, 151, 171–173, 183
materialism 90, 93, 95, 124–125, 127, 136, 186, 203
means of production 1–6, 8, 123, 137, 188

Narrative of the Life of Frederick Douglass 169–181
Nietzsche, Friedrich 5, 30–32, 34, 44, 146, 159, 194

O'Connor, Flannery 10, 182–209

213

Index

Pound, Ezra 94, 97
proletariat 5, 7, 32, 51, 96, 107, 122, 124–126, 129 138–139, 178–179, 183, 208

rags-to-riches archetype 132, 138
Riis, Jacob 53, 71, 78

Schocket, Eric 9, 65, 71, 74
self-made man 82, 122
slum tourism 72
socialism 3, 51, 53, 55, 82, 104
Spoon River Anthology (Masters) 89
strike (labor) 10, 47–62
The Sun Also Rises (Hemingway) 10, 141–156

The Theory of the Leisure Class (Veblen) 4, 125, 196

Toomer, Jean 10, 100–120
Trachtenberg, Alan 56, 60
Twain, Mark 9, 28–45, 115, 157–158

Veblen, Thorstein 4, 8, 37, 39–40, 125, 138, 146, 151–152

We Have Always Lived in the Castle (Jackson) 182–209
Weber, Max 1–3, 5, 9, 37, 106–108, 113, 126, 137–138, 144, 155, 188
Whitman, Walt 61, 89, 116
Winesburg, Ohio (Anderson) 10, 80–99
Wright, Richard 176

www.ingramcontent.com/pod-product-compliance
Lightning Source LLC
Chambersburg PA
CBHW020836020526
44114CB00040B/1222